Family, class and education

A READER

This Reader offers an analysis of the complex relationship between home background and school performance, ranging from the more traditional 'macro' studies of family, class and education to more recent 'micro' studies. Throughout, the intricacy and elusiveness of what we have tended to regard as a straightforward and 'commonsense' relationship is stressed, and the concluding chapter includes a plea for the more sophisticated, interdisciplinary analysis of what, in all industrial societies, is a key psycho-social process.

Family, class and education

A READER

Edited by Maurice Craft
Senior Lecturer in Education
University of Exeter

Longman

LONGMAN GROUP LIMITED

LONDON

Associated companies, branches and representatives throughout the world

This Reader © Longman Group Ltd 1970
Linguistic development and educability
     © Dennis Lawton 1970
Social class, values and behaviour in school
     © Barry Sugarman 1970

First published 1970
Second impression 1971
Third impression 1972

ISBN 0 582   48757 9 cased
              48758 7 paper

Printed in Singapore by
New Art Printing Co., (Pte.) Ltd

Contents

List of Contributors   vii

Acknowledgements   ix

Editor's Preface   xi

PART ONE: Overview

1. Family, class and education: changing perspectives   3
   MAURICE CRAFT

PART TWO: Demographic studies

2. Social class factors in educational achievement   31
   JEAN FLOUD

3. Educational opportunity and social selection in England
   and Wales: trends and policy implications   49
   JOHN WESTERGAARD and ALAN LITTLE

4. The influence of the home   72
   R. R. DALE and S. GRIFFITH

PART THREE: Contextual studies

5. The community environment of the school   91
   S. JOHN EGGLESTON

6. The subculture and the school   109
   JOHN BARRON MAYS

7. Two subcultures   127
   DAVID HARGREAVES

PART FOUR: Subcultural studies I

8. Parental encouragement   151
   J. W. B. DOUGLAS

9. The survey of parental attitudes and circumstances, 1964 158
   ROMA MORTON-WILLIAMS

10. The 'good home'
    FRANK MUSGROVE   184

vi

PART FIVE: Subcultural studies II

11. Parental factors in educational mobility   205
    ELIZABETH COHEN

12. Linguistic development and educability   224
    DENIS LAWTON

13. Social class, values and behaviour in school   241
    BARRY SUGARMAN

14. Social class and family life   255
    OLIVE BANKS

Author Index   265
Subject Index   268

Contributors

OLIVE BANKS
Reader in Sociology, University of Leicester

ELIZABETH G. COHEN
Associate Professor of Education and Sociology, Stanford University

MAURICE CRAFT
Senior Lecturer in Education, University of Exeter

R. R. DALE
Reader in Education, University College of Swansea

J. W. B. DOUGLAS
Director, M.R.C. Unit, London School of Economics

S. JOHN EGGLESTON
Professor of Education, University of Keele

JEAN FLOUD
Fellow of Nuffield College, Oxford

S. GRIFFITH
Head of Physics Department, Pembroke Grammar School

DAVID HARGREAVES
Lecturer in Social Psychology, University of Manchester

DENIS LAWTON
Senior Lecturer in Curriculum Studies, University of London

ALAN LITTLE
Director, Research and Statistics, Inner London Education Authority

JOHN BARRON MAYS
Professor of Social Science, University of Liverpool

ROMA MORTON-WILLIAMS
Principal Research Officer, Government Social Survey

FRANK MUSGROVE
Professor of Research in Education, University of Bradford

BARRY SUGARMAN
Research Fellow in Sociology, Farmington Trust Research Unit, Oxford

JOHN WESTERGAARD
Senior Lecturer in Sociology, London School of Economics

Acknowledgements

We are grateful to the following for permission to reproduce copyright material.

The American Sociological Association for an extract adapted from 'Parental Factors in Educational Mobility' by Elizabeth Cohen from *Sociology of Education* Vol. 38, No. 5 1965; B. T. Batsford Ltd for an extract 'Social Class and Family Life' from *The Sociology of Education* by Olive Banks; Miss R. M. Morton-Williams and The Controller of Her Majesty's Stationery Office for an extract based on Appendix III to Volume 2 of the *Plowden Report: Children and their Primary Schools* published by HMSO on behalf of the Central Advisory Council for Education 1967; Higher Education Research Unit of the London School of Economics for a figure from *The Utilization of Educated Manpower in Industry* by Blaug, Peston and Ziderman, published by Oliver and Boyd Ltd; Liverpool University Press for an extract 'The Subculture and the School' from *Education and the Urban Child* by John Mays; MacGibbon & Kee Ltd for an extract from *The Home and the School* by J. W. B. Douglas; Organisation for Economic Co-operation and Development, Paris for an extract 'Educational Opportunity in England and Wales: Trends and Policy Implications' by John Westergaard and Alan Little from *Social Objectives in Educational Planning*, and an extract 'Social Class Factors' by J. E. Floud from *Ability and Educational Opportunity* edited by A. H. Halsey; Prentice-Hall Inc. for a table from *Social Stratification: The Forms and Functions of Inequality* by Melvin M. Tumin, © 1967 Prentice-Hall Inc. New Jersey, U.S.A.; Routledge and Kegan Paul Ltd and Humanities Press Inc. for extracts from *Social Relations in a Secondary School* by David Hargreaves, *Down Stream* by R. R. Dale and S. Griffith, *The Social Context of the School* by John Eggleston, and 'The Good Home' from *The Family, Education and Society* by Frank Musgrove.

Editor's preface

The influence of 'home background' upon school achievement is a familiar theme in educational research, government reports, and journalistic comment. This collection of readings seeks to give greater precision to what is meant by home background, and to shed some light on its very complex relationships with a child's school performance.

In a field in which so much has been written the selection of papers is bound to be somewhat arbitrary, but in this volume several criteria have been used as guidelines: British studies have generally been preferred to American on the grounds of their more immediate relevance, although our debt to the massive transatlantic research in this field is willingly acknowledged and discussion of much American work is included; and secondly, the collection has been designed primarily for students and others beginning a study of this aspect of the sociology of education.

The layout of the book takes the reader from the more traditional 'macro' studies of family, class and education to more recent 'micro' studies, and this trend in research is taken as the central theme and is surveyed in the opening chapter. Throughout, the intricacy and elusiveness of what we have tended to regard as the straightforward and commonsense relationship of family, class and education is stressed, and the concluding chapter includes a plea for the more sophisticated, interdisciplinary analysis of what, in all industrial societies, is a key psychosocial process.

I am greatly indebted to the contributors of the various chapters and to their respective publishers, to Dr D. F. Swift for valuable comments on an earlier draft, to my wife for much help and advice, and to my secretary, Mrs Jacqueline Foote who cheerfully copes with my handwriting.

MAURICE CRAFT

University of Exeter
June 1969

PART ONE   Overview

I

Family, class and education: changing perspectives

Maurice Craft

This introductory paper begins by outlining the field to be considered in this volume, and then goes on to identify and illustrate three broad approaches to its analysis—the demographic, contextual and subcultural—each of which is further exemplified in subsequent chapters. This first paper argues that while demographic studies offer the essential definition of social class patterns of educational opportunity and achievement, explanations for these patterns must be sought in terms of attitudes and values (i.e. in contextual and subcultural studies), and that such knowledge can only be advanced by interdisciplinary enquiry, through the overlapping viewpoints of sociology and psychology.

A great many studies have considered the relationship of education and environment. Some of the most notable have listed a range of variables, from quality of school buildings to local crime figures, and have related them to school performance. Others have adopted a more group-centred approach and have placed greater emphasis on the social situation in which such environmental factors operate. Boocock (1966) for example, has reviewed four such social settings—the classroom, the school as a whole, the peer group, and outside school (which includes the socio-economic status of the child's family). This latter is our point of departure in this volume, and so it will be clear that the relationship of family and social class to educational performance is by no means the only pattern of social pressures upon the school child, nor is it always necessarily the dominant one. But successive researches have demonstrated beyond doubt that family, class and education form an important relationship, and in this opening chapter we shall examine three major approaches to its analysis: these have been labelled the *demographic, contextual* and *subcultural.* They are often used in combination but studies generally emphasise a particular viewpoint, and our purpose will be to examine and illustrate each in turn. Secondly, it will be suggested that researches into the family–class–education relationship are moving gradually from the demographic to the contextual and subcultural, that our perspectives are changing from a 'macro' to a 'micro' view. And thirdly, succeeding chapters, which have been chosen to illustrate this changing perspective, will be linked in turn to our theme.

DEMOGRAPHIC STUDIES

First, the arithmetical or *demographic* approach which is represented in Part Two of this volume. Such studies as that of Lindsay (1926) and Gray and Moshinsky (1938), and amplified in more recent years by numerous, often government-sponsored researches have documented the now well-known fact that working-class children (and particularly the children of unskilled manual workers) are under-represented in selective secondary and higher education; and that even at the same levels of ability they are far more likely than middle-class children to deteriorate in performance and to leave school at the earliest permitted age (Central Advisory Council for Education, 1954, 1959; Robbins, 1963; Douglas *et al.*, 1968; Schools Council, 1968). A similar wastage is found in many complex, industrial societies abroad. Svalastoga (1965), for example, reports that in the Netherlands the upper 5 per cent of the population produced 45 per cent of all male students (and 66 per cent of all female students) in higher education in 1958/59, while the lowest 68 per cent produced only 9 per cent of all male and 3 per cent of all female students. Svalastoga's summary continues:

> In the United States around 1950, the majority (58 per cent) of the ablest one-tenth in regard to I.Q. did not receive a college education. Among the top 23 per cent of Norwegian recruits as measured by I.Q. at age 19, nearly one half (48 per cent) had at most obtained ten years' formal education as of 1950 . . . [while] . . . in France (1953–54) the percentage of elementary school pupils of given social origin who proceeded to secondary education was found to range from 13 for agricultural labourers to 89 for professionals (p. 137).

More recent figures, relating to university recruitment in Sweden and in Japan (Coombs, 1968, pp. 190–1), and to school dropout in the

Irish Republic (see Table 1.1), clearly show the same social class variations.

TABLE 1.1.   *Social class and school-leaving age in S. Dublin.*

	Middle class %	Upper working class %	Lower working class %	Totals %
Left by 14 yrs	14	37	60	35
Left by 15 yrs	7	12	12	11
Left by 16 yrs	11	20	17	17
Left by 17 yrs	10	13	4	11
Still at school (in 1970)	57	18	7	27
	N = 176	N = 336	N = 113	N = 625

Source: Derived from a current personal research by the author.
See also O.E.C.D., *Investment in Education*, Dublin: Stationery Office, 1965, Chap. 6, Pt. 2.

But valuable as these demographic studies have proved to be in alerting policymakers to inequalities of opportunity and to waste of talent, they tell us very little about *why* these discrepancies exist. As Barry Sugarman (1966) has written:

> Given the kind of educational system and the kind of relationship between school and home which exists in most of the economically advanced countries of the West, differential educability is linked to social class background. But 'social class' is just a shorthand way of referring to a complex of factors which correlate with occupation. It describes the distribution or incidence of a phenomenon *but does not explain its occurrence in any causal sense* (p. 287; my italics).

Or as Kahl (1957) writes of able children who do not benefit from higher education in the United States: 'Statistically, the major explaining variable is the social-class level of the boy's family, although such a statement still leaves much unexplained about the way social class operates as a motivating force in an individual boy's life' (p. 282).

The *Early Leaving* Report concluded that an explanation of class variations in school dropout must be sought . . . 'in the outlook and assumptions of parents and children in various walks of life' (C.A.C.E., 1954, para. 97), that is, in terms of our three approaches, in *subcultural* factors. The trend in research has thus been away from the 'arithmetical' assessment of social class differentials in educational opportunity towards the study of 'educability', responsiveness to the school system in terms of attitudes and values, although studies of educability usually begin with a demographic definition of the problem.

One final example of the demographic approach to the study of family, class and education is provided by the educational economist; this is the charting of the relationship of education and income. Miller (1965), for example, demonstrates this very clearly for the United States, in Table 1.2.

TABLE 1.2.   *Relationship of education to earnings (1959 figures).*

School years completed	Average annual income	Expected lifetime earnings
Less than 8	$2550	$143,000
8	3769	184,000
9–11	4618	212,000
12	5567	247,000
13–15	6966	293,000
16 or more	9206	425,000 (approx.)

Source: Tumin, 1967, p. 57.

Thus, middle-class homes foster educational achievement and thereby ensure middle-class status for their children, a complete circle. Abrams has produced similar figures for Great Britain using a random sample of 6500 male heads of households over twenty years of age. He found that for those who left school at fifteen years, the median income in 1963 was £636; for those who left between sixteen and eighteen years, it was £1034; and for those who left at nineteen years or over, £1583. As Abrams (1964) points out, it seems that 'the private benefit of an additional two or three years at school beyond one's fifteenth birthday is worth £400 a year or £20,000 over the whole adult life of a man. Yet a further two or three years of education and the financial outcome is an income for life more than double that received by the ordinary man who left school at fifteen or less' (p. 26). Abrams goes on to demonstrate that these 'private benefits' of education vary during a man's lifetime and that although all incomes decline in old age, the *differential* tends to widen up to the point of retirement. This kind of data ('age–earnings profiles') is presented in Table 1.3.

In their current research with a sample of 3000 individuals in industry, Blaug and his colleagues (1967, p. 36) have already constructed *actual* age–earnings profiles which seem to follow a very similar pattern.

TABLE I.3.   *Hypothetical age–earnings profiles by levels of education.*

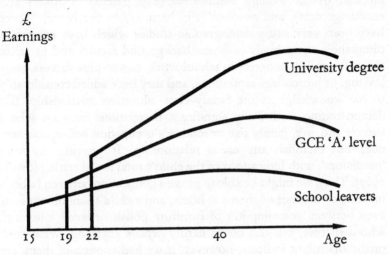

Source: Blaug, Peston, and Ziderman, 1967, p. 10.

This particular kind of demographic data thus appears to demon-strate how the social-class variations in secondary and higher education discussed earlier may be translated into differential 'life chances'. We have of course to recognise that we are not here measuring the effect of educational qualifications alone; social class of origin and intelligence have not been separated out. But what is perhaps more important from the point of view of this volume is that such demographic calculations tell us little of the subcultural processes (social class attitudes), or of the more intricate psychosocial processes of the individual family which together provide the motivation to excel and the implementary values which can turn school achievement into career success. The demographic studies can usually tell us 'what' and 'how many', but for the 'how' and 'why' we need to look farther afield.

It would, of course, be unfair to suggest that sample surveys work entirely in terms of *aggregates*. In many cases, the demographic ap-proach to the family–class–education relationship has usually involved an attempt to analyse the influence of such components as the child's sex, age, the size of his family of origin and his ordinal position within it, his parents' education and reading habits, his mother's occupation before marriage, his grandparents' occupations, home living conditions and so on. Fraser (1959) in a classic study of this kind related school performance to four types of home background factor—*cultural* (e.g. parental education), *material and economic* (e.g. income, overcrowding), *motivational* (e.g. parental attitudes and encouragement), and *emotional* (e.g. harmony in the home). There have been very many demographic studies which have sought to disentangle these kinds of home background factors and to relate them to a child's progress in school work, eleven-plus success, early leaving, or job/college aspirations, and they have added considerably to our knowledge of the family–class–education relationship. But demonstrating statistically significant correlations between school success and, say, family size or mother's occupation before marriage does not establish any *causal* relationship. It provides us with 'predictors', with indications of the child's total social setting (Swift, 1967). Thus, we might be able to prove a connection between father's income, or number of rooms at home, and a child's school work; or even between consumption of furniture polish or weed killer and school success, but this could hardly *explain* anything. What such predictors might indicate, however, if we had enough of them, are the shadowy outlines of a neighbourhood or a family's ideology or value system. This is what the sociologist would mean by the influence of the social environment and we shall pursue this further when we consider the *subcultural* approach. We have first, however, to consider what is perhaps an intermediate stage between the demographic and the subcultural viewpoints, the *contextual* approach.

CONTEXTUAL STUDIES

Contextual studies place emphasis on the influence of the *neighbourhood* or of the *school*. But because they provide this intermediate stage between the demographic and the subcultural viewpoints, contextual studies are of varied kinds depending on where each stands in relation to the extremes. Thus, at one end of the contextual continuum we find studies which, while focusing say upon a particular neighbour hood, are broadly demographic in treatment; and at the other there are those which are more subcultural and which highlight the influence upon an individual child's behaviour of the norms and values of a particular community or a particular school.

At the demographic end of the continuum we have Wiseman's 1964 and 1967 studies which related school performance to such neighbourhood predictors as birth and mortality rates, population density, illegitimacy, provision of play areas, percentage of corporation housing and amount of school breaking and entering. Perhaps the most extensive study of this kind was reported by Thorndike (1951) and which involved the testing of about half a million children drawn from every part of the United States. The resulting average intelligence and achievement scores for the children in each community studied were then related to twenty-four community variables covering aspects of population structure, educational level, occupational distribution, housing conditions, and economic level. The average intelligence of children tested in any community was found to correlate highly with adult educational level, degree of home-ownership, and high quality housing, while achievement was closely related to the percentage of professional workers and to the mean level of adult education—a perhaps not unexpected commentary on the relationship of family, class and education.

Clearly these more narrowly ecological studies seem to share the same advantages and disadvantages of the demographic researches discussed earlier. They quickly and efficiently provide a map of social and educational disadvantage, but they tell us little about how these handicaps are caught, or taught. Sexton's massive study (1961) of a quarter of a million children in all the three hundred schools in a major American city argued that the simple index of *father's income* was not only the best all-round guide to a family's way of life; but that average family income could be used to categorise schools, and schools grouped in this way were then shown to vary markedly in pupils' levels of ability, achievement, delinquency and many other school and community variables. Again, this was an ingenious contextual study of a demographic sort, although Sexton also offers a wide range of comment on the socio-psychological origins of these variations in an attempt to explain how and why.

Rogoff (1961), however, in another well-known contextual study might be placed a little further along the continuum because of the implications it raised. This research demonstrated that school performance and college aspirations were very closely related *to the type of area* in which the schools were situated—children in the larger suburbs performing better than those living either in small towns or in large cities. As we might expect, working-class children were found to rate lower than middle-class children in *all* kinds of neigh-bourhood (a demographic finding); but their achievement was better and their drop-out rate was lower in the larger suburbs (a contextual finding). Rogoff offered no hypothesis to explain these differences. They might be due to variations in quality of educational provision (schools, equipment, teachers), or in other community amenities (libraries, museums, sports facilities); this is one important aspect of contextual influence. Or they might reflect differences in the home motivational environment (in subculture, and in the ideology of individual families). We know that there is a degree of social selection in migration, the more ambitious and thrustful families seeking better jobs, homes and schools for their children (a point taken up later in respect of 'privatised' working-class families); in other words, the working-class children in the larger suburbs might be subject to significantly different home environmental pressures than those in the small towns and larger cities. This is a second important aspect of contextual influence which is clearly far closer to the subcultural end of the continuum.

British contextual studies in the sociology of education are relatively sparse, but Blyth (1967) offered a valuable review of relevant community researches in sketching the varying social settings of the English primary school. Here he discusses the implications for curriculum and organisation, the teacher's role and the school's value climate of local social structure and ideology, considering in turn a range of environments from villages to inner city suburbs. These inner neighbourhoods which generally show a higher incidence of almost every form of deviance and social malaise have, of course, been a focus of attention for sociologists for many years, but it is perhaps Mays's (1962) research (part of which appears in Chapter 6 of this volume) which has the most outstanding relevance for our discussion of family, class and education. This was a classic study of the interaction of school and community in several inner city districts in Liverpool, considering in detail the working-class sub-cultures in which schools function. But it is more a contextual study than an analysis of the motivational environment of individual families which we consider later in this chapter. Obviously the borderline between the two cannot be sharply drawn, but it is illustrated, perhaps, by the *Early Leaving* Report in its study of grammar school drop-outs:

Children in different social groups may start their . . . school life with different sets of unspoken assumptions about the length of school life. . . . But ideas are picked up not only in the home *but in the neighbourhood*. It is easy to imagine, for instance, that a headmaster may despair of keeping in the sixth form any boy from a particular street, not only because of the poor conditions in the houses but *because of the character and atmosphere of the street as a community*. There is no doubt of the strength of the pressure on even conscientious parents from neighbours who see no point in education beyond fifteen or sixteen, as the case may be; and if the pressure on the parent is strong, it is much stronger on the children. (C.A.C.E., 1954, paras. 98–99. My italics.)

Finally, the school itself. If neighbourhood provision is one major aspect of contextual influence, and neighbourhood subculture is another, a third is found in the value climate of the school. The Robbins Report (1963, i, 50) demonstrated that working-class children entering grammar schools were likely to *improve* their measured ability scores between the ages of eleven and fifteen years, while working-class children of the same levels of ability entering secondary moderns suffered a *deterioration;* the same was true of middle-class children. Similar evidence is reviewed by Elder (1965), p. 186 *et seq.* Douglas's most recent study goes into much more detail on this. His research shows how lower working-class children of high ability were far more likely to stay on in 'good' secondary modern schools (i.e. schools with over 600 pupils and/or good amenities; with over 20 per cent graduate staff, and/or a pupil–teacher ratio of less than 19 : 1), than in 'poor' ones, *even where parental interest* (a very powerful predictor) *is high* (Douglas *et al.*, 1968, p. 183). This seems to give contextual influences very great importance in a social group (the children of unskilled manual workers) already suffering the most severe social handicaps from birth onwards.

Comparable findings emerge if we break the school down into its constituent groups. For example, in streamed primary schools Douglas (1964) reported that allocation to upper streams was related to an improvement in test scores at each level of ability, while deterioration at each level followed allocation to low streams.

To some extent streaming embodies social-class selection for a greater proportion of children from large families and suffering poor maternal care were to be found in the lower streams of Douglas's sample at each level of ability and as a result of the polarisation discussed above, these social-class differences are reinforced. However, although such studies illustrate the contextual influence, it is not always easy to separate this from the effect of individual home background. For example, in Douglas's upper streams, while all children improved their average test scores between eight and eleven years, middle-class children gained far more than those from working-class homes; and in the lower streams working-class children suffered most. So the influence of the school context here appears to reinforce that of the individual child's home.

Perhaps the most intriguing question which runs through this discussion of the contextual influence of schools is how does it happen? As we have seen, the educational handicaps of a child with a working-class background can often be alleviated by allocation to a higher stream, or by membership of a particular primary or secondary school. In the latter case is this because of the better school buildings and facilities? Or better teaching and lower staff turnover? We have considered studies which would tend to support either hypothesis. Or are we now moving closer to the *subcultural* approach, does the social composition of a school—the proportion of upper working-class or middle-class children on roll—have something to do with it? A number of contextual studies seem to underline this more sub-cultural influence. Douglas (1968, pp. 179–80), for example, writes:

> Some primary schools recruit their pupils mainly from families of clerks and other middle-class workers, including those in the professions, while others recruit them predominantly from the manual working class. Between the ages of eight and eleven pupils in those primary schools which enrolled their pupils predominantly from the manual working class fell behind the rest in their test performance and at each level of ability were less likely to be allocated to grammar schools. These same pupils are likely to leave early and so seldom sit the G.C.E. examinations. At secondary modern schools, they are only two-thirds as likely to stay to the end of the 1961/62 session as are those of similar measured ability coming from primary schools with a largely non-manual intake. If they go to grammar schools, they are also at a similar disadvantage. The influence of the primary school is particularly strong for the manual working-class child; if he has been to a primary school that is predominantly middle class, he is more likely to succeed at secondary school, than if he had been to a primary school recruiting its pupils mainly from the manual working class.[1]

This seems a very clear statement, but it is perhaps not conclusive. Working-class children who attend largely middle-class primary schools may not themselves be from 'typically' working-class families. They may belong to aspiring, ambitious families who have

1. See Willmott (1963) for a discussion of some of the educational consequences of large, one-class housing estates.

moved because of favourable job opportunities,[1] or to be near a
school with a good reputation for eleven-plus successes. What
therefore appears to be a clear contextual influence may once again
be the result of the interaction of home and school environments. In
Jackson and Marsden's study of eighty-eight working-class grammar
school children, very many came from districts of mixed social class,
'and where there was an important minority of middle-class children
attending the local primary school'. They also came from *small
families*[2] and families which often had some middle-class connections
(Jackson and Marsden, 1962, pp. 92–3). So were they 'typical'
working-class children, or a selected group possessing some middle-
class characteristics?

The same basic question is raised by A. B. Wilson's (1959) highly
significant research in California, that of Jayasuriya (1960) in London
and that of Eggleston (1967) in Leicestershire. Both Wilson and
Jayasuriya found that working-class children perform better and have
higher educational and occupational aspirations in predominantly
middle-class schools; and Eggleston (reported in Chapter 5 of this
volume) similarly discovered that working-class children in middle-
class areas were more likely to stay on at school than those in working-
class areas. Were these 'typically' working-class youngsters, who
acquired higher aspirations through their contacts with middle-class
school friends; or did they come from aspirant working-class families
in the first place? Krauss (1964) suggests that both factors seem to
operate. He analysed the sources of college-going plans of working-
class school children in San Francisco and concluded that the two
major ones were, first, certain *family characteristics* (e.g. mother's non-
manual occupation; mother's experience of higher education; grandparents' non-manual occupation; siblings' or family friends' experience of higher education); and second, *peer group activity* (i.e. friends
with college aspirations) in a predominantly middle-class school.
Simpson's (1962) study, however, gives rather greater weight to the
influence of the home compared with that of the peer group. While
schoolboys (working-class and middle-class) with high occupational
aspirations were found to have received parental advice and to have
middle-class friends to a significantly greater extent than those without
such ambitions, the relationship of *parental advice* was clearly stronger
than that of peer influence.

1. See the discussion of 'embourgeoisement' below, pp. 16 *et seq.*
2. The significance of family size as an index of family values is considered below
on pp. 21 *et seq.*

In this discussion of the contextual approach we began with *neighbourhood* studies which utilised a largely demographic treatment, and moving along the continuum we have considered other contextual researches in which the subcultural element is greater. Rogoff's study prompted the thought that selective migration to the larger suburbs from both inner city districts and from smaller towns and rural areas might have produced an 'untypical' working-class population, one that was more ambitious and thrustful; and when we come to assess contextual influences in *schools* we are led to consider the same possibility, that successful working-class children who may often attend middle-class schools and have middle-class friends may be from untypical home motivational environments. Clearly the next step must be to examine what is meant by the labels 'working-class' and 'middle-class', and to focus more sharply on variations in value systems between and within the social classes, and within individual families.

SUBCULTURAL STUDIES

The subcultural approach is the main preoccupation of Parts Four and Five of this volume and attempts to seek explanations for the behaviour charted by demographic and contextual studies. Although it may well be that the 'how' and 'why' of the family–class–education relationship may be more profitably pursued in the subcultural area, this is an exceedingly complex field and offers no simple answers. It has already been suggested, for example, that family ideology interacts with the culture of the school, perhaps through the medium of the peer group, and perhaps also through selective migration; and that although there may be broad differences in ideology[1] between working-class and middle-class families, there will be variations within each group.

Heterogeneity within the working class

The stratification system is broadly related to the highly differentiated economic and occupational structure of an advanced industrial society—the managers and professionals, the clerks and supervisors, the skilled and unskilled manual workers. Similar modes of life generate class consciousness at each level and differences in social status and in power between each level. Although, of course, the variations in status and power between social classes are related to a

1. This point is qualified later in this chapter (pp. 18 *et seq.*).

society's political ideology as well as to its basic economic structure,[1] it is fundamentally the way a society earns its living, the complexity of its economic and occupational structure, that gives rise to its pattern of subcultures.

Secondly, in an open, democratic society such as our own there are many religious, ethnic and regional variations which will add further variety to this pattern of subcultures. We might therefore expect to find more or less subtle differences between the beliefs and aspirations of Jewish and Catholic doctors, or between labourers on South Devon farms and South London building sites, or between English-born nurses in Bath and West Indian-born nurses in Birmingham. This variety is not to be overstated; it is the contention of this volume that social-class differences override most other sub-cultural patterns and that Jewish and Catholic doctors, say, will have far more in common with each other than doctors will have with labourers overall. Nonetheless, as the working class amounts to some two-thirds of our adult working population and as we have such a highly differentiated economy and a pluralistic social and political ideology, we should hardly expect uniformity of subculture within this group and the same will be true of the middle class. Research has barely begun to analyse the mosaic of belief systems which underly these very crude labels—'working-class' and 'middle-class', but a number of beginnings have been made. Klein (1965), for example, in an extensive review of social class subcultures suggests three main groupings within the working class: the *deprived*, a group characterised by insecurity and deviation from a variety of social norms; the *traditional working class*, subdivided into 'respectables' and 'roughs', those who attempt to 'maintain standards' rather than 'let things slide'; and thirdly, a group whose style of life is *changing*, these are often residents in newer housing areas who are more home-centred and less oriented to kin and community, whose families are more democratic and child-centred, and who are altogether more individualistic and more questioning. This latter group (the 'status dissenters') are far more likely to be ambitious for their children and to see relevance in their schooling than the traditional working class, the 'status assenters' living in long-established, close-knit communities.

Carter's (1966) classification is similar. At the lowest level of the

1. Does a society, for example, legislate to moderate extremes of wealth and poverty? Does it permit sectional groups (professional, commercial, or trade union monopolies) to develop and maintain extensive powers?

working class are the *roughs* who have 'little regard for the "official" norms and values of society', who live for the present and whose families offer a generally disorganised pattern of life. Children from these homes may well regard school with irreverence and hostility, for in their experience chance seems a better explanation of achievement than rational planning and perseverance. Carter's second group is the *solid working class,* more organised and purposeful than the roughs, but where relations with school (and indeed many other areas of family decisionmaking) are the mother's responsibility and where education is undervalued for it seems largely irrelevant to the occupational experience of the group. The third group Carter labels the *home-centred, aspiring type,* far less easygoing than the solid working class and far more concerned with appearances and with 'getting on'. This third category subdivides into 'traditional respectables' and the 'newly affluent'; both tend to have smaller, planned families and to be ambitious for their children and keenly supportive of school activities, occasionally even putting excessive pressures on children to do well at school. The 'traditional respectables' may include many skilled manual workers, often foremen or chargehands, and clerical workers, while the 'newly affluent' who may show a somewhat greater concern for material possessions may include rather more semiskilled and unskilled men.

Despite their use of similar terms in slightly different ways, these two interpretations by Klein and Carter of the varied subcultures within the working class clearly overlap, and demonstrate a range of patterns of living and of belief from the most alienated to the most conformist. Rose's (1968) illuminating discussion in fact suggests a simple, fourfold structure: upper, middle, lower, and deviant (which is mainly a substratum of the lower working class).[1] But perhaps the most interesting analysis of working-class subcultures from the point of view of this volume is that developed by Goldthorpe and Lockwood, for it focuses on occupational and attitudinal trends of great relevance which have been touched upon in Klein's 'changing' group and arter's 'newly affluent'. This analysis describes three types of worker—*proletarian, deferential,* and *privatised.* Both *proletarian* and

1. Wilson (1963) in a study of new housing estates offers a classification of the working class ('solids', 'brittles', 'difficults') which is rather more concerned with the impact of the changed environment upon *family stability*. But an increasing number of working-class families are undergoing rehousing, and anxiety about changed financial obligations and about changed relationships and neighbourhood expectations may also be reflected in varying attitudes towards the value of education and relations with schools.

deferential are traditional working-class; but the former is found for example in mining, docking, and shipbuilding which give rise to close-knit long-established industrial communities fostering a profound class consciousness; while the *deferential* (who often work, for example, in rural areas, or in service occupations) are likely to have closer contact with employers or 'other middle-class influentials' and to lack this class consciousness. The *privatised* worker, on the other hand, employed perhaps in large-scale mass-production and living on the suburban housing estate, is said to have little involvement in work, workmates or local community. Work is purely to provide money and possessions for the home (Lockwood, 1966).

The enormous social and political implications of this 'privatisation' of the working class have attracted great interest. Are postwar conditions of full employment and social security giving rise to an 'embourgeoisement' of such manual workers? The conclusions of Goldthorpe and Lockwood's research in Luton are that they are not (Goldthorpe *et al.*, 1967, 1968a, 1968b). Apart from adopting a more 'instrumental', alienated attitude towards work, and a more isolated, home-centred orientation in general, the 'affluent' worker appears to seek middle-class affiliation neither socially nor politically. As the authors say, ' "middle classness" is not, after all, simply a matter of money', it is more a matter of attitudes.

From the point of view of education, the embourgeoisement thesis has great relevance, for the *privatised* worker will become more typical with the progress of technological advance and the trend to large-scale capital-intensive production, and with continued urban redevelopment. At very least, we might expect his greater home-centredness to include a more lively interest in his children's schooling, and in their preparations for a career rather than for a job. But it is also possible, on the limited evidence available so far, that we might find such homes to be extremely ambitious for their children. The privatised worker may not entertain his friends at home, participate in recreational associations, or vote Conservative to the extent of his middle-class peers; but he seems to share a number of fundamentally middle-class attitudes (or 'value orientations')[1], sometimes derived

1. The Luton study measured middle-class aspirations in terms of behaviour and expressed attitudes rather than of basic value orientations as discussed later in this chapter, and this approach risks measuring an *adjustment to* circumstances rather than more fundamental beliefs themselves. For example, if prospects of promotion are poor (as they normally are for manual workers), it is not too surprising that ambition among the Luton workers was found to be low. Nonetheless, nearly 40 per cent of the manual workers' sample had seriously considered starting up

perhaps from family or occupational white-collar connections.[2] These 'value orientations', or basic beliefs, are discussed in the following pages (and more fully in Chapter 13); but essentially they amount to a greater confidence in the possibility of effectively mastering the environment, as opposed to the far more widespread fatalism of traditional working-class families. In short, the 'privatised' worker will probably be more likely to plan for his children's future and to perceive the benefit of education.

Heterogeneity, achievement and values

So far this chapter has argued that demographic and contextual studies may chart the outlines of the relationship of family, class and education, and that they may demonstrate in detail the underachievement of working-class children. But it is in the *subcultural* area that we are more likely to find explanations, and we have begun by exploring the heterogeneity of the working class, the great variety of home motivational environments which working-class children may experience. Studies of the middle class would offer a similarly varied pattern (Klein, 1965; Raynor, 1969). All too often we make use of a simple, two-level model of social-class stratification which conceals this variety. Herriott and St John (1966), for example, writing of the United States summarise the traditional view as follows:

> The middle-class family is said to be child-centred, future-oriented and interested in achievement and mobility. It teaches children to respect property and to value neatness, thrift and

in business on their own account (compared with one-fifth of the white collar sample), and a third of these had actually made the effort at one time or another. It is conceivable that the class variation here reflects different perceptions of opportunity rather than major differences of orientation. Furthermore, the Luton workers were geographically mobile, they were prepared to 'follow the money' and had few ties to workmates or neighbourhood. A majority lived outside typically working-class areas (city centre, or council estates) and a number owned their own houses. On the face of it, this is a more activistic/individualistic/future-oriented group than one would expect to find in a more traditional working-class setting and in terms of basic value orientations, far more 'middle class'. The sample also had a number of family and occupational 'bridges' with the middle class—20 per cent came from white-collar families, a quarter had white-collar fathers-in-law, nearly half had wives who held (currently or in the past) white-collar jobs, and 10 per cent had themselves spent some of their working lives in white-collar work. In fact less than a third of the manual workers' sample had *no* such white-collar affiliation, and for these the level of Labour voting was correspondingly higher than for the others. (Goldthorpe *et al.*, 1968a, 1968b.)
2. And as the authors note, with the continued growth in white-collar occupations and in their employment of women, these white-collar connections will become increasingly common (Goldthorpe *et al.*, 1968b, p. 81).

punctuality. The lower-class family, on the other hand, is described as adult-centred, present-oriented, and interested in enjoying life with extended family and peers. It teaches children to admire toughness, physical prowess, generosity, and practicality (p. 7).

So far as attitudes to education are concerned, this two-level model argues that middle-class families are likely to value extended schooling and to recognise its career value, while among working-class families there is 'reduced striving for success . . . an awareness of lack of opportunity, and a lack of valuation of education, normally the major avenue to achievement of high status' (Hyman, 1953). But as I have suggested, reality is far less clearcut than this simple two-level model suggests. Matza and Sykes have suggested that the racial analogy is particularly appropriate here. Just as we now accept that 'pure' racial types are notional, we should similarly recognise that 'most values appear in most social classes; the social classes differ, however, in the frequency with which the values appear' (Matza and Sykes, 1961, p. 716). Thus, we would expect *most* middle-class families to be more concerned with, say, planning, and to place a higher valuation on extended education than *most* working-class families; but as we have seen in our discussion of subcultures within the working class, there are likely to be exceptions at each social level. In Kahl's (1953) classic study of intelligent working-class boys, those whose parents had come to recognise the career value of education had influenced them to seek a college course, while the drop-outs lacked this parental pressure.

But this more heterogeneous view of the value systems of the different social classes can be taken a little further. It has been argued, for example, that the western 'success' ethic is shared at all social levels, all seek high occupational achievement; but working-class children adjust their aims and come to terms with what seems possible in the light of their experience and that of their parents (Caro, 1966). As Hargreaves puts it in Chapter 7 of this volume: 'The working class may not be able to attain these goals [i.e. personal achievement], due to their restricted access to the means, but many of them accept the validity of the values, even though they may sometimes appear to reject them.'

Rodman (1963) has elaborated a theory of 'value-stretch', suggesting that the American working-class person 'without abandoning the value placed upon success, such as high income and high educational and occupational attainment, . . . stretches the values so that lesser degrees of success also become desirable' (p. 209). Other evidence supports this hypothesis. Using the simple, two-level model of social-class values, many researchers have found that working-class children have far lower educational and occupational aspirations than middle-class children; they will aim, say, to be plumbers rather than doctors. But following the alternative assumption that 'getting ahead' it valued by all but a marginal, alienated minority, other research has demonstrated that *compared with their fathers' occupations* many working-class children have high 'relative' aspirations (e.g. Empey, 1956).

Subcultural studies of the relationship of family, class and education have thus attempted explanations for the under-achievement of working-class children identified by the demographic and contextual approaches. The work of McClelland and other psychologists on 'achievement motivation' (or 'achievement need') might also be included in the subcultural category and is reviewed by Professor Musgrove in Chapter 10. Achievement motivation has been identified as a personality factor, a drive to persevere and excel which may be found to vary between individuals, ethnic groups, social classes, or even entire nations, and which is held to explain different levels of achievement (Berkowitz, 1964; Kahl, 1965; Pareek, 1968). But achievement motivation, the pursuit of high performance, might apply to any area of human activity, vocational, recreational, or even criminal; so while the study of family structures and child rearing practices which generate achievement motivation is very relevant to our theme, it seems a less profitable line of subcultural analysis than the study of basic beliefs, or *value orientations* to which we referred earlier (p. 18). This is the notion that fundamental beliefs (held either implicitly or explicitly) on three essential dimensions in particular—attitudes to time, to activity, and to individualism—will govern all one's basic decision-making. It may be that the position an individual, a social class, or a society takes in relation to these major value orientations is an outcome largely of the way that individual or social group earns his/its living. The daily work of a business executive or of a professional man, for example, requires the capacity to take initiatives, to plan ahead, and above all to assume that the future can be shaped. The labourer, on the other hand, whose work situation demands little initiative, and is fundamentally insecure (and maybe also physically dangerous) is more likely to assume that the future will just happen.[1]

1. Continued economic and technological development, and the steady decline in unskilled work will gradually change these occupational demands.

This concept of basic value orientations (discussed more fully by Barry Sugarman in Chapter 13) perhaps sheds some light on the mechanism by which working-class children, although supporting society's 'success' ethic (with the possible exception of a small, alienated group), often come to terms with a lower level of educational and occupational aspiration and achievement than their ability would justify. The environment is basically *not* thought capable of mastery, achievement comes as much through 'luck' or 'influence' as through careful planning, cultivated skill, or perseverance (Katz, 1964). A passive acceptance of the limitations of the environment seems an appropriate response to years on the housing list, or insecure and poorly-paid employment, especially when a more 'activistic' role requires either geographical or social mobility (or both) and a weakening of the traditionally close bonds with family and friends. Similarly, among those working-class children who may be hardworking and perfectionist at school (i.e. who may possess high 'achievement motivation'), lack of these vital 'implementary' values—activism, future-orientation, individualism—may cause some of the most able to drop out at the earliest school-leaving age, or to take dead-end jobs (Rosen, 1956).

Clearly, the full importance of these basic value orientations to the relationship of family, class and education has to be more extensively explored. We know, for example, that mother's secondary school education or white-collar job before marriage, or father's supervisory role in the factory, or a cousin's grammar school or college achievement are very often related to a working-class child's school performance. Is this because of the knowledge of possible educational and career avenues, or the experience of success, that these models provide? Or are these 'predictors' indices of the family possession of more activistic/future-oriented/individualistic 'implementary' values (as was suggested in our discussion of embourgeoisement)?[1] The same question arises if we consider family size. As Professor Musgrove points out in Chapter 10, many studies have shown that children from smaller families do better at school and stay on longer. This was documented in detail by the Crowther Report which clearly demonstrated that *at each social level*, ability scores fall and early drop-out increases in the larger families (C.A.C.E., 1959, ii, 125–9), and subsequent studies have reiterated these findings (Douglas, 1968, chap. 17; Schools Council, 1968). Is this because of the educative qualities of small families? Or is it related to the basic beliefs of parents

1. See footnote on p. 17.

2

who have decided to limit their families; is it an outcome of those assumptions about planning and about mastery of the environment which may even be largely unconsciously held, the 'implicit culture' of the small family?

The answer to this question cannot be a simple one, although recent enquiries offer some supportive evidence (C.A.C.E., 1967, i, para. 90; Douglas, 1968, p. 128). On the one hand, as Denis Lawton argues in Chapter 12, the possession of relatively well-developed linguistic skills is obviously fundamental to school success, and it has been suggested that the smaller the family the more likely is a child to possess this 'elaborated' verbal code, perhaps because of his greater contact with adults. So smaller families may well have more educative qualities in these terms. On the other hand, family size is linked to social class (even for Roman Catholics), the higher the social class the smaller the family (see Table 1.4). So we cannot separate a family's 'educative qualities', as defined above, from its (class-linked) value system, i.e. from the decisions and the assumptions underlying them, that have shaped it.[1] Indeed, the possession of an 'elaborated' linguistic code is itself more than simply a matter of vocabulary or of dialect; as Bernstein (1965) has argued, the 'elaborated' code (found

TABLE 1.4.   *Social class and family size among Irish Catholics.*

Family size	Middle class %	Upper working class %	Lower working class %	Totals %
Small family (1–3 children)	24	23	14	22
Average family (4–7 children)	62	56	53	57
Large family (8+ children)	14	21	33	21
	100 (171)	100 (336)	100 (113)	100 (620)

$\chi^2 = 16.25$ 4 D.F. $P < 0.005$.

Source: Derived from a current personal research by the author in Dublin.

1. Or, for that matter, from such cruder class-based correlates as poverty or overcrowding. For all these kinds of reasons, family size is probably our best available predictor of school success, for whatever reason. As Jean Floud writes in Chapter 2, 'once the grosser material handicaps are eliminated and parents' attitudes come into their own as independent variables, the size of the family rather than its socio-economic status, emerges as potentially *the most important single indication of the educative quality of home environment*' (p. 43; my italics).

more often in the middle class) and the 'restricted' code (found more often in the working class) are linguistic forms generated by the life experience of these particular subcultures. They reflect not simply the differing cognitive skills required, say, by dockers or dentists, but at a far deeper level they reflect (and reinforce) quite different assumptions about the social environment, about social relationships, and about getting things done.

So when we begin to probe the home motivational environment of the school child and to analyse social-class differences, we seem never to be far from a consideration of value orientations, basic attitudes to achievement, to time, and to individualism. As I have suggested, this appears to be true if we consider family size or language; and similarly if we study social-class differences in child-rearing practices (which are considered by Professor Musgrove in Chapter 10 and also by Olive Banks in Chapter 15)[1], or if we try to assess the effect on a child's school achievement of his parents' social adjustment and 'ideology', an important area discussed in Chapter 11 by Professor Cohen. As Marsden (1967) writes: 'Parents guide their children's education by what they are, what they do consciously, and, possibly more important, *what they do unconsciously*' (p. 38; my italics) But one cannot argue that there is a simple causal relationship. We have as yet merely identified the outlines of a pattern of motivational variables whose mode of interaction is highly complex and largely unknown.

CHANGING PERSPECTIVES

This chapter began with a review of the more traditional *demographic* approach to the relationship of family, class and education, moving on to the *contextual* view where concern with attitudes and values becomes more apparent, and discussing, finally, the distribution of social-class *subcultures* and some of the constituents of the motivational environment of individual families. This progressive narrowing of focus is represented in the succeeding chapters and reflects a changing perspective in research into family, class and education.

Barber's (1961) commentary on social-class differences in educational life-chances in many ways summarises this trend, as he considers first 'economic' factors, and then such subcultural areas as child-rearing patterns and variations in attitudes and aspirations, including the influence of what he calls 'social structures' (i.e. the *contextual* pressures of schools and neighbourhoods). More recently,

1. See also the useful review by Zigler (1968).

Swift (1968) has argued a similar case, and calls for a more sophisticated conceptualisation of what we mean by social class when we are
assessing its influence on educational achievement. How exactly does
social class operate as a motivational context, what are the mechanisms? This search for mechanisms, as Olive Banks points out in
Chapter 15, is leading sociologists into the study of the intricate
processes of family socialisation, and this, as she rightly states,
requires 'more than the sociological approach alone. It is an interdisciplinary concept and requires interdisciplinary methods, and in
particular an emphasis on the relationships between personality and
social structure.'[1] At a general level this is a familiar point of debate.
Inkeles (1959), a sociologist, has argued very persuasively that the
perspectives of sociology and psychology are complementary, that
'adequate sociological analysis of many problems is either impossible
or severely limited unless we make explicit use of psychological
theory and data in conjunction with sociological theory and data'
(p. 250).

Naturally each discipline has its own distinctive point of focus,
sociology in the structure and functioning of social systems and
psychology in that of the individual; and some areas of human
knowledge and experience are relatively more susceptible to the one
form of analysis than to the other. But social class in particular, once
we get beyond statistical mapping operations, takes us into the area
of *personality* and requires an interdisciplinary approach. Instead, the
specialisation of research workers has provided us with merely a
series of limited snapshots. As Himmelweit (1966) has put it:

> Quite often the sociologists and social psychologists study the
> same phenomenon, but do so from different points of view; this
> results, in the one instance, in an oversimplified model of
> motivation and learning and, in the other, in a neglect of a
> subtler understanding of the way in which social forces impinge
> upon the individual's outlook and behaviour (p. 25).[2]

The case for greatly extending the collaboration of sociologists and
psychologists in social science research (and, perhaps more important,

1. An alternative approach but one involving major methodological problems
might be called the 'autobiographical', and is represented, for example, by
Goldman (1968).
2. See also Lipset and Bendix, 1959; Inkeles, 1964; Wiseman, 1964; Lavin, 1965;
Westwood, 1967; Lawton, 1968; Young and McGeeney, 1968; and in particular
Swift, 1965, who offers an illuminating commentary on the conflicting viewpoints
of sociology and psychology, and on the need for interdisciplinary enquiry.

for a broader-based training for each) would seem to be a very strong one. Indeed, it seems unlikely that our knowledge of the complex relationship of family, class and education can advance substantially without it.

REFERENCES

ABRAMS, M. (1964), 'Rewards of education', *New Society*, **4**, no. 93, 26.
BARBER, B. (1961), 'Social class differences in educational life-chances', *Teachers College Record*, **63**, no. 2, 102–13.
BERKOWITZ, L. (1964), *The Development of Motives and Values in the Child*, Basic Books.
BERNSTEIN, B. B. (1965), 'A socio-linguistic approach to social learning', *Penguin Survey of the Social Sciences*, ed. J. Gould, Penguin Books, pp. 144–68.
BLAUG, M., PESTON, M. H. and ZIDERMAN, A. (1967), *The Utilisation of Educated Manpower in Industry*, Oliver & Boyd.
BLYTH, W. A. L. (1967), *English Primary Education*, Routledge, vol. 2.
BOOCOCK, S. S. (1966), 'Toward a sociology of learning: a selective review of existing research', *Sociology of Education*, **39**, no. 1, 1–45.
CARO, F. G. (1966), 'Social class and attitudes of youth relevant for the realisation of adult goals', *Social Forces*, **44**, 492–8.
CARTER, M. (1966), *Into Work*, Penguin Books.
CENTRAL ADVISORY COUNCIL FOR EDUCATION (ENGLAND) (C.A.C.E.) (1954), *Early Leaving*, H.M.S.O.; C.A.C.E. (1959), *15 to 18* (Crowther Report), H.M.S.O.; C.A.C.E. (1967), *Children and their Primary Schools* (Plowden Report), H.M.S.O.
COMMITTEE ON HIGHER EDUCATION (1963), *Higher Education* (Robbins Report), H.M.S.O.
COOMBS, P. H. (1968), *The World Educational Crisis: A systems analysis*, New York, O.U.P.
DOUGLAS, J. W. B. (1964), *The Home and the School*, MacGibbon & Kee.
DOUGLAS, J. W. B., ROSS, J. M. and SIMPSON, W. R. (1968), *All Our Future*, Peter Davies.
EGGLESTON, S. J. (1967), 'Some environmental correlates of extended secondary education in England', *Comparative Education*, **3**, no. 2, 85–99.
ELDER, G. H. (1965), 'Life opportunity and personality: some consequences of stratified secondary education in "Great Britain" ', *Sociology of Education*, **38**, no. 3, 173–202.
EMPEY, L. T. (1956), 'Social class and occupational aspiration: a comparison of absolute and relative measurement', *American Sociological Review*, **21**, 703–9.
FRASER, E. (1959), *Home Environment and the School*, U.L.P.
GOLDMAN, R. J., ed. (1968), *Breakthrough*, Routledge.
GOLDTHORPE, J. H., LOCKWOOD, D., BECHHOFER, F. and PLATT, J. (1967), ' The affluent worker and the thesis of embourgeoisement: Some preliminary research findings', *Sociology*, **1**, no. 1, 11–31.
GOLDTHORPE, J. H., LOCKWOOD, D., BECHHOFER, F. and PLATT, J. (1968a), *The Affluent Worker: Industrial Attitudes and Behaviour*, Cambridge U.P.
GOLDTHORPE, J. H., LOCKWOOD, D., BECHHOFER, F. and PLATT, J. (1968b), *The Affluent Worker: Political Attitudes and Behaviour*, Cambridge U.P.
GRAY, J. L. and MOSHINSKY, P. (1938), 'Ability and opportunity in English Education', *Political Arithmetic*, eds., L. Hogben *et al.*, Allen & Unwin.
HERRIOTT, R. E. and ST JOHN, N. H. (1966), *Social Class and the Urban School*, Wiley.
HIMMELWEIT, H. T. (1966), 'Social background, intelligence and school structure: an interaction analysis', *Genetic and Environmental Factors in Human Ability*, eds. J. E. Meade and A. S. Parkes, Oliver & Boyd, pp. 24–41.

HYMAN, H. H. (1953), 'The value systems of different classes: A social psychological contribution to the analysis of stratification', *Class Status and Power*, eds. R. Bendix and S. M. Lipset, Glencoe, Free Press, pp. 426–42.

INKELES, A. (1959), 'Personality and social structure', *Sociology Today*, eds. R. K. Merton, L. Broom and L. Cottrell, Harper & Row, vol. 2, 249–76.

INKELES, A. (1964), *What is Sociology?* Prentice-Hall.

JACKSON, B. and MARSDEN, D. (1962), *Education and the Working Class*, Routledge.

JAYASURIYA, D. L. (1960), quoted in Sugarman (1966), see below.

KAHL, J. A. (1953), 'Educational and occupational aspirations of "common man" boys', *Harvard Educational Review*, 23, no. 3.

KAHL, J. A. (1957), *The American Class Structure*, Holt, Rinehart & Winston.

KAHL, J. A. (1965), 'Some measurements of achievement orientation', *American Journal of Sociology*, 70, 669–81.

KATZ, F. M. (1964), 'The meaning of success: some differences in value systems of social classes', *Journal of Social Psychology*, 62, 141–8.

KLEIN, J. (1965), *Samples from English Cultures*, Routledge, 2 vols.

KRAUSS, I. (1964), 'Sources of educational aspirations among working-class youth', *American Sociological Review*, 29, 867–79.

LAVIN, D. E. (1965), *The Prediction of Academic Performance*, Wiley.

LAWTON, D. (1968), *Social Class, Language and Education*, Routledge.

LINDSAY, K. (1926), *Social Progress and Educational Waste*, Routledge.

LIPSET, S. M. and BENDIX, R. (1967), *Social Mobility in Industrial Society*, Univ. of California Press.

LOCKWOOD, D. (1966), 'Sources of variation in working-class images of society', *Sociological Review*, 14, no. 3, 249–67.

MARSDEN, D. (1967), 'School, class and the parent's dilemma', *Class*, ed. R. Mabey, Blond.

MATZA, D. and SYKES, G. M. (1961), 'Juvenile delinquency and subterranean values', *American Sociological Review*, 26, 712–19.

MAYS, J. B. (1962), *Education and the Urban Child*, Liverpool University Press.

MILLER, H. (1965), *Rich Man Poor Man*, New York, Signet Books.

PAREEK, U. (1968), 'A motivational paradigm of development', *Journal of Social Issues*, 24, no. 2, 115–22.

RAYNOR, J. M. (1969), *The Middle Class*, Longmans.

ROBBINS REPORT (1963). *See* Committee on Higher Education.

RODMAN, H. (1963), 'The lower-class value stretch', *Social Forces*, 42, 205–15.

ROGOFF, N. (1961), 'Local social structure and educational selection', *Education, Economy and Society*, eds. A. H. Halsey *et al.*, Glencoe, Free Press.

ROSE, G. (1968), *The Working Class*, Longmans.

ROSEN, B. C. (1956), 'The achievement syndrome: a psychocultural dimension of social stratification', *American Sociological Review*, 21, 203–11.

SCHOOLS COUNCIL (1968), *Young School Leavers*, H.M.S.O.

SEXTON, P. C. (1961), *Education and Income*, New York, Viking Press.

SIMPSON, R. L. (1962), 'Parental influence, anticipatory socialisation, and social mobility', *American Sociological Review*, 27, 517–22.

SUGARMAN, B. N. (1966), 'Social class and values as related to achievement and conduct in school', *Sociological Review*, 14, no. 3, 287–301.

SVALASTOGA, K. (1965), *Social Differentiation*, New York, David McKay.

SWIFT, D. F. (1965), 'Educational psychology, sociology and the environment: a controversy at cross-purposes', *British Journal of Sociology*, 16, no. 4, 334–50.

SWIFT, D. F. (1967), 'Family environment and 11+ success: some basic predictors', *British Journal of Psychology*, 37, 10–21.

SWIFT, D. F. (1968), 'Social class and educational adaptation', *Educational Research in Britain*, ed. H. J. Butcher, University of London Press.

THORNDIKE, R. L. (1951), 'Community variables as predictors of intelligence and academic achievement', *Journal of Educational Psychology*, 42, no. 6, 321–38.

TUMIN, M. M. (1967), *Social Stratification*, Prentice-Hall.

WESTWOOD, L. J. (1967), 'The role of the teacher—II', *Educational Research*, 10, no. 1, 21–37.

WILLMOTT, P. (1963), *The Evolution of a Community*, Routledge.

WILSON, A. B. (1959), 'Residential segregation of social classes and aspirations of high school boys', *American Sociological Review*, 24, 836–45.

WILSON, R. (1963), *Difficult Housing Estates*, Tavistock.

WISEMAN, S. (1964), *Education and Environment*, Manchester University Press.

WISEMAN, S. (1967), 'The Manchester Survey', Central Advisory Council for Education (England), *Children and their Primary Schools*, H.M.S.O., vol. 2, pp. 347–400.

YOUNG, M. and MCGEENEY, P. J. (1968), *Learning Begins at Home*, Routledge.

ZIGLER, E. (1968), *Social Class and the Socialisation Process*, New York, Teachers College, Columbia University (cyclostyled).

PART TWO   Demographic studies

2

Social class factors in educational achievement*

Jean Floud

This paper was prepared for an international conference called by the Organisation for European Economic Cooperation in 1961, to discuss the mobilisation of talent in industrial societies. It focuses on educational opportunity in postwar Britain, outlining the marked social class variations in access to grammar schools and universities primarily in quantitative terms, but also in terms of the quality of home environment and of the relationship of the middle-class expectations of teachers and of the capacity of working-class pupils to respond to them. The paper's demographic analysis is developed in Chapter 3 and its subcultural implications are examined in detail in Parts Three, Four and Five. But as an authoritative statement by a leading postwar sociologist that is still valid in all essentials, it forms a reference point for studies in this field.

The best contribution that the educational system can make to the economic problem is to send forward recruits to the labour force, potentially mobile, with or without further education as may be necessary, within the widest possible range of occupations, whether by guidance, direction, or merely in response to the prevailing pattern of economic incentive.

To state the problem thus abstractly is to understate the difficulties. It is safe to say that the greater the degree of industrialisation, the more are young people limited in their choice of employment by their educational attainments and the more difficult it is for adults to move

* Reprinted from A. H. Halsey, ed., *Ability and Educational Opportunity*, Paris: O.E.C.D., 1961, pp. 34–7, 91–109, by kind permission of the author and the publisher.

outside the range of occupations for which their formal educational attainments equip them. Quite apart, therefore, from the primary difficulty of ensuring that ability translates itself into the appropriate educational achievement, it is important to devise educational arrangements which will not gratuitously reinforce this endemic tendency to rigidity in the supply of labour in a modern economy.

We may begin with the fundamental problem, which we may express in this way: how may differences in educational performance be reduced to differences of natural endowment? Some pupils will always do better than others, but it is desirable that the order of inequality should be, as it were, a natural one, unmarred by factitious and irrelevant social differences. No matter that such an objective is 'only an ideal' and must in practice remain for ever unattainable; the important thing is that it should guide policy and that we should actively seek to approach it.

In all modern western societies, the phenomenon of *social class* is a prime source of, so to speak, 'unnatural' inequalities in education; that is to say, of inequalities which do not rest on differences of endowment.[1] It is the purpose of this paper to explore the manifold ways in which it makes its obstructive influence felt, and to suggest practical measures for the consideration of policy-makers and administrators who, because they believe in the natural right of individuals to education, or because they want 'talent' to find its own level in the labour market, are anxious to bring ability, educational opportunity and performance into something like perfect relationship.

Social class interferes with this relationship in a number of ways: at any given level of ability, it is both cause and consequence of inequalities of educational opportunity, in the sense of unequal chances of access to educational institutions or facilities; or, again at a given level of ability, it may influence the volume and direction of pupils' energies and, hence, their educational output; or, finally and more radically, it may affect the very structure of ability itself. It follows that it is susceptible of investigation and amenable to policy in very varying degrees. Until 1945, roughly speaking, the problem of social class in education was seen, by social investigators and policy-makers alike, primarily as a *barrier to opportunity*. The problem was an institutional one: how to secure equality of access for children of

---

1. Other important sources of such inequalities readily suggest themselves: e.g. sex, geographical locality, ethnic or religious affiliation. To the extent that they are related to the more complex phenomenon of social class they are touched upon in this paper: some of the others were dealt with elsewhere in the conference.

comparable ability, regardless of their social origins, to institutions of secondary and higher education designed for, and still used in the main by, the offspring of the superior social classes. In so far as social class was seen to influence educational *performance* the problem was conceived of as a material one: how to mitigate the handicaps of poverty, malnutrition and overcrowding by using the schools as social agencies—by distributing free milk and meals to necessitous children and developing the school medical services. Only in the post-war period has the continuing attempt to democratise secondary and higher education in unfamiliar conditions of full employment and widespread prosperity confronted us with the need to formulate the problem more subtly and to see social class as a profound influence on the *educability* of children.

Here we are not concerned with snobbery in education—with invidious social differences in school or overt social bias in selection procedures—but with the existence of fundamental differences as between the social classes in ways of life, values, attitudes and aspirations, as well as in material circumstances. So far as education is concerned, these class differences, which reflect a social distribution of probabilities in the life experiences of children of different social origins, can be translated as probabilities that they will respond differently to school, even at the same level of measured intelligence. The important thing to know is, first, what are the probabilities of response to schooling as we now organise it or offer it, and second, within what limits can we change or redistribute these probabilities given defined social, political or economic aims and certain resources. I will try to elucidate these points and illustrate them as well as I can, in the main from British experience.

SOCIAL CLASS AND EDUCATIONAL OPPORTUNITY

The educational systems of most European countries have grown up in the image of out-moded social-class systems. That is to say, they reflect a stage of economic and social development in which education was a corollary, rather than a determinant, of social-class position. Various types of independent and publicly-maintained schools have grown up to serve the different social classes and have developed distinctive and restrictive relations with the universities and with the occupational structure. These relations have been modified by the democratising tendencies of recent years. Both in France and in England, for example, the social composition of the traditionally middle-class grammar-type secondary schools has been transformed since 1945.[1] In both countries the way has been opened up for working-class children into the universities and the liberal professions, as well as into the higher ranks of industry and commerce; the social role of the secondary schools as agents of interchange between the classes (social mobility) has become of considerable importance.

But in neither country was the school system designed for the purpose of selecting and promoting talent; and there are a number of difficulties in adapting its aims and organisation to the new task of occupational and social selection thrust upon it by the twin pressures of national economic need and parental anxieties on behalf of their children's future in the labour market. There is no parity of industrial or social status among secondary schools of different types. Only a minority of schools in either country retains pupils for advanced work to the age of eighteen or over, and has a direct connection with the universities and other institutions of full-time further education. These are selective schools, either because they charge fees, or because public provision of this type of schooling is limited and places must be competed for, and are awarded to the most able candidates.

The selective schools are the prime source of recruits for all non-manual occupations and they have a virtual monopoly of entry to the high-ranking professional and managerial occupations. That the supply of trained talent should thus be, to all intents and purposes, dependent on separately organised schools of high social and educational status, catering for a selected minority of able pupils, in itself makes for rigidity.

For historical reasons the provision of selective school places varies considerably as between localities and these differences are associated with differences in the social composition of local population.[2] Broadly speaking, the higher the proportion of non-manual workers in the local population, the larger the proportion of the eleven-year-old age group admitted to grammar schools. The relationship of the provision of places to the distribution of ability is loose to the point of arbitrariness. Age groups of children at the eleven-plus in different localities may show similar proportions with I.Q.s of 130+ but

1. See Christiane Peyre, 'L'origine sociale des élèves de l'enseignement secondaire en France', pp. 6–34 in *Ecole et Société*, ed. Pierre Naville, Paris, 1959; Jean Floud, A. H. Halsey, and F. M. Martin, *Social Class and Educational Opportunity*, Heinemann, 1956.
2. In England the provision ranges from 10 per cent to 50 per cent of the age-group; a comparable degree of geographical inequality is illustrated for France with the aid of a more complex index by Christiane Peyre, *op. cit.*

marked discrepancies in the proportions admitted to grammar school. Since these discrepancies are related to the social composition of the age group the effect is to make inequality of opportunity cumulative, with the bizarre result that the less rigorous the selection (the larger the proportion admitted to grammar schools) the greater the rate of success (the larger the proportion of those admitted staying at school for advanced work and proceeding to universities).

The very need to select for entry to secondary schools organised separately makes for rigidity. The supply of places in the selective secondary schools is bound to be relatively inelastic, and quite apart from short-run and localised changes in demand brought about, for instance, by migration, the task of keeping pace with long-term demographic fluctuations is a very formidable one. The result is that relative 'class chances' of access to selective schools and the universities to which they lead are not easily equalised or even greatly improved in relation to each other.

In France, a leap in the numbers of working-class children entering the secondary schools, which resulted in the quadrupling of their proportionate strength in the annual entry between 1936–7 and 1943–4, has been followed by a relative slackening in their contribution, which after 1946 remained stable at about 12 per cent in face of a greatly increased total intake to the schools.[1] Data for England and Wales are fuller than for France, and the difficulties better illustrated from the experience of attempts over half a century to democratise the traditionally selective system of secondary and higher education. That the social composition of the secondary grammar schools has been severely modified by the progressive opening of all places to competition, can be seen from the following rough comparison of the occupations followed by the fathers of boys entering them before and after the Second World War.

TABLE 2.1. *Social origins of boys entering secondary grammar schools before and after 1944. England and Wales.*

Occupations of fathers	In percentage	
	1930–41	1946–51
Professional and managerial	40	26
Clerical and other non-manual	20	18
Manual	40	56

Source: Prewar figures from D. V. Glass, ed., *Social Mobility in Britain*, Routledge, 1954, Table VII, p. 129. Postwar figures from *15–18* (the Crowther Report), vol. 2, H.M.S.O. 1960, Table X, p. 130.

1. See Christiane Peyre, *op. cit.*

Comparable information is not available for the universities, but the changes there too have been marked, although on a smaller scale.

However, although the proportion of grammar school pupils and of university students coming from working-class homes has grown considerably, the percentage of all children at this social level who pass into the grammar schools and universities remains small; and changes in the relative 'class-chances' for admission to these institutions have been much less striking than might appear from the changes that have taken place in their social composition. The figures in Table 2.2 illustrate these points.

The postwar increase by 50 per cent in the proportionate attendance at selective secondary schools and universities is shown in column 3. From columns 1 and 2, however, it appears that while the proportion of the relevant age-cohorts of working-class boys passing into the grammar schools has increased by 50 per cent since the war, the figure is still very low—rather less than one in six as compared with nearly one in two of children from non-manual homes. At the university level, the chances of working-class boys are virtually unchanged, although those of boys from other families have more than doubled. Only one working-class boy in fifty proceeded to the universities in the postwar period, as compared with one in five of boys from other families.

It should be made clear that these trends cannot be accounted for by overt social bias in the selection process. There is conclusive evidence[1] to show that awards of places in grammar schools and universities are made today (as they were not before 1945) to children of all classes on equal intellectual terms; that is to say that the social distribution of available places closely reflects the social distribution of measured intelligence. It is nevertheless not the case that the differences in overall 'class chances', revealed in Table 2.2, can be attributed simply to social class differences in measured intelligence, well attested though these be. They must be accounted for in part by the pressure of population in the postwar years, and in part by the wide local variations in grammar school provision, associated with variations in the social composition of the population. That social-class differences in ability as measured by intelligence tests are by no means alone responsible for the existing social-class inequalities of educational opportunity is convincingly demonstrated in the section of the Crowther Report, dealing with the distribution of latent ability.

1. Cf. Jean Floud, A. H. Halsey, and F. M. Martin, *op. cit.*

TABLE 2.2. *Changes in the social distribution of educational opportunity. Secondary and university education of boys reaching the age of eleven before and after the Second World War, in England and Wales.*

		Percentage attending		
		Working class[1]	Other[2]	All
1931–40	Independent efficient or grammar[3]	9·8	38·9	14·7
	University	1·7	8·5	3·7
1946–51	Independent efficient or grammar[3]	14·5	48·5	23·0
	University	1·6[4]	19·2[4]	5·6[5]

Source: Figures for national samples of boys reaching the age of eleven, 1931–40, derived from D. V. Glass, ed., *op. cit.* Tables 1 and 2, pp. 18–19; those for the 1946–51 group from *15–18* (Crowther Report); Tables 3a and 9, pp. 122 and 130 respectively. I am indebted to my colleague, Simon Pratt (Ford Unit for Research in the Economics and Administration of Education, University of London Institute of Education) for the corrected percentages of those attending universities.

1. i.e. Sons of fathers following manual occupations, whether skilled, semi- or unskilled.
2. i.e. Sons of fathers following non-manual occupations, whether professional, managerial or other 'white-collar'.
3. Independent secondary grammar schools (both private proprietary and 'public' endowed schools) inspected by the Ministry and certified 'efficient'.
4. The class distributions in columns 1 and 2 are based on the findings of the National Service survey reported by the Crowther Committee (*15–18*, vol. 2, Table 3a, p. 121). The chances of working-class boys are probably over-estimated and those of other boys under-estimated in the figures given there, owing to differences of practice as between independent and other schools with regard to deferment of military service. The Report states (p. 109) 'Deferment operated heavily throughout all types of school other than the independent efficient schools'. The figures in columns 1 and 2 have been arbitrarily corrected to reduce the error from this source.
5. The overall chance of a boy going to a university is calculated as the number of men of all ages entering universities in the given years, divided by the size of the age-group most likely to correspond—i.e. an average of those reaching the age of 18–20 in those years. Students commencing first diploma courses (about 4·5 per cent of all students) have been excluded. But the figure of 5·6 per cent overall is nevertheless likely to be on the high side, since no account could be taken of the 10 per cent of all students in England and Wales who are recorded in the reports of the University Grants Committee, without distinction of sex, as living outside the United Kingdom. England and Wales are more likely to have a net import than export of men students. However, it is likely that any error is proportionally reflected in the figures in columns 1 and 2.

Table 2.3, compiled from data provided in the Report, shows the social differences in opportunity which prevail in England even as between children at the same general level of ability.

TABLE 2.3.   *Social class differences in the schooling of Army recruits (1956–58) at two levels of ability.*

	Father's occupation									
	Professional and managerial		Clerical and other non-manual		Skilled manual		Semi-skilled manual		Unskilled manual	
	Group		Group		Group		Group		Group	
Secondary schooling	I	2	I	2	I	2	I	2	I	2
	%	%	%	%	%	%	%	%	%	%
Independent or grammar	89·4	58·6	86·8	32·4	76·0	22·1	77·0	18·0	55·0	14·0
Technical	6·8	10·5	7·5	14·2	10·8	11·0	9·0	11·3	22·2	12·3
All selective	96·2	69·1	94·3	46·6	86·8	53·1	86·0	29·3	77·2	26·3

Source: Compiled from Table 2a, *15–18* (the Crowther Report), vol. 2, p. 120.

In the second order of ability, 58·6 per cent of the Army recruits in the sample whose fathers were of the professional and managerial class had attended grammar or independent schools. At the same level of ability, only 22 per cent of the sons of skilled workers had done so —and it is not the case, as might be hoped, that more of them had attended technical schools instead. Even in the first order of ability, the social differences in schooling are marked. It seems that the post-war movement of educational reform has brought the abler sons of the skilled working class into the grammar and technical schools. But ability and opportunity are still in imperfect relationship, with social class as the intervening variable.

ABILITY, SOCIAL CLASS AND EDUCATIONAL PERFORMANCE

We come now to the second important aspect of the relations between social class and education—its influence, at any given level of ability, on the volume and direction of pupils' energies and consequently on their output or performance in school.

It must be admitted at the outset that although the relations between ability, social class and educational performance are known in broad terms they have not yet been precisely worked out. In the first place, we do not yet know how the relations hold as the variables fluctuate. McClelland remarks pertinently in the course of an attack on the supposed linearity of the relationship of intelligence-test scores to school performance:[1] 'Let us admit that morons cannot do good school work, but what evidence is there that intelligence is not a threshold type of variable; that once a person has a certain minimal level of intelligence, his performance beyond that point is uncorrelated with his ability?' And he urges 'the desirability of plotting carefully the relationship of ability-test scores to performance criteria *over the entire range* in order to check for threshold, deceleration, or other curvi-linear relationships'. We evidently need a thorough investigation of the relationships between these three variables throughout the whole range of each.

In the second place, in so far as we have established these relations, we do not as yet know what they might mean. What are the differences of family environment underlying the closer dependence of school performance on home background than on I.Q.? The influence on performance of two features of the family—its size and socio-economic status—has been repeatedly and conclusively demonstrated. A brief discussion of these will illustrate the state of our knowledge.

Class as a socio-economic handicap

There is a well-known positive relationship between socio-economic status, as judged by father's occupation, and intelligence-test scores; but there is a significantly closer relationship between father's occupation and success in school. This may express anything from the crude impact of gross material or economic handicap to imponderable, cultural determinants of motivation.

Absolute poverty needs no discussion. Fees cannot be paid, nor can adolescent earnings be foregone by the family; malnutrition and overcrowding in the home are obvious impediments to learning. General social reform is the only answer to these conditions; they cannot be lived down in school. However, they need not be exacerbated by allowing the traditional association of poor homes with poor schools to persist; and they may be mitigated in the case of the small minority of talented children who survive their circumstances or rise above them, if scholarships and maintenance allowances are generously awarded. Even with such a programme of educational aid, however,

1. D. McClelland *et al.*, *Talent and Society*, New York, Van Nostrand, 1959, pp. 12–14.

the authorities must be prepared for wastage of talent, in the shape of under-achievement in the primary schools and a more or less substantial 'refusal-rate' in respect of places offered in secondary schools and universities to the able children of impoverished families.

Relative poverty or material hardship is less easy to define and deal with, mainly because the question of incentives enters in once a certain crippling level of absolute poverty is left behind. Income probably behaves as a threshold variable; at a certain low level it acts as a direct impediment to a child's educational chances, even where parents are favourably disposed; at a certain high level it liberates, making it possible for parents to implement without difficulty their interest in their children's education. At any level between these extremes, however, it does not act as an independent variable at all. It follows that in circumstances such as those prevailing in Britain, where absolute poverty, at any rate among the families of young children, is at a minimum, but where an income of any size is obtained by the fathers of only a fraction of any age-group, the attitudes of parents and children towards education are of prime importance in the under-development of talent and should be deliberately cultivated if an improved educational harvest is desired.

La famille éducogene

Parental attitudes are the principal ingredient in the subculture which a social class represents from the point of view of the school. They are at once symbol and source of social differences in the educational performance of children at the same general level of ability.

The French have coined the apt phrase *la famille éducogene* to describe families providing for their children an educative environment including, in particular, supporting social and intellectual pressures in the same direction as those exerted by the schools. For obvious reasons, such families are proportionally more numerous at the top of the social scale, and it is possible also that they are qualitatively superior as well; but the notion is to some extent relative.

At any given social level, *la famille éducogène* as so far identified by investigators, need not be more prosperous, though it tends to be smaller than average; it is likely that the parents will have had some education beyond the compulsory minimum; the mother before marriage may have followed an occupation superior to that of the father; and the climate of opinion in the home will be educationally favourable by such elementary criteria as willingness to visit the school and talk with teachers, and a knowledgeable approach to educational facilities. The children of such families will tend to be more successful on average, both as regards competition for entry to selected schools and universities, and as regards propensity to stay the course once admitted.

Table 2.4 illustrates these points. It is true that such figures are open to the objection that they merely reflect differences of intelligence among parents which are adequate to account for the different success rates of their children in the secondary selection examination. But investigations which have taken intelligence as well as family environment into consideration in trying to account for differences in school performance, show the closer dependence of the latter on family environment.

These findings must cause one to take another look at the correlation between socio-economic status and school performance. It may be differently expressed as a social distribution of *familles éducogenes*— by saying that such families are proportionally more numerous with each step up the social scale. The question then arises: what factors make for a change in this distribution? (Under what conditions can we expect a weakening of the correlation between socio-economic status and school performance?) Before turning to this question we must briefly note the bearing of family size on educational performance.

Family size and educational performance
It is a well-established fact that children from small families *at all social levels* tend, on the average, to perform better both in intelligence tests and at school. There seems to be little doubt that, as a recent investigator put it, 'the presence of a large number of siblings (or some factor related to it) is an adverse element as far as educational attainment is concerned, quite apart from the low intelligence usually associated with large families'.[2] This relationship obviously has its economic aspect even in the Welfare State. It has also been suggested, more subtly, that the child of a large family learns the verbal skills, so decisive both in intelligence tests and in school performance, less effectively from his peers than does the child of a small family from adults, and carries the handicap at least until the age of eleven.[3] But

1. E. Fraser, *Home Environment and the School*, University of London Press, 1959. See also A. Girard, 'Mobilité sociale et dimension de famille; enquête dans les lycées et les facultés', *Population*, 1951, pp. 103–24.
2. E. Fraser, *op. cit.*
3. J. D. Nisbet, *Family Environment: A Direct Effect of Family Size on Intelligence*, London, Eugenics Society, 1953.

TABLE 2.4. *Awards of places in secondary grammar schools in relation to various features of children's home background in an English locality, 1952.*

	Awards of grammar school places to children of fathers following various occupations							
	Skilled manual		*Unskilled manual*		*Non-manual*		*All 11-year-olds, 1952*	
Features of home background	No. of children	% Award	No. of children	% Award	No. of children	% Award	No. of children	% Award
1. *Income* of chief wage earner rated:								
High[1]	378	19	81	9	208	34	667	22
Low	213	16	215	13	194	31	622	20
2. *Father's education:*								
(a) Secondary:								
Selective	82	21	23	13	205	42	310	34
Other	541	16	286	12	231	24	1058	17
(b) Further:								
Some	160	26	27	22	223	38	410	40
None	472	14	286	11	244	28	1002	16
3. *Parents' attitudes towards education:*								
(a) Discussed child's education with primary teacher:								
Yes	268	27	95	22	287	38	650	31
No	364	10	217	7	179	20	760	12
(b) Preference expressed for:								
Grammar school	304	29	135	21	322	47	761	31
Modern school	328	6	178	4	145	19	651	8
(c) School leaving age preferred:								
18+	145	35	44	27	188	49	377	41
16–17	250	16	102	17	188	28	540	21
15 (compulsory minimum)	226	6	159	3	81	7	466	5
4. *Family size:*								
1–2 children	277	21	122	17	255	35	654	26
3–4 children	245	12	126	11	169	31	540	18
5+ children	108	17	64	2	42	21	214	13

Source: Jean Floud, A. H. Halsey, and F. M. Martin, *Social Class and Educational Opportunity*, Heinemann, 1956, pp. 104–7.

1. The definition of 'high' income varied according to social class status:
    Non-manual: £10 per week or over.   Manual: £7.10 per week or over.

there must be more to the matter than this. Quite apart from class differences in strength of the influence of family size on children's verbal development, which have not been investigated but are probably considerable, there is some evidence to the effect that the educational disadvantages of a large family are less marked for the children of Catholic parents, even at the bottom of the social scale.[1] If generally true, this would cast doubt on the notion that the significance of a small family for educational performance should be sought in some distinctive quality of educational value in the environment it provides. It would lend colour to the suggestion that for children at a given social level, relative size of family is, generally speaking, symptomatic of parental attitudes and family pressures favourable to a child's educational progress—the best index, in fact, of *la famille éducogène* in all cases where religious principles do not prohibit the expression of these favourable attitudes in family limitation.

We thus arrive at the suggestion that once the grosser material handicaps are eliminated and parents' attitudes come into their own as independent variables, the size of the family, rather than its socio-economic status, emerges as potentially the most important single indication of the educative quality of home environment. However, a frontal attack on the problem of the determinants of family size at different social levels is notoriously difficult. We must be content in the short run to examine some of the more accessible differences of family culture, of which size is for the time being a general indication, and of which parents' attitudes towards their children's education and subsequent occupations are a particular manifestation.[2]

SOCIAL CLASS AND THE DEMAND FOR EDUCATION

Here we return to the question raised above of the conditions under which the correlation between socio-economic status and success in school may be weakened by the spread of *la famille éducogène*. Parents' attitudes towards education are, in the short run, class-typed. What is the effect of social policy on these attitudes? Do 'middle-class' educational attitudes spread hand-in-hand with 'middle-class' prosperity? To some extent this will happen, especially since the spread of prosperity is bound up with a scale and pace of economic

1. Jean Floud, A. H. Halsey, and F. M. Martin, *op. cit.*
2. For some indication of the position in the United States, see J. A. Kahl, 'Educational and occupational aspirations of "common man" boys', *Harvard Educational Review*, Summer, 1953.

development which itself generates a public thirst for educational qualifications. Affluence does not breed *la famille éducogène*, but it provides both incentives and the means for such families to become widespread. Evidence has already been gathered of a postwar transformation of the attitudes of parents in England to their children's education. The Crowther Committee, in its recent report, urges the Government to ride on the crest of this wave of public interest and to raise the school-leaving age to sixteen, noting that parents do not in general allow their children to receive less education than they themselves have had, so that the process of extending educational opportunity is cumulative from one generation to the next.

However, even under conditions in which the demand for education is rising generally, social-class influences may continue to distort the pattern of *effective* demand. Thus, the rising demand from working class families for a selective and extended education for their children, their success in competition for places in the grammar schools in which this demand can be met, and the upthrust of advanced courses in the secondary modern schools catering overwhelmingly for working-class children, are common-places of the English educational scene. Yet the fact remains that there is quite severe class-based wastage and early-leaving from these grammar schools.[1] Table 2.5 illustrates this.

TABLE 2.5. *Contrasts in the occupational composition of the grammar school leavers up to, and over, 16.*

	School composition	
Parental occupational group	Leavers up to 16 %	Leavers at 17 and 18 %
Professional and managerial	17	39
Clerical and other non-manual	17	20
Skilled manual	51	34
Semiskilled manual	9	5
Unskilled manual	6	2
Total = 100%	863	579

Source: 15–18 (Crowther Report), vol. 2, p. 132.

1. For relevant evidence of a comparable situation see A. Girard, 'L'enquête nationale sur l'orientation et la sélection des enfants d'âge scolaire', *Population*, 4, 1954.

HOMES AND SCHOOLS AND THE PROBLEM OF EDUCABILITY

The social as distinct from the purely academic character of the process of attrition at the secondary stage which is illustrated in Table 2.5 is well established. Thus, for instance, it has been strikingly demonstrated that changes in the rank order of children on entry to the English grammar school are not random but are systematically related to their social-class origins, so that the proportion of children in the top one-third of the performance hierarchy who are drawn from working-class families falls from about two-thirds on entry to around one-third at the end of the seven-year school course.[1]

It is important to realise, however, that social selection disguised as academic selection is a process at work in all schools. By the time children reach the threshold of secondary education at the age of eleven, those drawn from certain social groups have as a whole already begun to outstrip scholastically those from families at the other end of the scale, and the same process is continued among those selected for grammar schools during their time there.

It is not merely that children from the higher social classes are more intelligent than others (in the sense that on average they score better in tests of intelligence). Table 2.5 reflects the further striking fact that improvement in school performance between eleven and sixteen within the highly select group of grammar school pupils, which raises many from the bottom group on entry to the top group on completion of the course, is most common among the children of professional and managerial workers; while the corresponding deterioration which causes many placed in the top group on selection to fall to the lower group on completion is most common among the children of semi- and unskilled workers.[2]

This seems to indicate a problem of social assimilation. The grammar schools grew up to serve the middle classes, and although before 1945 a highly selected minority of able working-class children was satisfactorily assimilated, the much larger postwar contingents have proved difficult. But American experience, essentially similar, but less well defined in the context of a non-selective school system, makes it clear that the problem is not specific but general, and must be thought of in broader terms.

We select the most likely candidates for success in the way of life that our schools represent, and we know something, although not as much as we need to know, about the kind of families which produce

1. *Early Leaving*, H.M.S.O., 1954.
2. *Ibid.*

children who are, as it were, apt for success in schools as we now organise them. But when we are confronted with children of proven initial capacity, as measured by whatever standards we use in selecting them, who in the event fail 'to give teacher what he wants', we are brought up against our ignorance of the fundamental conditions of success in our schools. We need to ask ourselves, what exactly does teacher want, and how far are his demands justifiable, given certain educational, social, political or economic assumptions and aims?

'What teacher wants' can be thought of quite explicitly in terms of curriculum content and classroom skills—Latin, say, or verbal and arithmetical facility. But it must also be thought of in more subtle terms if we are to understand the processes of social selection in education. Teachers may take for granted and find it reasonable to demand of all children the social equipment with which the average middle-class child tends to come to school; a certain capacity to assume responsibility, a relative independence of mind and breadth of interests. They may demand assumptions about life on the part of their pupils which are in fact 'middle-class' assumptions; such as that life is one long progress towards ever deferred gratifications; that the present is always at a discount and the future a premium; that one must have always a career rather than a job; that the popular pleasures purveyed by the mass media are at best worthless and at worst sinful.

Schools, in fact, make all sorts of tacit social and cultural demands on children to which they are not all equipped to respond, and it is worth making the point that the tendency for the gap between the demands and assumptions of the school and the skills and assumptions that the children bring with them is widening. This is partly because the social composition of our secondary schools is becoming increasingly representative of the population at large and they contain a substantial minority, in some areas a majority, of pupils from working-class homes. It is also because the effect of current competitive pressures is to load examination syllabi and push minimum standards of acceptable performance ever higher. Every year the dice are loaded more and more heavily against children from underprivileged homes and in favour of those who come with an initial set of cultural advantages in the shape of parental supports and pressures, which are in the same direction as those which the school expects them to be. The children from culturally impoverished homes can spend today less and less time on the pursuits which might conceivably mitigate the effects of their impoverished background, and the schools have at least two jobs to do in present circumstances. They have not merely to instruct their pupils up to an ever-rising standard of competence; they have also to tackle for an increasing proportion of their pupils all sorts of educational tasks normally undertaken in a middle-class home by parents with at least some degree of education analogous to, or comparable with, that to which the child aspires or is entitled by virtue of his ability.

If to equalise opportunity in the interests of maximising the flow of talent is the aim of policy, then the implications of our growing understanding of the relations between home and school are very radical—much more radical than was foreseen when governments first began to remedy material defects in children's homes by distributing free milk and meals. As family environments change demographically, economically and culturally, together with the structure of opportunities in the labour market, the organisation of education must respond to the same pressures so that full advantage can be taken of the changing patterns of demand.

The necessary measures may be primarily political and administrative in character—it may be a question of re-organising schooling along 'comprehensive' or 'common school' lines, if it can be shown that this will make for a longer average school life and greater fluidity in the supply of labour. But other measures may be indicated. Thus, recent work on social-class differences in linguistic capacity indicates that the handicap which reflects itself in the poorer average educational performance of working-class children is deeply rooted in the social structure of working-class community and family life.[1] In groups of working-class children, particularly those from semi- and unskilled families, scores on verbal tests are grossly depressed in relation to scores at the higher levels of non-verbal tests. It seems that the very nature of his ability is profoundly influenced by the social environment of the child; and that the linguistic handicap of working-class children becomes a more general intellectual handicap at the secondary stage of education. Successful learning may, therefore, be dependent on different educational measures for children of different backgrounds. Bernstein[2] infers the proposition, for instance, that the more humble the origins of pupils the smaller the optimum number in class. One might also infer the need for financial reallocation as between primary and secondary education so as to make extremely small classes the rule in the early stages of primary education rather

1. Cf. B. Bernstein, 'Social structure, language and learning', *Educational Research*, 3, 3 (June 1961), 163–76.
2. *Ibid.*

than, as is now customary, at the advanced stages of secondary education. A truly radical and single-minded policy might also find a use for boarding-schools.

However, here is not the place to do more than indicate the radical implications of the policy or equality of opportunity in the present state of sociological knowledge. Suffice it to say that it involves us in the need for a most elaborate inspection of what actually goes on in schools, of what the assumptions and values are that have been embodied in their organisation, of what tacit as well as explicit demands they make on pupils. At the same time, we need a very much deeper knowledge than we have now of the social and cultural environment of children of different social origins, and of the extent to which they are correspondingly more or less capable of responding to the intellectual and social demands with which school confronts them.

3

Educational opportunity and social selection in England and Wales: trends and policy implications*

This chapter develops the demographic analysis presented by Mrs Floud in Chapter 2 by bringing together the published evidence from a variety of large-scale postwar enquiries, and providing an overall picture of the way in which social selection operates in the British educational system. Their findings support those of Floud and others, and indicate the long-term persistence of clear social-class variations in educational opportunity and achievement in this country. The authors note the importance of subcultural influences in these social-class differences, but argue that such material factors as school provision are more immediately accessible to change and this could help modify inequalities of opportunity. Some of these recommendations were echoed by the Plowden Report and others are now government policy in secondary education.

John Westergaard
and Alan Little

Educational policy has become a major subject of public debate in England and Wales since the Second World War. Far from resolving conflict, the reforms associated with the Education Act of 1944 provided the starting point of a new, more intensive and sustained series of controversies. The pressures and themes of this debate are reflected in the string of official enquiries undertaken during the past decade. At the same time, the division of labour between these various enquiries has itself testified to those continuing divisions of educational structure and provision which have been a major focus of controversy.

* Reprinted from *Social Objectives in Educational Planning*, Paris, O.E.C.D., 1967, pp. 215–32, by kind permission of the authors and the publisher. An earlier version appeared in the *British Journal of Sociology*, Dec. 1964.

Thus the Crowther Report[1] and its forerunner, *Early Leaving*,[2] were directed mainly to selective secondary education beyond the minimum school leaving age; the Newsom Report[3] to the education of the majority of children in secondary 'modern' schools; the Robbins Report[4] to the advanced education of a small, even though growing, minority in universities, technical colleges and training colleges. Another committee is due to report in 1966 on the age of transfer from primary to secondary education in the public sector; and a Commission was established early in 1966 to advise on means of 'integrating' major schools of the private sector with the publicly maintained schools. Between them, the reports published so far have provided a mass of information about the workings of the educational apparatus. The three first mentioned were sponsored by the same official body. Yet none of these governmental enquiries has been designed to review educational provision as a whole.

Public debate has centred precisely on the divisions within the structure of English education—on inequalities of provision and opportunity; on the contrasts between promise and performance in postwar educational policies. It is these contrasts, too, which form a large part of the background to the current demands for, and official moves towards, some kind of unification of public secondary education in 'comprehensive' schools.

The 1944 Act provided for the establishment of secondary education as a stage in the education of all children, not a style of education reserved for the elect; the abolition of all remaining fees in publicly maintained schools; the raising of the minimum school leaving age to fifteen; and the administrative unification of primary and secondary education in the public sector. In so far as different types of secondary education were provided, these were to enjoy 'parity of esteem'. Access to them, moreover, was to depend on aptitude and parental preference, not on the accidents of social origin and financial capacity. In the event, different types of secondary education were provided by most authorities. The demand for 'parity of esteem' could not be reconciled with the realities of the educational and social structure: with the continuing advantages of money and staff enjoyed by the grammar schools; above all, with the fact that the grammar schools equip their children with the means of access, either directly or

1. Ministry of Education, Central Advisory Council for Education, England, *15 to 18*, H.M.S.O., 1959.
2. *Idem., Early Leaving*, H.M.S.O., 1954.
3. *Idem., Half our Future*, H.M.S.O., 1963.
4. Committee on Higher Education, *Higher Education*, H.M.S.O., 1963.

through higher education, to the middle and upper levels of the adult occupational hierarchy. For all improvements of facilities, staff and syllabi, the post 1944 secondary 'modern' schools supply the labour for the mass of ordinary and low-paid, and for males predominantly manual, occupations; they have therefore continued to play much the same kind of social role as the pre-1944 'senior elementary' schools.[1]

Structural differentiation was thus built into the postwar educational system. The independent schools were left virtually intact by the changes associated with the 1944 Act. And the different channels of public secondary education were directed to different socio-economic levels of the world of work after school. Nevertheless selection for these different channels was intended, in principle, to be blind to differences of social background among the children; to take account only of scholastic ability and hence, by inference, of prospective occupational aptitudes. The forward link between education and destination in adult life was reinforced; the traditional backward link between education and social origin was to be cut—in intention, and with respect to the public (but not the private) sector of education.

Not surprisingly, much of the debate has turned on the question of how far this intention has been realised; how far 'equal opportunity' has been achieved for children of 'equal merit', irrespective of their class of origin. In turn, preoccupation with this question has reflected a variety of concerns: a concern with the efficient utilisation of human resources of talent and skill; a concern with 'fair shares', with the equitable distribution of those educational services which are both scarce and 'profitable' in adult life; and a more general concern with the consequences of educational selection for the overall patterns and trends of social mobility in the society at large. The latter two kinds of concern, closely linked as they are, are accentuated by recognition of the increasing importance of formal education as a prerequisite of

1. For general analyses of the 1944 reforms and their historical and social background, see especially O. Banks, *Parity and Prestige in English Secondary Education*, London, 1955; and D. V. Glass, 'Education and Social Change in Modern England', in M. Ginsberg, ed., *Law and Opinion in England in the Twentieth Century*, Stevens & Sons, 1959 (reprinted in A. H. Halsey *et al.*, eds., *Education, Economy and Society*, Collier–Macmillan, 1961). In our summary characterisation of the divisions within the public sector of secondary education, we have ignored the small number of 'technical' schools, intermediate between grammar and modern schools. We have also ignored comprehensive schools, which were too few to be taken into account during the period to which our analysis relates, and the current plans for which take such a diversity of forms that no firm predictions about their future character and role can as yet be made.

occupational achievement, and therefore as an 'avenue' of social mobility.

Much information is, of course, available on class differences in access to education in postwar Britain. But the evidence from different sources has not yet been brought together to provide an overall picture of the operation of social selection in education, from school to university; and at the same time to allow a comparison with prewar years.[1] It is the purpose of this paper to do that, and only that. No new data are reported. The calculations are based entirely on published information. And their scope and accuracy reflect not only the limitations inherent in the original data, but also those which arise from the attempt to use diverse data in combination. Classifications in the source material do not always fully coincide; assumptions have had to be made on certain points where direct information is incomplete; and the analysis shows only selection for education of a grammar school type and in universities, since comparable evidence is not available on recruitment, for instance, to technical schools, independent schools not recognised by the Ministry of Education as efficient, and institutions of further and higher education other than universities.[2]

EDUCATIONAL OPPORTUNITY IN THE 1950S

Three national surveys provide the basis for a composite picture of social selection in education during the 1950s: the report on *Early Leaving* (1954); the Crowther Report (1959–60); and R. K. Kelsall's *Report on an Enquiry into Applications for Admission to Universities* (1957). Each contains information on the educational experience and social

1. An earlier attempt to compare class differentials in educational opportunity before and after World War II was included in J. Floud 'Social class factors in educational achievement', reproduced in Chapter Two of this volume. While using some of the same sources, however, that analysis was less detailed and reliable on a number of points, and also covered a shorter period, than the present one. The Robbins Report, *Higher Education* (Appendix I, Cmnd 2154-I, pp. 52–4) uses some of the same prewar data as we for a brief comparison of access to universities then and now, but does not deal with prewar access to secondary education. Within these limitations, the general conclusions from both analyses tally with ours.

2. At most some 10 per cent of the seventeen-year-old children still at school in the late 1950s were in schools not covered by the data. The proportion of the 'university age group' receiving full-time higher education outside universities was about 4 per cent: class differentials in access to such education were in the same direction, though not quite so sharp, as those in access to university education. (See the Robbins Report, Appendix I, pp. 39–42; and the present article, *infra*.)

backgrounds of roughly the same generation: children born in the late 1930s, who entered secondary education around 1950 and reached university entrance age in the middle to late 1950s. Moreover, the social class classifications used in the three reports are identical or very similar.

Table 3.1 is based on these sources, and relates to England and Wales: Scotland is excluded. The figures of boys' secondary schooling derive from the Crowther Report's sample analysis of national service recruits; the figure of girls' secondary schooling from those for the boys, adjusted to allow for the slight sex differences in educational experience at these stages indicated by the Early Leaving Report; and the university entrance figures from data in the Kelsall Report showing the social-class composition of 1955–56 undergraduate entrants. It is assumed, however, that 4 per cent of the age group entered universities. In fact, this proportion was not achieved until 1958, the mid-1950s figure being nearer 3·5 per cent. Chances of university entrance are thus slightly overstated.[1]

The table confirms, first, that at each successive stage of education, progressively smaller numbers of children survive to enter the next stage. One in four of this generation was at secondary grammar school at thirteen; one in ten was still at school at seventeen; while only one in twenty-five went on to university. Secondly, that as this process of elimination goes on, so the relative prospects of survival as between children of different social origin become steadily less equal. At eleven to thirteen a professional or managerial family's child had nine times as high a chance of entering a grammar or independent school as an unskilled worker's child. Some years later, at seventeen, he had nearly thirty times as high a chance as the other of still being at school. The data do not allow separate identification of the professional and managerial group at university entrance (although calculations from other figures in the Kelsall Report indicate that, of the rather smaller group with fathers in the Registrar General's Social Class I, some 29 per cent entered universities). But if the children of the two non-manual groups are taken together, their chances of selective secondary or higher education were seven times higher than those of unskilled workers' children at the stage of entry to grammar

1. The Crowther Report data exclude boys who, for medical or other reasons, did not do national service. The Kelsall Report's figures on the social composition of university entrants have been translated into figures of differential class chances of university entry on the assumption that the entire age group contained the same proportionate representation of social classes as the Crowther Report's national service sample.

3

TABLE 3.1. *Proportions obtaining education of a grammar school type and in universities, among children of different classes born in the late 1930s.*

Sex and father's occupation	Per cent in grammar schools and equivalent at ages 11–13			Per cent still in grammar schools and equivalent at age 17			Percentage entering universities
	In maintained and direct grant schools	In independent efficient schools	Total both types	In maintained and direct grant schools	In independent efficient schools	Total both types	
BOYS							
Professional and managerial	40	22	62	24	19	43	16·5
Other non-manual	30	4	34	13	3	16	2·5
Skilled manual	17	—	17	5	—	5	2·5
Semiskilled	12	—	12	3	—	3	1·5
Unskilled	7	—	7	1·5	—	1·5	·5
All boys	20	3·5	23·5	8	3	11	5·5
GIRLS							
Professional and managerial	42	20	62	25	14	39	8
Other non-manual	31	3	34	14	1·5	15	1
Skilled manual	17	—	17	5	—	5	1
Semiskilled	12	—	12	3	—	3	·5
Unskilled	7	—	7	1	—	1	—
All girls	20	3	23	8	2	10	2·5
BOYS AND GIRLS							
Professional and managerial	41	21	62	24·5	17	41·5	12
Other non-manual	30·5	3·5	34	13·5	2	16	1·5
Skilled manual	17	—	17	5	—	5	1
Semiskilled	12	—	12	3	—	3	1
Unskilled	7	—	7	1·5	—	1·5	·5
All children	20	3	23	8	2·5	10·5	4

Note. Percentages have been rounded to the nearest half digit.   — = less than 0·3 per cent.   For sources, see text and footnote, p. 53.

and independent secondary schools; twenty times higher at the sixth-form stage at seventeen; and twenty-five to thirty times higher at the stage of admission to universities. One in every four of the non-manual, middle-class children who entered a grammar school type course at eleven-plus eventually went on to a university; but only one in fifteen to one in twenty of the grammar school entrants from unskilled working-class homes did so.

As is already known, such marked social differences in educational opportunity can only to a limited extent be attributed to social differences in the distribution of measured 'intelligence'. A local study approximately contemporary with the present data thus suggests that, if selection were based solely on I.Q., class differences in chances of grammar school entry at eleven-plus would be of roughly the order shown in the first column of Table 3.1.[1] But that column excludes independent schools—which, as is evident from the second column, provide additional opportunities for middle-class children, but are virtually closed to working-class children. The disparities widen during the stage following entrance to selective secondary education. This results mainly from the fact, repeatedly demonstrated by recent research, that in the publicly supported grammar schools middle-class children complete the full course far more often than do working-class children. This conclusion stands even when the comparison is confined to children of similar measured ability.[2] The disparities are widened still further because the independent schools retain more of their children to seventeen and beyond than do the publicly supported grammar schools.

However, if a working-class child survives the secondary school course to seventeen or beyond, his academic performance and his chances of entering a university are then much less affected by the cultural, economic and other forces which in the years before have eliminated so many of his age mates of similar social origin. Table 3.2 shows that among sixth-formers leaving school at seventeen or more in 1960–61 (a slightly more recent generation than that hitherto discussed) the proportion who left with at least the minimum qualifications for university entry varied somewhat by social class. But the disparities are generally small. They are noticeable mainly among girls, while among boys only the sons of semi- or unskilled

1. J. Floud *et al.*, *Social Class and Educational Opportunity*, Heinemann, 1956, pp. 42–61.
2. Cf. J. Floud *et al.*, *op. cit.* (e.g. pp. 111–33); Ministry of Education, *Early Leaving*, 1954 (e.g. p. 18); *idem*, *15 to 18*, vol. 2 (e.g. pp. 118–19); *Higher Education*, Appendix I (e.g. p. 43).

workers fall below the average level of achievement.[1] The same point is still more evident when intellectual ability is held constant. The Robbins Report thus shows that among the ablest children selected for grammar schools who stayed on until eighteen, the proportions leaving with two A-levels were practically identical as between those from professional and managerial homes (79 per cent) and those from semi- and unskilled manual working-class homes (81 per cent).[2] Factors conditioning early school leaving and 'under-performance' to age sixteen to seventeen may not influence the performance of 'survivors' after age seventeen.

TABLE 3.2. *Children of different classes leaving school at age 17 or more in 1960–61: percentage who left with at least two A-level passes—i.e. minimum requirement for university entry.*

Father's occupation	Boys	Girls	All
Professional and managerial	53	41	48
Clerical	50	39	45
Skilled manual	51	33	43
Semiskilled and unskilled	39	24	32
Unknown	41	29	35
All	50	36	44

Note. Calculated from Ministry of Education, *Statistics of Education 1961*, Supplement to Part Two, Table 12. The data do not include the small numbers of children aged seventeen or more who left secondary modern schools or independent schools not recognised as efficient.

Of course, those who acquire the minimum qualifications for university entry do not necessarily seek or obtain admission. The same data as used for Table 3.2 show that of the boys and girls leaving school at seventeen or older in 1960–61 with two or more A-levels, at least one-third came from manual working-class homes; another 9 per cent could not be classified, and must have included some of working-class origin. By contrast, according to the Kelsall Report, only one-fourth of university entrants in 1955–56 were from manual workers' families. The difference cannot be explained by any increase

1. Such class differentials as Table 3.2 shows do not arise from better sixth-form examination performances in independent schools than in publicly supported schools. On the contrary—as might be expected from the more stringent process of academic selection in schools of the public sector—the proportion leaving at 17+ with at least two 'A' level passes was 49 per cent for the latter, compared with 38 per cent for the former.
2. *Higher Education*, Appendix I, p. 45 (from Ministry of Education statistics).

in the working-class share of university places between 1955 and
1961.[1] It is likely that qualified working-class sixth-formers rather
more often than those from middle-class homes fail either to seek or
to obtain entry to universities, and go instead to technical colleges,
colleges of education or directly into the labour market. Nevertheless,
the class differentials at work among those who have survived to this
stage of the educational process, all in all, are fairly slight. They are
certainly of little account by comparison with those which, earlier
on, result in the elimination of some 96 out of every 100 manual
working-class children from formal full-time education before the
age of seventeen.

These points are worth further consideration. Table 3.3 derives
from the Robbins Report's analysis of the post-secondary education
of children born in 1940–41, in relation to class background and to
intelligence as measured at eleven. Two conclusions stand out. First,
in the highest ability group, fewer children from manual than from
non-manual homes received some form of higher education. But the
overall difference is fairly small, because the marked disparity in the
proportions entering university as full-time students is partly com-
pensated by a larger proportion of manual than of non-manual
children who receive a higher education outside universities.
Secondly, such non-university education does not, however, provide
an alternative channel for manual workers' children in the next
highest ability group. Among these children, with I.Q.s of 115–129,
twice as many of the non-manual as of the manual group again
receive a full-time university education—but rather more of them also
obtain higher education of other kinds (though not of part-time
education by itself). It is clear that in discussions of 'class opportunities' for higher education, a distinction must be drawn between
different types of higher education; and that the various factors
determining opportunities may operate differently at different levels
of ability.

Table 3.3 relates to all children with I.Q.s of 115 or more, not just
to those among them who stayed at school until seventeen or eighteen.
Earlier, however, it was suggested that if a working-class adolescent
stays at school until that age, his final school results and subsequent
educational path are rather little affected by those factors that
previously eliminated so many of his class (and ability) peers. This

1. The Robbins Report's evidence on university entry in 1960 compared with
earlier years indicates no such increase in the working class share (e.g. Appendix
I, p. 54).

may be true also of his academic performance, if he enters a university. A survey of students admitted to universities in 1955 thus showed that the proportion obtaining first or second class honours was virtually the same (just about one-half), whether the students came from manual or from non-manual backgrounds, and the same for both men and women.[1] Clearly, we must distinguish between factors determining the level of education reached and factors determining performance at any given level. Social class strongly influences the level reached; but (as measured by broad classifications of parental occupation) it appears to have no marked effect on performance at the upper level of secondary and in higher education.

TABLE 3.3.   *Higher education of 'able' children of different classes born 1940–41.*

I.Q. at 11	Father's occupation	Full-time degree-level	Other full-time	Part-time only	Total
		Per cent obtaining higher education of following kinds			
130+	Non-manual	37	4	10	51
	Manual	18	12	10	40
115–	Non-manual	17	17	4	38
129	Manual	8	7	9	24

Source: Higher Education, Appendix I, p. 42.

There are other inequalities of educational opportunity besides those of class—inequalities between the sexes, for example. But these —so far as the present data go—are of little importance until sixth-form level. In each social class, as many girls as boys are admitted to grammar schools or the equivalent at eleven-plus; and as many stay on till seventeen. But fewer sixth-form girls than boys leave with the minimum qualifications for university entry; and fewer—even among the qualified—in fact gain admittance to a university. Moreover, the disparity between the sexes widens as one goes down the social scale. The resources—cultural, economic, psychological—necessary for a working-class child to overcome the obstacles on the way to a university place are very rarely expended on behalf of a girl. At the extreme of the scale, an unskilled manual worker's daughter has a chance of only one in five or six hundred of entering a university—a

1. J. G. H. Newfield, 'The academic performance of British university students', *Sociological Review,* Special Monographs No. 7, October 1963.

chance a hundred times lower than if she had been born into a professional family.[1]

PREWAR AND POSTWAR EDUCATIONAL OPPORTUNITY

Floud's analysis of the 1949 social mobility data provides the most comprehensive information available on the educational experience of the generations who were at school between about the turn of the century and the outbreak of the Second World War.[2] There are some difficulties in comparing this information with that just presented for the 1950s, because the occupational classification of the earlier material does not correspond precisely with those of the later sources. But the discrepancies are small enough to allow an approximate comparison, when individual categories are combined into rather broader groupings. The same difficulties necessitate that the comparisons of opportunities for secondary education and for university education be kept separate. Table 3.4 thus compares prewar and postwar access to selective secondary schools, Table 3.5 prewar and postwar opportunities for university education.

The progressive expansion of opportunities for education of a grammar school type is evident from Table 3.4. Twice as many children born in the late 1930s went into grammar or independent secondary schools as of those born before 1910. The expansion has been continuous—although slowest as between the two 'middle' generations, children born in the 1920s being affected by crisis measures taken during the 1930s. Expansion after the second world war is thus the continuation of a long-term trend. This, of course, is well known; but it is sometimes forgotten. What is less well known is that expansion benefited the children of all social classes—not just those of the less prosperous groups. Moreover, this was true not only during the decades before the Second World War, as Floud has already shown. But it has been equally true of the expansion following the 1944 Act. The point is crucial, though obvious. The widening of educational provisions does not in itself reduce social inequalities in educational opportunity; it does so only if the expanded facilities are

1. These class-related inequalities of opportunity between the sexes are somewhat lower if access to *all* forms of full-time higher education, not just to universities, are considered. Teachers' training colleges include a high proportion of women among their students, and recruit from further down the social scale than universities. See, e.g., *Higher Education*: Appendix 2B: Students and their Education (pp. 69 ff), and also discussions of the 'slum school' in *Half our Future*.
2. J. Floud, 'The educational experience of the adult population of England and Wales', Chapter 5 of D. V. Glass, ed., *Social Mobility in Britain*, Routledge, 1954.

TABLE 3.4. *Proportions in different classes obtaining education of a grammar school type among children of different generations.*

Sex and father's occupation		Per cent obtaining secondary education in grammar and independent schools			
Pre-war genera-tions (Hall-Jones groups)	Postwar generation (Crowther Report groups)	Born pre-1910	Born 1910 -19	Born 1920 -29	Born late 1930s
BOYS:					
1–3	Prof./manag.	37	44	54	62
4–5	Other non-manual and skilled manual	7	13	15	20
6–7	Semi- and unskilled	2	4	9	10
All boys		12	16	19	23
GIRLS:					
1–3	Prof./manag.	37	50	50	62
4–5	Other non-manual and skilled manual	7	13	16	20
6–7	Semi- and unskilled	1	3	5	10
All girls		11	16	17	23
BOYS AND GIRLS:					
1–3	Prof./manag.	37	47	52	62
4–5	Other non-manual and skilled manual	7	13	16	20
6–7	Semi- and unskilled	1	4	7	10
All children		12	16	18	23

Sources: For pre-war generations (born before 1930), Jean Floud, *op. cit.* (see page 59). For postwar generation (born late 1930s, secondary schooling during 1950s), same sources as for secondary school data in Table 3.1.

Note:

(i) Hall-Jones groups 1–3 appear to be slightly more broadly defined than the 'professional and managerial' group of the Crowther Report classification; conversely, Hall-Jones groups 4–5 appear to be rather more narrowly defined than the 'other non-manual and skilled manual' category of the Crowther Report classification.

(ii) The figures for the postwar generation include only those independent schools which are recognised as efficient by the Ministry of Education, and thus slightly understate the chances of selective secondary education in that generation, mainly for middle class children.

(iii) No prewar figures are available on the numbers of children from different social classes who continued school till seventeen, as distinct from entering a school (grammar or independent) in which they might stay on till seventeen.

made proportionately more accessible to those children previously least able to take advantage of them. To some extent this has happened. As between the generations born in the 1920s and in the late 1930s, the chances of entering a grammar school or the equivalent rose by about two-fifths for children of the lowest social group, by about a fourth for those of the middle group, and by only about one-fifth for those of the upper group. The relative differential between top and bottom was reduced over that period from a ratio of more than seven to one, to a ratio of about six to one. Again, the process has been continuous, not one confined to the postwar era: the corresponding ratio for the generation born before 1910 was about thirty-seven to one. Clearly, however, this long-term trend towards a reduction of social differentials in educational opportunity at the secondary stage is moderate and limited. The differentials remain sharp. Indeed, if the proportion *not* going to grammar-type schools is taken as the measure of changing educational opportunity, the persistence of inequalities stands out still more clearly. Less than two in every five children from homes in the upper social group failed to obtain education of a grammar school type in the 1950s, compared with almost two in every three in the first decades of the century—a reduction of nearly half. By contrast, no less than nine in every ten of the lowest social group were still deprived of a grammar school education in the 1950s; the proportion so deprived was barely a tenth smaller than thirty or forty years before. Conclusions concerning reductions in class differentials will thus be conditioned by the relative weight one attaches to the proportion achieving, as compared with the portion who fail to achieve, selective secondary schooling. But even on the more favourable basis, the reduction is neither very large nor a unique phenomenon of the period after the 1944 Act.

A university education remains the privilege of a very small proportion of young people, even though the proportion has increased over time. Moreover, the expansion of the universities has if anything, benefited the children of middle-class people and skilled workers more than those from semiskilled and unskilled workers' homes (see Table 3.5). Since the figures are small, and the comparisons between them over time rather rough, too much weight must not be attached to them. Nevertheless, there are certainly no indications of any narrowing of class differentials in access to universities over the generations. In terms of the broad categories distinguished here, the social class composition of the student body in the universities has remained roughly the same during the past three to five decades— this despite expansion, maintenance grants for students, and the changes which have occurred in secondary school provision.

The pattern of sex differentials in educational opportunity has

3*

TABLE 3.5. *Proportion in different classes entering universities, among children of different generations.*

Father's occupation		Percentage reaching universities among								
Pre-war generations (Hall-Jones groups)	Postwar generation (Reg. Gen.'s social classes)	Boys born			Girls born			All born		
		Pre-1910	1910–1929	Late 1930s	Pre-1910	1910–1929	Late 1930s	Pre-1910	1910–1929	Late 1930s
1–4	I and II: Professional, managerial, 'intermediate'	4·5	8·5	19(15)[1]	2	4	9·5(7)[1]	3	6	14·5(11)[1]
5	III: Skilled manual and remaining non-manual	1	1·5	3·5(3)[1]	—	—	1(1)[1]	0·5	1	2·5(2)[1]
6–7	IV and V: Semiskilled and unskilled	0·5	1	1	—	—	0·5	—	0·5	0·5
	All	2	3·5	5·5	0·5	1·5	2·5	1·5	2·5	4

1. Hall-Jones group 5 may include a somewhat smaller segment of lower grade non-manual workers than Registrar General's Social Class III. The figures in brackets show the position as it would be if all non-manual workers in Social Class III were allocated to the top rather than to the middle group.

All figures are rounded to the nearest half digit. — indicates a per cent of less than 0·3.

Sources: For pre-war generations (born before 1930), Jean Floud, *op. cit.* (see page 59). For postwar generation (born late 1930s, reaching university age during second half of 1950s), estimates are based on data from Kelsall, *op. cit.* (as for Table 3.1, except that here the parental class distribution of the age group has been assumed to correspond to that of all males aged 20–64 in 1951; if this assumption had been modified to take account of class differentials in fertility and mortality, social inequalities in postwar access to universities would be slightly greater than they appear here).

hardly changed. As in the latest generation, so too among those born before 1910, boys and girls had about the same chances of entering a grammar school or the equivalent (Table 3.4); but girls had a very much smaller chance than boys of entering a university (Table 3.5). In fact, the sex ratio among university students has remained remarkably stable—at about three girls for every seven boys—over the generations covered by the data. In this field, at least, female emancipation has made no further progress: the increased educational opportunities for girls reflect the general expansion of facilities, not a narrowing of sex differentials.

It may be asked whether there have been further changes since the early and middle 1950s, to which the latest data used here relate. Have the reforms associated with the 1944 Act perhaps had consequences which, while not visible in the experience of the early postwar generations of school children, may become apparent in the case of those children who entered the secondary schools in the late 1950s and early 1960s? There is not sufficient comprehensive and comparable information available for a precise answer. But there is no reason to believe that any striking changes have taken place during the last few years.

An estimate for children leaving school in 1960–61 might seem to suggest some further reduction of class differentials in access to selective secondary schooling since the middle 1950s.[1] But since the

1. Ministry of Education data on school leavers aged seventeen-plus in 1960–61 (*Statistics of Education,* Supplement to Part 2, Table 12) have been used in the estimate below for the generation born about 1943. It was assumed that those data could be taken to indicate roughly the numbers of children staying at school to seventeen-plus out of a hypothetical age group intermediate in size between the seventeen-year-olds of 1959 and 1960. Additional assumptions were made concerning the class composition of the age group, and of school leavers for whom fathers' occupation was not reported. These assumptions, however, make the comparison inexact, and also overstate the overall expansion in numbers staying at school till seventeen-plus.

Father's occupation	*Percentage staying at school to 17+ among children born in*	
	*late 1930s**	*about 1943*
Prof./Manag.	42	52
Clerical	16	15
Skilled	5	9
Other manual	3	5
All	10	14

* From Table 3.1 of text.

estimate is rough, the small differences between it and the material presented in the text may be fortuitous. More striking is the broad similarity of results, which may be taken as confirmation of the general trend. There is also some evidence in a contrary direction—to suggest that social inequalities in educational opportunity may even have widened in recent years, rather than narrowed. A large-scale national follow-up survey of children born in 1946 thus indicates marked social differentials in the chances of admission to grammar and technical schools as between children of similar measured ability.[1] These children entered the secondary schools in the *late* 1950s; in contrast, previous postwar work had suggested that class differentials in access to—though not survival in—the publicly supported grammar schools during the *early* 1950s largely reflected class differences in the distribution of measured ability.[1] If the retrogression thus indicated has occurred, this could be the result of an increased use of general records, teachers' assessments and traditional examinations as the criteria of selection for secondary schools, in place of standardised ability tests. That such informal or conventional selection procedures discriminate still more in favour of middle-class children than do the standardised tests of ability on which much criticism of the 'eleven-plus' has focused, is suggested by at least one study.[2] However, in the absence of further evidence, it would be unsafe to assume that any changes which may have taken place in the social distribution of educational opportunity since the early and middle 1950s—for better or for worse—have been more than marginal.[3]

SOCIAL MOBILITY

Consideration of the trends in educational opportunity in England and Wales may help to throw some light on the wider question of trends, past and prospective, in social mobility. The belief, common

1. J. W. B. Douglas, *The Home and the School*, MacGibbon & Kee 1964 (Chapter 6 and Appendix III, pp. 153–8).
2. J. Floud and A. H. Halsey, 'Intelligence Tests and Selection for Secondary Schools', *British Journal of Sociology*, March 1957.
3. The Robbins Report includes data for the generation born in 1940–41, but not (except on university entrance—see page 57) of such a kind as to allow direct comparison with the material analysed here for those born in the late 1930s and earlier. The Report, however, concludes from a brief analysis of some recent trends that there has been little reduction of class differences in educational achievement: *op. cit.*, Appendix I, pp. 52–4.

in Britain, as in many other countries of Western Europe, that economic, political and educational changes must have increased the volume and chances of individual movement up and down the social scale in the course of this century, has hitherto found little or no support from empiral research.[1] But the evidence available has related generally to the patterns of social mobility prevailing yesterday. By its nature it has been able to say little about the patterns which may prevail tomorrow—in those generations which have only recently entered upon their working careers, or have still to do so. Thus in England and Wales, as Glass pointed out in the early 1950s, the provisions associated with the 1944 Education Act might eventually increase the frequency of social mobility.[2]

In fact, this does not now seem likely from the results of the present analysis. True, class differentials in educational opportunity have diminished somewhat—with respect to entry into the grammar schools—since 1944. But this moderate reduction of the inequalities in access to selective schooling is no new phenomenon. It is the continuation of a long-term trend no less visible before 1944—indeed during the whole period since the turn of the century. Yet, as we know, rates of social mobility did not rise to any noticeable extent during that period. Evidently, the small but continuous widening of the educational 'channel' was roughly counter-balanced by a corresponding contraction of other avenues of social mobility. This is precisely what might be expected. For as professionalisation, bureaucratisation and technical complexity in work have proceeded, so access to occupations of the middle and higher levels has increasingly demanded formal educational qualifications. Career prospects and social position have come to depend less on experience and training acquired on the job, more on the education obtained in

---

1. For Britain, see especially D. V. Glass, ed., *Social Mobility in Britain*, Routledge, 1954 (Chap. VIII). Evidence on mobility trends over time in different countries has still to be brought together systematically; this aspect was not dealt with in S. M. Miller's 'Comparative social mobility', *Current Sociology*, 9, no. 1, 1960, by far the most comprehensive and rigorous international comparison of recent mobility rates. But general reviews of relevant European and American material are contained, e.g., in G. Carlsson, *Social Mobility and Class Structure*, Lund, 1955 (pp. 110–13) and S. M. Lipset and R. Bendix, *Social Mobility in Industrial Society*, Heinemann, 1959 (especially pp. 33–8, 90, 121–43). See also for more recent American data, E. Jackson and H. J. Crockett, 'Occupational mobility in the United States', *American Sociological Review*, February 1964. There may, of course, be exceptions to the general finding of constant mobility rates in this century, cf., e.g. the Danish data in K. Svalastoga, *Prestige, Class and Mobility*, Copenhagen, 1959 (pp. 349–52).
2. D. V. Glass, ed., *op. cit.*, pp. 21–3.

childhood and adolescence.[1] The range of occupational statuses over which promotion—or demotion—may be expected in the course of a normal working life has probably therefore narrowed. To that extent increased 'educational mobility' will have been matched by decreased 'career mobility'.

There is no reason to suppose that this process—a slow trend rather than any abrupt shift—has come to an end. It is therefore improbable that the modest reduction in educational inequalities which has occurred since 1944, any more than the earlier trend of which it is an extension, will be sufficient to outweigh the simultaneous gradual restriction of career promotion and demotion as a mode of social mobility. Only a fairly drastic modification of the factors which continue to prevent a more even distribution of educational opportunities would alter this prospect.

CONCLUSIONS

The preceding analysis therefore gives as accurate a comparison of prewar and postwar educational opportunities as it seems possible to present from available data. The results are easily summarised. Social inequalities in access to selective secondary education have been somewhat reduced over the past fifty to sixty years. But the reduction has, in the first place, been small—so small as to disappear should one choose to look at the differentials in failure to obtain a grammar school type education, rather than at the differentials in successful admission to such an education. In the second place, the reduction of social inequalities is not a new, post-1944 phenomenon, but the continuation of a long-term, gradual trend. And in the third place, it has been confined to entry into selective secondary education, while access to the universities has remained more or less unaffected. The

1. For British evidence showing a decline over time in the proportion of industrial managers or directors who started their careers at the bottom of the ladder, as clerks or manual workers, with little formal education, see Acton Society Trust, *Management Succession,* London, 1956 (e.g. pp. 14–18); R. V. Clements, *Managers: a Study of their Careers in Industry,* Allen & Unwin, 1958 (pp. 154–61); and C. Erickson, *British Industrialists: Steel and Hosiery 1850–1950,* Cambridge U.P., 1959 (pp. 56, 129). In the Civil Service, demands for improved opportunities for promotion have contributed to increased recruitment of administrative class officials from the middle ranks; see R. K. Kelsall, *Higher Civil Servants in Britain,* Routledge, 1955 (especially Chapter 3). But exceptional factors are probably involved here—e.g., the public scrutiny to which a government bureaucracy is subject, difficulties in recruiting civil servants in recent decades. Among other work, R. Bendix, *Work and Authority in Industry,* New York, Wiley, 1956; Harper Torchbooks, 1963, includes some American evidence on trends in the recruitment of industrial management (especially pp. 226–36).

general increase of grammar school places has benefited children of all social classes, but working-class children proportionately rather more than others. The general increase of university places has perhaps, if anything, benefited children of the upper and middle strata more than those from the lower stratum. Certainly, the overall expansion of educational facilities has been of greater significance than any redistribution of opportunities.

The persistence of marked social inequalities in educational opportunity is in line with a good deal of other evidence on the relative constancy of class divisions in our society. While average levels of living have increased in absolute terms, and crude economic insecurity has been reduced, relative differences between the strata remain sharp, for example, in the distribution of wealth and welfare, in the incidence of infant mortality, and in patterns of fertility.[1] Some of these or other social differentials may perhaps be in process of modification. Boundary lines between the strata are inevitably imprecise; and there is considerable movement of individuals across them— though probably no more now than fifty years ago. Nevertheless, the social classes constitute genuine groupings, 'quasi-communities' distinct from each other in their typical life chances and styles of living.

To recognise this, however, is not to assume that particular patterns of inequality are fixed, or embedded in so tightly interlocking a complex of economic and cultural factors as to defeat attempts either to identify particular causes or to pursue particular policies designed to reduce such inequalities. Differentials in educational opportunity coincide with many other social differentials: their causes need still

1. The accumulated evidence on the persistence of class differentials in these and other respects is voluminous and scattered widely through the literature. The following are some of the central or most recent studies relevant in this connection: J. L. Nicholson, 'Redistribution of income in the United Kingdom', in C. Clark and D. Stuvel, eds., *Income and Wealth: Series X*, 1964; H. F. Lydall, 'The long-term trend in the size distribution of incomes', *J. Royal Statist. Soc.*, Series A, 122 (1), 1959; *idem* and D. G. Tipping, 'The distribution of personal wealth in Britain', *Bulletin Oxford Univ. Inst. Statistics*, February 1961; B. Abel-Smith and P. Townsend, *The Poor and the Poorest*, G. Bell, 1965; General Register Office, *Registrar General's Decennial Supplement for England and Wales, 1951: Occupational Mortality*, London, 1954, 1958; J. N. Morris and J. A. Heady, 'Social and biological factors in infant mortality', *Lancet*, 12 February – 12 March, 1955; N. R. Butler and D. G. Bonham, *Perinatal Mortality*, E. and S. Livingstone, 1963; D. V. Glass and E. Grebenik, *The Trend and Pattern of Fertility in Great Britain* (Royal Commission on Population Papers, vol. 6), London, 1954; Census of England and Wales, 1951, *Fertility Report*, London, 1959 (Data on fertility and mortality from, or relating to the period around, the Census of 1961 had not been published at the time of writing). For a general review of this and other evidence, see J. H. Westergaard, 'The withering away of class: a contemporary myth', in P. Anderson and R. Blackburn, eds., *Towards Socialism*, Collins, 1965.

to be separately traced. A good deal of recent work has pointed to the important—and almost certainly increasing—role of cultural, rather than crude material, factors in perpetuating educational inequalities: class differences in educational aspirations, occupational orientations, language, intellectual climate, and so on.[1] Fruitful or promising as much of this work has been, it should not blind one to the continuing influence also of other factors, less subtle in their operation—and more immediately amenable to change through deliberate policy.

Among this latter group of factors in England and Wales are the gross economic facts of educational provision—the continued existence of a private school system, closed to most of the population; the persistence of wide differences in educational provision between different areas; and the low level of total educational provision in a society which—like most European countries—reserves formal schooling beyond a fairly rudimentary stage for a small minority of its young people. The effect which this latter feature, in particular, may have on the social distribution of such educational facilities as exist has still to be explored in precise terms. But almost certainly it helps to give the patterns of educational inequality the character of a self-perpetuating cycle. The education of the great majority of children finishes at fifteen or shortly after. As a result the working-class child who strives or is encouraged to stay on at school is deviating from the pattern of early entry into the labour market which is the typical experience of his age-mates of the same social background. Because successful completion of a full grammar school course is thus at present inevitably exceptional, it is not surprising to find hints in the evidence available that the working-class child who manages it fairly often comes from a family which, by virtue of origins, style of life or aspirations, is somewhat detached from the general working class environment.

IMPLICATIONS FOR POLICY

Policies designed to reduce the persistent inequalities of educational opportunity—whether in the interests of economic efficiency or distributive justice—must clearly take account of such factors. At the simplest level, they may take the form of measures to eliminate those inequalities of sheer material provision which can be seen in a

1. See, e.g., J. W. B. Douglas, *op. cit.*; B. Jackson and D. Marsden, *Education and the Working Class*, Routledge, 1962; and the work (as yet suggestive rather than conclusive) of B. Bernstein, cf. 'Some sociological determinants of perception', *Brit. J. Sociology*, 1958.

sense as the 'accidental' product of local variations in resources inherited from the past, in financial and staff recruitment capacities, and in the specific interpretation and implementation of national educational policies. The existence of such inequalities—in terms of class sizes, physical facilities, basic educational equipment, staff qualifications and turnover, as well as the number of places available in the selective streams of secondary education—has been clearly documented in recent years.[1] To eliminate inequalities of provision of this kind is to do no more than to remove anomalies. Such measures will involve no changes in national educational policies—except probably for some direct or indirect reduction in the autonomy of local educational authorities; but only the more even and consistent application of those policies. Still less will they entail any attack on those underlying features of social structure in which many of the obstacles to effective educational opportunities are rooted. But by the same token, measures of this kind—while urgently needed, and essential as a basis for wider reforms—can be expected to have only limited effects on social selection through education.

A second, and in principle more radical, set of measures would be those directed to the structure of the educational system, and to the priorities and assumptions which are expressed in that structure. Such measures could take the form of a reallocation of resources from the 'privileged' to the 'deprived' sectors and streams of the educational system; even a reversal of priorities, to discriminate positively and substantially in favour of the deprived sectors and, within these, in favour of the socially and culturally most handicapped children. They could also take the form of policies intended to minimise the structural divisions of the educational system, and to postpone their operation until later stages of the typical school career. The elimination of 'streaming' by merit in the primary schools; the effective introduction of 'comprehensive' education at the secondary stage, involving a postponement of selection for courses of varying academic and vocational content until a late age, and accompanied by a substantial rise in minimum school leaving age; not least, of course, the abolition of private education—all these would belong in the latter category. If fully implemented, they would mark—and pre-suppose—a basic change in educational philosophy. Even if they were intended only, or primarily, to even out the terms upon which

1. See, e.g. *The State of our Schools*: Report of the National Survey of School Conditions, National Union of Teachers, 1963. *The School Building Survey 1962*, Dept. of Education and Science, H.M.S.O., 1965.

children of different social and cultural backgrounds compete with each other, they would in effect entail an acceptance of an extended common education as the right of all children, and as a prerequisite of subsequent academic and vocational selection. Current official moves towards 'comprehensive' secondary education and a closer 'integration' of the major independent schools with the public sector might be interpreted as steps in this direction. But it is doubtful whether the force behind these moves will be sufficient—or indeed is intended—to produce such basic changes in the structure and objectives of the educational system. The major private schools are to be 'integrated', not abolished; and the pressures for the retention of 'streaming' within the walls of the new comprehensive schools—as in the primary schools—are quite evidently powerful.

Even if such a fundamental shift in the character and orientation of English education were to take place, its ultimate effect on the patterns of social selection might be rather limited. The abolition of private schooling would clearly close a major loophole, through which the children of wealthy parents are now able to escape the impact of the national principle of equality of opportunity. But these children would carry many advantages with them into the competition within the public sector. Comprehensive education at the secondary stage, and a substantial rise in the minimum age of school leaving, would indeed postpone the process of competitive selection. But the effect could be to shift the social inequalities of educational opportunity to the higher ages at which selection would then operate (and where at present, as we have suggested, competitive social pressures are not so strongly felt); rather than to reduce those inequalities drastically. A comparison with the United States, where the school leaving age is high and secondary education follows a far more 'comprehensive' pattern than in Europe, is suggestive. An estimate for the early 1950s indicated that the chances of graduating from a university or college varied from over 40 per cent for children from professional and semi-professional families to some 6 or 8 per cent for children from manual workers' and farmers' homes.[1] The range of variation is not very dissimilar to that found in England and Wales, at about the same time, with respect to the proportions staying on at school to seventeen or more (Table 3.1)—with the big

1. D. Wolfle, *America's Resources of Specialised Talent,* New York, Harper; London, H. Hamilton, 1954, (p. 162). For a recent attempt at an international comparison of social selection in secondary and higher education, see J. Ben-David, 'Professions in the class system of present-day societies', *Current Sociology,* 12, no. 3, 1963–64 (Chapter 3).

difference that the American figures relate to college graduation. Of course, the comparison is rough; it may indeed suggest a somewhat narrower range of variation in the United States; and, given the very sharp class—and colour—related local differences in effective educational provision, the 'comprehensive' character of American secondary education is to some extent more nominal than real. Even so, the comparison gives some indication of the limitations which the structure of the wider society may be expected to impose on the effects of changes—however radical in conception—confined to the educational system itself.

This is not to argue against such changes: far from it. Their impact on patterns of social selection is neither precisely predictable, nor likely to be negligible. Moreover, to provide an extended common education for all children can be seen as a policy objective of intrinsic merit, which does not need to be justified on other grounds. The point is merely this: that the persistent class differentials in educational opportunity in the final analysis are anchored in equally persistent divisions of the society at large. Very sharp reductions in those differentials are therefore unlikely to be achieved without broader changes in the class structure itself—changes affecting both the economic foundations of the structure, and the related cultural divisions which imprint themselves upon the patterns of educational experience and achievement.

4

The influence of the home*

The authors of this chapter analysed the entry of a coeducational grammar school over a period of five years and identified thirty-nine 'deteriorators', children who had suffered demotion from a high to a low academic stream. A group of 'improvers' was also studied for comparison. This chapter forms an important part of the authors' report and is included here as a second example of the demographic approach. While in Chapter 3, Westergaard and Little offer a large-scale map of educational disadvantage, here in Chapter 4 Dale and Griffith attempt to disentangle some of the components or 'predictors'. Subsequent chapters seek to probe further into the determinants of the relationship of family, class and education so clearly charted by these demographic studies.

R. R. Dale and S. Griffith

Throughout our investigation the relationship between the nature of the home and the attainment of the pupil was frequently and sometimes forcibly brought to our attention. For a long time teachers have been aware of the influence of the home on individual pupils, but the influence's strength and pervasiveness were not fully appreciated. The concept of social class gathers under its umbrella many of the factors in the home which are associated with pupil attainment; it also lends itself easily to objective classification and analysis. We shall begin therefore, with this constellation in general and then deal with some of its component factors. First, however, we should perhaps point out that defective home backgrounds are not the sole prerogative of any one social class, nor are the 'defects' limited to those of a material kind; they clearly include the intellectual and the emotional.

* Reprinted from *Down Stream*, Routledge, 1965, pp. 14–30, by kind permission of the authors and the publisher.

As assessed clinically these defects played a major part in the deterioration of twenty-five of the thirty-nine deteriorators, contributed substantially to the deterioration of four other pupils, and had a slighter effect on four others. In two other cases, where the home was an asset, there was recovery from deterioration, and one of these eventually even improved on his status at entry. The improvers also were blessed with good homes. In two cases the principal factor in deterioration has been classified as 'emotional upset' and not under 'home background' because, although the cause of the upset may in one way be said to have originated in the home, yet the home could do nothing about it and was otherwise a good home. In one case the child suddenly discovered that he or she was illegitimate and in the other the mother suddenly died at a critical time in the child's career.

SOCIAL CLASS

The association between severe deterioration in attainment and the character of the home was first noticed clinically. The authors therefore prepared Table 4.1 in which the occupations of the fathers of the pupils were classified for

(*a*) one whole year of entry
(*b*) the improvers for years 1 to 6 inclusive
(*c*) deteriorators for years 1 to 5 inclusive.

The improvers included all pupils who conformed to a promotion criterion; they are presented here because they bring the social-class factor into even greater prominence. It should be noted that the one year of entry will in itself contain some deteriorators and some improvers. Readers are reminded that Class 1 is professional and high administrative, and Class 7 unskilled manual workers.

TABLE 4.1. *Classification for social status from parental occupation*

Parental occupation category:	1	2	3	4	5	6	7
No. of pupils—one year	6	9	10	9	41	21	6
No. of improvers— years 1 to 6 inclusive	0	6	7	8	15	0	0
No. of deteriorators— years 1 to 5 inclusive	0	0	0	2	15	12	10

In the table the deteriorators tend to congregate in the skilled, semi-skilled and unskilled manual working classes, i.e. thirty-seven out of thirty-nine are in these categories; on the other hand, the improvers do not go below the skilled manual class.[1] The fathers of twenty-two of the thirty-nine deteriorators were unskilled or semiskilled, i.e. 56·4 per cent, whereas only 26·5 per cent of the pupils in a whole year's entry (including future deteriorators) belonged to these classes. This finding is confirmed by other researches, notably the Ministry of Education report *Early Leaving,* page 18, where it is stated that:

> Deterioration which has caused many who were placed in the top selection group at eleven, to be found at sixteen in the lowest academic categories, is most common among the children of unskilled workers (54 per cent) and semiskilled workers (37·9 per cent).

At the other end of the table none of the thirty-nine cases of deterioration gathered from five years of entry, came from the professional, executive and inspectional classes, whereas thirteen out of the thirty-six improvers came from these classes. Even in the middle of the scale, Class 4, or the lower supervisory workers, contains eight out of the thirty-six improvers but only two out of the thirty-nine deteriorators

In an attempt to isolate more specifically the particular influences associated with deterioration we included a detailed examination of a number of factors in the social-class 'constellation'. Our findings on two factors appear to be of special significance and are treated more fully than the others, on which we have less conclusive evidence. The first of these is the education of the parents.

PARENTAL EDUCATION

We began with a control group consisting of the total entry for two years and tabulated the pupils according to stream and education of parents. This information is given in Table 4.2.

There were 108 families out of 181 with one or more parents who were taught at a grammar school. It should be noted in passing that whereas 83 per cent of children in the A stream had at least one parent who was educated in a grammar school, this proportion declined to 63 per cent in the B form and only 28 per cent in the C form (cf.

1. Statistical comparisons (chi-square) of the social class distribution of deteriorators compared with the one-year entry (itself 'contaminated' with improvers and deteriorators) gives a significant difference well beyond the 0·025 level. The comparison between deteriorators and improvers gave a highly significant difference. That between improvers and the one-year entry was significant beyond the 0·05 level. Yates's correction was used in each case.

TABLE 4.2.   *Streaming in relation to education of parents (percentages)*[1]

	A stream	*B* stream	*C* stream
Number of children (years 7 and 8)	64	63	54
(*a*) No parent attended grammar school	15·1	31·5	53·4
(*b*) Only mother attended grammar school	32·3	38·7	29·0
(*c*) Only father attended grammar school	51·2	39·5	9·3
(*d*) Both parents attended grammar school	61·8	32·4	5·9

1. The difference between (*a*) and (*b*) is significant beyond the 0·05 level, and those between (*a*) and (*c*), and between (*a*) and (*d*) beyond the 0·001 level.

Whalley, 1961, pp. 138–40 and pp. 45–57). From these figures alone one cannot say that the differences are produced solely by a decline in parental encouragement, as such factors as the correlation between social class and academic aptitude are also involved. The case study evidence, however, on progress in the grammar school, points strongly to parental influence as a major factor. The differences are most pronounced when both parents attended a grammar school, and when only the father attended a grammar school. When only the mother attended a grammar school the differences, as shown in the table, do not appear as great, but one would not care to make a definite finding from a single instance and with such small numbers (cf. Douglas, 1964, p. 43).

We then examined the parental education of the deteriorators and found to our surprise that in *only one case amongst the thirty-nine was there a parent educated in a grammar school,* whereas we have seen that in the control sample of a one-year entry there were 108 out of 181 families with one or more parents who were taught at a grammar school.[1] The research of Jones (1962) gives general support to these findings. His research produced a statistically significant association between deterioration and neither of the parents having been educated at a grammar school, and between deterioration and the mother not having been educated at a grammar school, but the difference caused by the father not receiving a grammar school education was not statistically significant, though the trend was the same. Further support for the influence of the mother on the educational progress of the child comes from our examination of the parental education of the full thirty-six improvers discovered in the entries of years 1 to 6. Both the parents of one-third of the improvers were educated at a

1. The difference is statistically highly significant.

grammar school, only the mothers of another third (30·6 per cent) were so educated, and in the case of 19·4 per cent of improvers only the father was so educated. In only 16·6 per cent of the cases did neither parent attend a grammar school. We are supported in this finding by the work of Greenald (1955), who concluded that there was some association between improvement and the parents' further or grammar school education.[1]

The scarcity of grammar school parents amongst the deteriorators does not, of course, imply an inevitable lack of academic culture in the home; but it does mean that all these parents have missed the experience of grammar school life and studies which could help them with their children's difficulties; and it cannot be easy for them to understand fully what the school requires of them as parents. Lewis (1952) writes: '. . . it was often more difficult for a boy from a poorer home to "fit in" as naturally as a boy whose parents had been to grammar schools, and where their own backgrounds and interests were not unlike those of the schoolmasters the boy would meet in school.' Thus in seven cases of the thirty-nine there was evidence of the reading of light novels by one or both parents, the other parents read newspapers and periodicals only. Another survey, reported in *Allocation Studies No. 5* (1955) of the National Foundation for Educational Research, has similar findings. It gives the results of interviews with 191 parents in a suburb of London; it states that

> . . . reading at the level of illustrated and feature magazines was related positively to improvement (22) and reading at the level of comics and women's papers to deterioration (31). For two-thirds of the sample, the type of newspaper taken in the home was approximately independent of trend of achievement; although in a small group where no paper at all was taken, there was a trend towards deterioration.

A number of researches have now demonstrated this finding, e.g. Metcalfe (1950, p. 63): 'The provision of (good) books in the home proved a significant factor' (for academic progress). Fraser (1959), pp. 43–6, comes to the same conclusion.

The second factor selected was size of family.

FAMILY SIZE

While we were examining the association between family poverty and deterioration in attainment we came across important differences

1. Cf. also the important book by Fraser (1959), pp. 41–3.

concerning family size. This is an aspect of the question which merits much more attention. As Stott (1956) states:

> When one examines the home background of delinquents or even of children who are backward at school, one cannot help remarking how frequently they are members of large families, and recent studies confirm that the numbers coming from such families are indeed disproportionate.

Even when social class is held constant, this effect of family size can be seen at work (cf. Floud *et al.*, 1956, Table 21).

Not only is a large family more likely to draw near the poverty line, and therefore be unable to pay for facilities such as books and the comfort of a fire for homework, but also interruption by other children in the family may help substantially towards the deterioration of a grammar school pupil. Four of our deteriorators suffered badly from such interruptions. Nor can the parents give as much attention to any one of five or six children as they could to an only child.

The difference between the size of the families of the deteriorators and those of a control group is shown in Table 4.3. This table was

TABLE 4.3.   *Size of family.*

	6 or more %	5 %	4 %	3 %	2 %	1 %
	Number of children in family					
One-year entry (95 pupils not counting deteriorators)	—	8·7	21·7	17·4	39·1	13·0
Deteriorators in the survey (39) (years 1 to 5)	18·0	5·1	28·2	15·4	20·5	12·8

prepared by noting the number of children in the family of each deteriorator, towards the end of the pupil's first year of attendance.

It will be seen that whereas 51 per cent of the deteriorators belonged to families where there were four or more children, only 30 per cent of the non-deteriorators were similarly placed and in the entry year considered in Table 4.3 there was no family of a non-deteriorator which had more than five children. The average size of the families of deteriorators was 3·9 whereas that of the thirty-six improvers was 2·1. Greenald (1955) came to the same conclusion. He reported that a family size of four children or more was associated with a downward trend in academic performance, in both middle and working classes. Academic improvement was associated with only children, particularly among the working class. In this study 67 per cent of the improvers were the first-born of a small family; the figure for deteriorators was 48·7 per cent.[1]

In order to ascertain more clearly the interrelationship between social class, size of family and pupil attainment the data was reorganised as it appears in Table 4.4.

TABLE 4.4. *Size of family and social class deteriorators compared with improvers*[1].

Children in family		Social class					
		2	3	4	5	6	7
1	Deteriorators				2	2	1
	Improvers	(1)	(4)	(3)	(5)		
2	Deteriorators					3	3
	Improvers		(3)	(3)	(7)		
3	Deteriorators				3	2	1
	Improvers		(4)	(2)	(1)		
4	Deteriorators			1	4	2	4
	Improvers				(2)		
5	Deteriorators				1	1	
	Improvers						
6	Deteriorators				2	1	
	Improvers						
More than 6	Deteriorators				2	1	1
	Improvers	(1)					

1. Improvers are in brackets; they are from years 1 to 6, whereas deteriorators are from years 1 to 5.

The dotted line is drawn to include all but one of the thirty-six improvers. When one reads from left to right, there are no improvers below social class 5 (skilled manual) and when one reads downwards there is only one improver from families of more than four children. In this exceptional case the father was a professional man (social class 2). Within each social class the family size of the improvers is smaller than that of the deteriorators; in social class 4 (lower supervisory) it is 1·9 compared with 3·0, and in social class 5 (skilled manual) it is 2·0 compared with 4·9. The other classes do not overlap, but for social

1. The differences are statistically significant.

class 3 (supervisory) the average size for improvers was 1·4, and in social class 2 (executive) it was 3·6 (because of the exceptional family of 9); for deteriorators in class 6 (semiskilled) the average size was 3·6 and for those in class 7 (unskilled) 3·4. As the number of deteriorators was only thirty-nine, and there were only thirty-six improvers, we record this information mainly to enable comparisons to be made with the results of other investigations.

Once again, however, we feel it necessary to remind readers of the 'floor' and 'ceiling' effects due to our definition of improvers and deteriorators. A large proportion of the higher social-class children were in the A stream on entry, because of their high place in the entrance examination. They were therefore more 'at risk' than those from the lower social classes, except that they were not included as deteriorators if they went down only to the B stream. Pupils in the A stream could not, however, become improvers. On the other hand, there was a large proportion of pupils of low social class in the lowest stream. It was therefore statistically easier for them to produce improvers, whereas they could not, by definition, become deteriorators. Our working definitions, therefore, tend to produce an underestimate of the association between social class and attainment in the grammar school.

In the remaining sections of this chapter we present evidence on other aspects of the home background, without, however, being able to compare it with evidence derived from a control group of pupils who made normal progress. Lacking the necessary financial resources and manpower we were unable to do this. Though we visited the homes of some of the improvers, the visits were too few to afford an adequate basis for statistical comparison. None the less, we present the results here because we consider that they are interesting, and valuable as clinical evidence.

HOME FACILITIES

One of the most obvious differences between the social classes, for our purposes, is in the facilities—or handicaps—which help or hinder the pupil while doing homework. Though this provision is sometimes merely a reflection of the attitude of the parents towards education, and the priority which they give to other things, such as radio, television and entertaining, it is often largely determined by limitations of accommodation and by finance. Its importance is illustrated by the finding of one research worker (Metcalfe, 1950) that those factors which do influence school progress are such as affect home-work facilities. We ourselves found that in twenty of the thirty-nine homes of deteriorators there was normally no fire in any room other than the kitchen or living-room, and in nine of these cases there was also fairly constant interruption from other members of the family, mainly children. One of these and another pupil (aged eleven-plus) were regularly kept in charge of their youngest brothers and sisters for the evening. The industrious type of child would often triumph over these difficulties, but not all children are industrious. While interviewing the parents in the homes the visitor became acutely aware that almost always it is not one single factor which is responsible for a pupil's lack of progress, but an interacting combination of factors, though one or two major factors are often clearly discernible.

There is a suggestion in *Early Leaving* (1954), p. 40, for assisting boys and girls who have poor opportunities for doing homework, viz:

> Boys and girls who had poor facilities for doing homework at their own home might be accommodated after school hours at (*a*) the grammar school, or (*b*) the primary school which they attended before entering the grammar school, or (*c*) some other convenient centre, e.g. Public Library, Youth Club.

Suggestion (*b*) would have been helpful in thirteen 'cases' of this survey; the others were far removed from the suggested facilities. If they could have stayed at the grammar school after the afternoon session, eleven local 'cases' would have benefited; suggestion (*c*) would have been difficult in this area because of lack of accommodation.

It is heartening to see that in Bootle since 1955 'a new branch library includes a successful children's homework centre equipped with study carrels, individual desk lights and a plentiful stock of reference books'. Similar experiments are being tried in other large cities.

In most regions the presence of a television set in the only room where there is a fire increases the handicap of the working-class child compared with the child of a professional or executive father. The problem has been so serious in some cases as to impel the Head to send a circular letter to parents asking for their cooperation in ensuring that children are enabled to do their homework in a warm room. without interruption. Other Heads have made the request at Speech Day or through a Parents' Association.

POVERTY

Lack of money does not, of itself, produce unstable academic performers. There was, however, as we have already seen, a deterioration of an undue proportion of the grammar school children of working-class families; in this deterioration the financial factor sometimes played its part. For example, two boy deteriorators had been told early in their school life by one or both of their parents that the financial state of their family could not keep them at school beyond the minimum age for leaving. Both of these boys worked for money in the evenings and on Saturdays. Another boy was possibly conscious of the financial struggle at home; he used to buy his own clothes with his wages as errand boy. There was financial stress, also, at the homes of an additional two boys, so that they took paid 'errand' work at an early stage in their grammar school career.

Financial difficulties also produce premature and early leaving, even though a maintenance grant is given to parents of children who remain at school after their fifteenth birthday. Two of our girl deteriorators because of the more or less permanent illness of the father (though their mother was working) considered their financial position very carefully, did not find the grant sufficient, and left school. But there is no evidence to show that, even if the grant had been doubled in value, these and the other deteriorators who were premature and early leavers would have remained at school. This aspect of early leaving is emphasised in a Report of the Association of Education Committees (1952): 'The amount and incidence of maintenance allowance play an insignificant part.' The Report continues: 'The chief attraction to the early leaver is undoubtedly the money to be received from entering paid employment.'

Another factor, of which readers should be reminded, is that within each social class, deteriorators tend to come from larger families; it is by no means unlikely that financial difficulties played a part here.

Other research also shows the influence of financial stringency. Ault (1940) concludes that 'unemployment or casual employment of father' is one of six causes of backwardness in secondary school work. Fraser (1959), pp. 46–9, working in Aberdeen, also found poverty to have an appreciable effect, even when intelligence level had been taken into account.

Further evidence of the impact of poverty on scholastic progress is provided by the National Foundation for Educational Research, *Allocation Study*, No. 5, 1955. It states:

Where there has been financial difficulty there is a trend towards deterioration . . .; further: That being an only child is likely to be associated with improvement, especially among the working-class pupils, and that belonging to a family of four or more is more likely to be associated with improvement or deterioration than with progress at the predicted level.

PARENTAL ATTITUDE

We include a short section on parental attitude to the pupil's education because we consider it to be of central importance. Disappointingly, however, we have little new evidence to offer. This is because we were convinced that the only reliable method of obtaining direct and reasonably valid information was by interviewing the parents of *all* the entrants before they had been more than a few months at the grammar school. Only at this stage would the attitudes of the parents be unaffected by the progress—or lack of progress—of their offspring. Later on the encouraging attitude of the parents—if it existed at all—might be undermined by the persistent failures of the deteriorators, while the support of the parents of successful pupils would be strengthened. Our resources were quite inadequate for interviewing on this extensive scale, and we therefore offer only some indirect evidence, and quote a few findings from other sources.

The most obvious indication of parental encouragement of academic progress is seen when parents give high priority to the provision of good facilities for quiet study and homework. This is a first essential, and a good test where the parents are financially able to make the provision. We have seen that in twenty of the deteriorators' homes no fire was provided in a separate room for studying. This was so from the time a fire was first needed in the autumn, so here there is no 'backwash' effect of a pupil's failure. Most of the parents could have afforded this expense if they had seen the necessity of it and adjusted their priorities.

The parents, of course, need to give much more than facilities; constant encouragement—even in the face of failure—is needed. This is much more likely to occur if parents themselves have attended a grammar school and realise what is required of the child, and have a practical insight into the part which they themselves need to play. In our study only one of the seventy-eight parents of the deteriorators had attended a grammar school, and the case studies given later contain plenty of evidence of parental ignorance about homework requirements, of lack of discipline regarding homework, of too frequent attendance at the cinema and social functions, and so on. The parental attitude is also reflected by the premature and early leaving of the deteriorators. Out of eleven deteriorators of the year 1 entries, nine left without sitting for the Ordinary level of the G.C.E.; out of seven deteriorators of the year 2 entries, four left after three years at the grammar school; and three more left without sitting for a G.C.E. It is realised, as mentioned above, that the lack of success would, in itself, be an incentive to the parent to withdraw the child (cf. Dale, 1957). Collins (1955) also emphasises the waste involved in this premature leaving: '. . . decrease (of premature leaving) requires primarily the development of certain attitudes towards continued education rather than the refinements of selection techniques and the adjustment of grammar school places'. There must be an attitude of mind in the parents which takes for granted the continuation of the child's study as far as the Ordinary level of the G.C.E., and possibly beyond.

The *Early Leaving* Report (1954) shows in Table 20 that 24 per cent of the number of girls leaving school prematurely did so because only the parents wished it; 40 per cent left beause only the pupils wished it . . . and one wonders how much influence the parents' attitude had on this 40 per cent. The investigation by Floud *et al.* (1957, p. 80) adds further evidence.

> The (grammar) schools may find that one in seven (in Middlesbrough) and one in twelve (South-west Hertfordshire) of the children admitted each year (regardless of social origin) are handicapped by the likelihood that their parents will withdraw them at the age of fifteen and the certainty that their parents will not resist any inclination on the children's part to leave school at this age. They may also have to face the fact that approximately another one in four in South-west Hertfordshire and one in three in Middlesbrough will be in the same position at the age of sixteen.

Though premature leaving (i.e. before taking the General Certificate at Ordinary Level) and early leaving (before taking a Sixth Form course) have both been reduced since these figures were published, and reflect a change in public opinion and parental attitude, there is still a long way to go.

DISHARMONY IN THE HOME

The evidence for harmony or discord in a home is often circumstantial and sometimes hearsay. Very few parents show mutual repugnance before a visitor. Although the field worker visited the homes of the deteriorators and knew the children well, we cannot be at all certain that we have included every instance of serious discord. Our cases are limited to those of a more serious type which cannot be concealed. But in ten cases out of thirty-nine, there is convincing evidence of the psychological turmoil produced in some children by disharmony in the home. These included indisputable records of serious discord in the families of two boy deteriorators just before their entrance to the grammar school, with disastrous effects on their work; another had a father who was physically vicious especially when drunk; the parents of a girl deteriorator were unmarried, and the father was morally unstable and often drunk; the illness of the father was the cause of unfortunate relationships at another boy's home; yet another boy had a home life which can only be described as 'tempestuous'; we have similar incontestable evidence of pronounced discord in another four cases. Further evidence of the same kind is provided by one sixth-form pupil, who was a brilliant student up to the sixth form and then had a serious psychological upset on account of a difficult relationship with one of the parents and also between the parents themselves. The student was persuaded to move from the home to 'digs'. This resulted in a marked recovery and the student managed to pass in two advanced subjects and went on to do well at the university.

We are aware that the evidence would have been strengthened if the homes of the deteriorators had been compared with those of the non-deteriorators, but the difficulty of obtaining satisfactory evidence prevented this being done. However, on the clinical level, the case study material points to disharmony in the home as a far from negligible factor in the production of deteriorators. It would indeed be surprising if this were not so. Other researchers have similar findings. Metcalfe (1950) also found that emotional disturbance is detrimental to school progress. She suggests that the uncooperative parent not only makes no effort to provide conditions and materials for home study or for physical wellbeing, but by his indifference, or even opposition to the demands made by the school, subjects the child to conflict and frustration and so sets up the state of emotional disturbance which is a significant factor in hindering scholastic and personality success. Fraser (1959, pp. 60–4) also found that an abnormal home background was important in lowering the attainment level, even when intelligence had been allowed for.

There are, however, cases where deterioration does not occur under these circumstances. We have in mind one pupil whose home conditions, well known to the investigator, were far from ideal—the father having a decidedly irresponsible attitude to his home. The child had a strong desire for university education, a factor which enabled her to pursue her studies with commendable single-mindedness; but it must be admitted that the mother was a better influence than the father.

EMOTIONAL DISTURBANCE

It is, of course, difficult and often impossible to separate this factor from the home background. We did, however, find five cases where the emotional disturbances did not appear to be produced by disharmony, poverty, or lack of facilities in the home. These severe disturbances were due to a girl's sexual precocity, a boy's discovery of his illegitimacy, the temperamental unbalance of a boy (leading later to confirmed serious illness), the death of a girl's mother, and the prolonged and difficult illness at home of a boy's father. These emotional factors contributed substantially, in our opinion, to the academic deterioration of all five pupils, but in only three of them did it appear to be the principal factor. There is no 'proof', in the scientific sense, that this is so; one is merely making a judgment from the data.

COMMENT

The evidence presented in this chapter has demonstrated the cardinal importance of a good supporting home background for the satisfactory academic progress of children. While conducting the case studies and while examining the evidence we have been impressed by the frequency with which a child suffers not merely from one handicap in the home but from an accumulation of them. John, who is the son of an unskilled manual labourer, has several younger brothers and sisters, and lives in a small house in a poor neighbourhood where the attitude to education is by no means as favourable as elsewhere. There is not enough money to pay for a second fire, there is no second living-room in which homework could be done, and there is no table in a bedroom either. John does his homework in the crowded living-room on the edge of the table, subject to frequent interruptions from other children. If he experiences difficulties in the work he is unable to call in help from his parents. If his homework is unfinished when father or mother want to listen to the radio or to watch television, he either finishes it under difficulties or gives up the struggle. His parents do not know whether the work is finished or not, nor do they show any particular interest. Sometimes John is left in charge of the younger children while his parents have a night out at the pub or the cinema. Sometimes a gang of his friends, who are all at the secondary modern school and have little or no homework, come and tempt John to go out and play before his own work is completed. They perhaps go to the cinema together twice a week. When John is put into a lower stream at the end of the first term at the grammar school, neither parent thinks of going to see the Headmaster to discuss John's deterioration, or if they do think of it, they cannot summon up the initiative or courage to do it. John leaves early because he is 'doing no good at school', the family needs his earnings, and his friends are leaving the secondary modern school and flinging their money about on girl friends and bicycles while John has 2s 6d a week pocket money and—no girl friend.

On the other hand David is the son of professional parents who have themselves been educated in a grammar school. They provide him with facilities for doing homework in a separate room and light a fire when necessary. There is therefore little interruption from other members of the family or from television and radio. If he has trouble with his homework he can turn to either his mother or father for help, and many books of reference are available. His cultural background is constantly a help to him at school and in his homework. Mother or father may even inspect his homework regularly or occasionally. If he appears to be losing ground his parents arrange an interview with the Headmaster to discuss the matter. If he is absent from school for a long period the parents arrange for a tutor to visit the home to give special help with subjects such as English and Mathematics. David's friends all expect to be at school till they are eighteen and many of them expect to go on to a university. David also receives a lot of attention from his parents because there are only a few children in the family. He himself aims high in order to do at least as well as his parents, and his parents encourage him to do so.[1]

Not all working-class pupils are as badly off as John and not all pupils of professional-class parents are as well off as David, but the trends are there, and to endeavour to hide them would do a real disservice to the working classes themselves. It has become axiomatic that educational progress depends greatly on social reform.

1. Cf. Dept. of Education and Science, *Education under Social Handicap*, Report on Education No. 17, H.M.S.O., December 1964.

REFERENCES

ASSOCIATION OF EDUCATION COMMITTEES (1952), *Early Leavers from Grammar Schools,* London.

AULT, H. K. (1940), 'An investigation into the causes of backwardness in geography', unpub. M.A. thesis, London.

CENTRAL ADVISORY COUNCIL FOR EDUCATION (ENGLAND) (1954), *Early Leaving,* H.M.S.O.

COLLINS, H. (1955), 'Premature leaving from grammar schools', *British Journal of Educational Psychology,* **25,** part 1.

DALE, R. R. (1957), Review, in *British Journal of Educational Studies.*

DOUGLAS, J. W. B. (1964), *The Home and the School,* MacGibbon & Kee.

FLOUD, J. E., HALSEY, A. H. and MARTIN, F. M. (1956), *Social Class and Educational Opportunity,* Heinemann.

FRASER, E. (1959), *Home Environment and the School,* U.L.P.

GREENALD, G. M. (1955), 'An inquiry into the influence of sociological and physical factors on the trend of achievement in grammar school pupils', unpub. M.A. thesis, London.

JONES, C. V. (1962), 'An enquiry into the causes of gross discrepancy between the performance of pupils in the 11-plus examination and their performance at the end of the first year in a Welsh grammar school', unpub. M.A. thesis, Swansea.

LEWIS, B. R. (1952), 'Some relationships between comparative success and failure in grammar schools and certain aspects of personality', unpub. M.A. thesis, London.

METCALFE, O. (1950), 'The influence of socio-economic factors on school progress and personality development', unpub. M.A. thesis, Birmingham.

THE NATIONAL FOUNDATION FOR EDUCATIONAL RESEARCH (1955), *Allocation Study,* no. 5.

STOTT, D. H. (1956), *Unsettled Children and their Families,* University of London Press.

WHALLEY, G. E. (1961), 'The effect of social class on the academic progress of boys within a boys' grammar school', unpub. M.Ed. thesis, Durham.

PART THREE Contextual studies

5

The community environment of the school*

S. John Eggleston

The demographic studies of Part Two quantified the outlines of the family-class-education relationship, both in terms of large-scale flows of talent and of the environmental components of individual families. The subcultural studies of Parts Four and Five build upon these foundations in their search for causal relationships, for mechanisms. Between the two approaches are contextual studies, where social-class variations in educational opportunity and achievement are examined in relation to particular neighbourhoods or particular schools. In this chapter, Professor Eggleston discusses the distinctive social climates of various kinds of urban locality and how these influence school achievement.

The distinctive characteristics of a *community* are well known. They are embodied in the small, localised, self-contained group with shared values and ways of life which constitute a *culture* catering for *all* the needs of all the individual members. These tightly-knit human groups of which one is unmistakably either an insider or an outsider have disappeared from large areas of modern Western society. In Britain they are to be found regularly only in the highlands and moorlands and in the Celtic fringes. In America they commonly exist only in the southern mountain regions or in the 'bible belt' areas of Utah and Idaho.

COMMUNITY AND ASSOCIATION

Nostalgia for the self-identification and security which a community offers is often expressed in phrases like 'We must recapture that lost sense of community' or 'We are trying to create a community feeling'.

* Reprinted from *The Social Context of the School*, Routledge, 1967, pp. 11–36, by kind permission of the author and the publisher.

But the very words show a realisation that the social order in which we live is largely based on something other than community. Community has been replaced by *association*. The relationship based on living together, which is appropriate to the shared and recurring tasks of the largely autonomous small communities of agrarian societies, is replaced by a complex network of contractual agreements or collaboration for specific tasks in modern industrial societies. Rational agreement rather than 'natural' grouping becomes the norm, and schools are an important example of the change, being established to perform important parts of the processes of preparing and selecting the young for adult status. Except for the education of a very few young people destined to be members of elite groups such as rulers or priests, these are processes which would have been taken care of without any kind of school system in the community. If schools had existed there they could at best have played only a marginal part in the process of *socialisation*—the transmission of the adult way of life to each new generation. Instead, most of the young people would have become adults solely as a result of the informal educative influence of the adults in the homes and the fields. There would have been no need for schools to help pupils to identify their talents so that they could enter an adult occupation which matched them. *Selection* would have taken place at birth, for in the community 'following father's footsteps' is a convenient and acceptable way of ensuring the required continuity in the labour supply. (In sociological terms, adult occupational role would have been *ascribed* to individuals rather than having been *achieved* by them.) The physical, moral and social *welfare* of the young would have been the sole responsibility of the parents aided informally by the other adults in the community. In short, the *social functions* of socialisation, selection and welfare were once left to the informal processes of the community. In modern industrial society, formal educational systems play an important part in their performance.

THE CATCHMENT AREA AS A COMMUNITY

Yet the present-day school serves an identifiable local group of parents and their children. At one level, this 'catchment area' can be regarded as no more than a fortuitous geographical grouping of individuals who happen to live in an area which a local education authority has allocated to a particular school, an artefact of educational administration. But all who know schools will have some evidence

that many catchment areas have more in common than just the avail-
ability of a particular school and have distinctive features which
differentiate the schools they serve. In modern Britain, the incidence
of social class and urbanisation has led to geographical groupings
which are by no means randomly ordered. We find local areas of
housing where inhabitants have much in common in their way of life.
The geographical mobility which is associated with the occupational
mobility of industrial societies leads not to dispersion, but to greater
concentrations of 'similar' people. The 'new' middle-class workers
and their families move to the new middle-class suburbs, and the
'downtown' central areas of towns and cities become housing areas
for the lower occupational and lower status groups of society. The
movement is reinforced by selective public housing policies where
'respectable' working-class families are given priority over the
'rough' in the allocation of new suburban council houses. Recent
studies have confirmed that new homogeneous groups which are
sharply differentiated from each other arise in mass society (Goldthorpe and Lockwood, 1963b).

As a consequence of all this the schools often find themselves
serving areas which have many of the characteristics of the old
communities, even to the inflexibility of social norms. The school
may find itself closely bound to such a catchment area, and the old
community pressures which were once felt directly by the individual
child may now be experienced through the school. The bonds may
be even greater if the local educational authority adopts a policy of
neighbourhood schools and arranges specially homogeneous
catchment areas—such as the new council or private housing estates
which are often 'allocated' to new primary schools. Alternatively, the
schools may be used as instruments in the integration of the local
population as in Cambridgeshire and elsewhere when the local
secondary school becomes part of a community college in which
many of the activities of the adults are also centred.

CATEGORISATION OF CONTEMPORARY COMMUNITY LIFE

Sociologists have attempted to categorise the manifestations of
community life in modern Britain in several dimensions. Frankenberg, in a valuable review of community studies in Britain, uses the
rural-urban dimension (Frankenberg, 1966). Another possible
dimension is that of socio-economic status, distinguishing communities at different positions in the class structure-differences which

can be seen in the occupation, the 'life-styles' of the areas and the values and attitudes associated with them. If we use this dimension we can set up a continuum of community types. At one end would be the 'twilight' zone slum areas of the big cities, with an overcrowded lower working-class population that has been variously described as 'rough', 'deprived' and 'underprivileged'. Moving along the socio-economic scale we would come to the 'solid' working-class areas of the kind sometimes represented in 'Coronation Street' and elsewhere. Beyond this would be 'home centred, aspiring' areas. One would contain the old-established 'respectable' working-class families, another the newly affluent young workers and their families. Moving into the non-manual areas, we would find the lower-middle-class groups, predominantly in the lower income clerical occupations, the new 'executive' housing areas with young and occupationally mobile populations and, finally, the established well-to-do middle-class areas of low density housing.

THE CONCEPT OF 'IDEAL TYPE' APPLIED TO COMMUNITY

In this chapter we shall consider two of these areas, one at each end of the continuum. The first will be the 'twilight' zones, the second the 'new middle-class' suburbs. In this consideration we shall be presenting the two areas as *ideal types*—in which *all* the identifiable characteristics of lower working-class or new middle-class areas are assumed to be present and *none* of the characteristics of other types of area exist. Such ideal types are useful devices to aid clarification and comparison of social facts, but it must always be remembered that in real life no single community will match up to all the characteristics described even briefly.

The 'Twilight' Zones

For a graphic account of a twilight community and its schools we may turn to the annals of the Crown Street area of Liverpool recorded by Mays (1962). Here in the old central areas of Liverpool, decaying houses have long been vacated by the well-to-do or even the relatively prosperous artisans, and have been refilled to overcrowding by an unskilled, nomadic and cosmopolitan population. The schools match the neighbourhood, and generally are old like the houses. Despite efforts by the teachers, the churches and the local authority, they are frequently ill-equipped.

For many of the children in these areas, the only relevance of the school is that it is seen to share the same material handicaps as the community. The social values of the school have little relevance to those of the community; indeed at best the school seems to achieve a kind of bilingualism and 'biculture' whereby children have one set of language and values for the home and one for the school. Here the learning environment provided by the family is quite apart from the learning environment provided by the school. Mays talks of the underlying belief of a minority that school is not really very important, that education is something imposed on them from above, with which they are forced to comply to some extent, however alien and unnecessary it may appear to be. But even amongst the majority of parents who are not hostile to education, he found prevailing attitudes of inertia and a lack of enthusiasm. Whilst they accepted that the children should attend school and acquire a minimal skill in the basic subjects, there was little acceptance or understanding that children should be encouraged to develop their innate abilities to the utmost extent.

The consequences of all this appeared in the teachers' comments. They reported that most of their children lacked a basic interest in school subjects and had little foresight and very slender ambitions. Their failure was seen to be not only due to innate disability but also to poor attainments resulting from a complex of social factors.

The pictures which emerge are the familiar ones of universal leaving at minimum school-leaving age, negligible transfer to grammar schools, minimal parent–teacher contact (though with some notable exceptions), and a high turnover of teaching staff which increases the already difficult conditions in the schools. In these schools the social tasks of education, though nowhere more necessary, were often less effectively performed than elsewhere, because the conventional ways of performing them were largely inappropriate to the environment of the school. The socialisation experience offered by the school was irrelevant, because nowhere did it effectively link with the informal socialisation of the community. The selective function of the school was almost non-existent as the school failed to bring its pupils forward to any achievement which could be rewarded with improved prospects. The majority of the children who leave the Crown Street schools fill the unskilled manual jobs which carry the lowest social prestige; only a minority become semiskilled and a smaller minority skilled. Most of the girls take jobs such as shop assistants and process workers in factories, while the boys will become coal-heavers, van drivers, dockers and builders' labourers. Only the welfare function of the school is seen to be relevant, but here the need for medical and social services is so great that the resources of the school are often swamped.

One of the reasons for the situation of schools in the areas of low socio-economic status is seen to lie in the existence of 'culture conflict' between teachers and the community. This is well expressed by Mays (1962), who writes:

> The teachers in the school find themselves at the nexus of two distinct cultures with a correspondingly difficult role to play. Being themselves mainly conditioned by the grammar school tradition and the middle-class system of values, they have to make a drastic mental readjustment to be able to deal sympathetically with the people whose attitudes and standards are so different (p. 180).

The important point about this *culture conflict thesis* is its emphasis on the two-way relationship between school and community. The hostility and low attainment of the pupils are seen to spring not only from the culture of the twilight area but also from the culturally based responses of the teachers to it. A number of research studies, some of which will be referred to later in this chapter, suggest that the critical responses of many teachers to aspects of the cultures of low socio-economic status areas may be one of the most significant causal factors in the social problems of the schools.

The 'twilight' zones are often referred to in popular writing as areas of *cultural deprivation*. This is a misleading term—it will be apparent already to the reader that the subculture of the twilight zone is likely to ensure a full and distinctive way of life for its members. What is usually meant is that the subculture of the area differs from the more general cultural patterns of the larger society—of which the education system is a part. In consequence the child from such an area may be at a disadvantage because his cultural background may not be in harmony with that of the education he receives. But it is important to remember that, though in this sense he may be *culturally handicapped* he is unlikely to be culturally deprived.

The 'New Middle-Class' Areas

The contrast with communities at the other extreme of the socio-economic scale—the 'new middle-class' areas—is marked. Here we are in a world of superior material environment, inside and outside the home. The community offers open spaces, play areas and clean air. The homes offer uncrowded accommodation reserved for the young, separate rooms for homework, gardens and other facilities for home entertainment unknown to the downtown child. But it is in the prevailing attitudes to education that these communities are so widely at variance with those we have just been considering. Far from a minimal support for education, the enthusiasm for the work of the school is great. Parents have a personal knowledge of the social advantages of schooling, and strive to ensure such advantages for their children. This leads them to take an active interest in the selective procedures, such as streaming, eleven-plus and public examinations, and to modify the learning environment of the family in order to maximise their children's chances. Thus active parental support reinforces the already advantageous home environment provided by books and conversation, physical and emotional care and the parents' own personal experience of an education which 'meant something'. The enthusiasm spreads over from individual homes to form part of the norms of the community, which becomes actively concerned with educational issues such as school improvement and the expansion of educational expenditure. Moreover, as Blyth (1965) notes, the

> protected environment is carefully fostered by the district itself, for it gives the children a relaxed and friendly world to live in, it maintains the status of the school and the teachers and it upholds the reputation of the district itself, and the status of those who succeed in living there (Vol. ii, 90).

The values of the home and the community are the values of the school; the values which the home and the community rewards are those which the school fosters. The contrast to Crown Street is complete. Staying on is the norm, parent–teacher communication is full and harmonious, teacher turnover is low and the whole process of education is further facilitated by the new and attractive schools built to serve the new and attractive houses. In some middle-class catchment areas the support tends to overwhelm the schools. One teacher in such an area recently told the author 'I just can't travel on the bus to town any more. Every time I sit down a parent comes and sits next to me and asks me about their child's prospects. There's no escape.' In the middle-class suburb, the range of informal and formal pressures applied by the community may seem to bring us to a point nearer the American situation of direct community control than is characteristic of our system. But the extent of this influence is more apparent than real. The isolation from direct community surveillance is still assured by the fundamental differences in the administration of education discussed in Chapter 4 [of *The Social Context of the School*]. The concord springs more from the coincidence of values between the teachers and the community than from the local community control characteristic of the United States.

OTHER 'IDEAL TYPES'

So far we have been describing 'ideal types' of twilight or middle-class communities. It is also possible to set up other ideal types within the socio-economic continuum. One of many is set up by Swift (1964), who makes an important distinction between two ideal types of middle-class environment. His first is the traditional one which 'sees the middle-class family providing a cultured, stimulating environment which leads to a mature interest in school work, verbal facility and habits of thought which make school work easy and pleasant'. The second ideal type is one which has none of the advantages of the first, but in which one or both parents is characterised by frustrated ambition.

> These parents value the education system for its role in social climbing, they believe (on the basis of their own experience) that ability alone is not rewarded except insofar as it is manifested in certificates, they also have a clear and accurate picture of the prestige hierarchy and their actual (as opposed to rightful) place within it (Swift, 1964, p. 7).

Yet another ideal type of catchment area is the one largely composed of the 'new' manual workers and their families. These are the workers, often highly paid, who are commonly to be found in new large-scale industrial plants. These workers tend to lack the collective loyalties of the older working-class groups and see themselves as being in limited contractual relationships with employers. They have been labelled the 'privatised' manual workers by Goldthorpe and Lockwood (1963a). But as these writers point out, the superficial similarities to the middle-class way of life overlay fundamental differences in social behaviour and values, including attitudes to education.

It must be emphasised once again that in our discussion of ideal types of community we have been presenting aids to understanding rather than descriptions of social reality. In real communities the characteristics of any one type are never entirely absent from any other. Thus the severely distressed 'twilight children' described by Clegg (1966, pp. 19–21) are to be found not only in the twilight zones but in all others too.

The contrast between typical 'downtown' and suburban schools is drawn by many writers. It is used by Conant (1961, pp. 1–2) to give emphasis to one of the most important features of the discussion— the ways in which the community attitudes and values are brought to bear on the schools. He shows that in the superior suburban high schools, from which 80 per cent or more of the students enter some sort of college, the most important problem for the parents is to ensure the admission of their children to prestige colleges; and there is great concern over good teaching of academic subjects. Here, the teachers' problem is to adjust the family's ambitions to the boy's or girl's abilities. In the slums, where as many as a half of the children leave school early, the problems are almost the reverse. The task with which the teachers in the slum must struggle is twofold, on the one hand to prepare students to get and keep jobs as soon as they leave school and, on the other hand, to raise the ambitions of those who have academic talent.

COMMUNITY INFLUENCE AND THE SCHOOLS

The differences may be transmitted to the schools in a variety of ways. A world of difference is conveyed between the following statements by parents reported by Jackson and Marsden (1962):

> The lad was at home with me when the exam (the eleven-plus) were on, so he never took it. I were poorly in bed, and then the lass, she'd been off school—it were the same, I'd been poorly in bed again—and they sent for her to take the exam. Well, it was ridiculous. They came across from the school and said that the exam were on and could she go in for it. She were very clever too and she'd probably have passed. All her friends were surprised because she hadn't passed to go to grammar school because she were cleverer nor them, but she'd been away three month and her mind weren't on it—it were silly her going really (p. 230).

This stands in striking contrast with Patricia's parents. When Patricia passed the selection examination she said:

> I was called by myself into father's office and he had the lists on his desk. 'Look at that,' he said, 'you've come right at the top.'

I was at the very head of the list of all the children in the school who'd passed. 'Now you can do anything you want,' he said. 'You can do anything.' (*Ibid*, p. 30.)

But community influence is sometimes brought to bear on the school in less direct ways than the attitudes of individual parents. There may be direct community influence on local educational structure, on buildings and facilities and on courses and curriculum. The influence may become more direct as teams of parents are marshalled to build swimming pools, organise fêtes and run school societies in more and more schools and as more parents join local Associations for the Advancement of Education and exert collective pressure on schools and local education authorities. The most powerful direct action still remains open to parents—the power to obtain alternative education by buying it in the private school sector or by moving elsewhere. Both of these modes of action are increasingly possible. The growth of the private sector of education, particularly of the 'private grammar school' with its small classes and recorded successes at A level and University Entrance opens up private alternatives to more parents. The diversity of local education authority provision and the mobility of middle-class parents in the modern occupational structure means that parents not only can move to a different area if they feel their children's prospects are thereby enhanced, but also that they are likely to get something different if they do. Such moves are not always based on adequate information. A family recently moved from a comprehensive school catchment area of Coventry to an area of Leicestershire where the two-tier comprehensive plan is in operation. In this plan, the upper-tier schools are popularly called grammar schools. The father explained to the author 'We've done it for the lad's sake, you know. We didn't go much on this comprehensive lark. We came to Leicestershire because here everyone can go to the grammar school.' But even when full information is possessed, direct action by parents is likely to lead to even sharper differences between school catchment areas, because such action is very likely to be taken by the middle-class parents and very unlikely to be taken by the parents of the twilight zones.

Yet another way in which the conditions of the catchment area can widen the gap is shown by Douglas (1964, p. 38). He notes that in areas where housing conditions are unsatisfactory, children's test scores are relatively low. Whilst this is so in each social class, the middle-class children, as they get older, reduce this handicap, but the manual working-class children from unsatisfactory homes fall even further behind; for them overcrowding and other deficiencies at home have a progressive and depressive influence on their test performance.

THE RESPONSE OF SCHOOLS TO THEIR CATCHMENT AREAS

What of the response of the schools to these community differences? The problems of the schools in the middle-class suburbs are relatively simple ones. It may be that over-enthusiastic or over-ambitious parents come to be restrained, sometimes with difficulty. Sometimes the school fails to restrain them and the parents end victorious. Jackson and Marsden (1962, p.31) tell the story of Helen, whose headmistress said she had to drop mathematics, but her father disagreed. Helen reported 'There was an awful scene. And all I could say was, my father says I've got to.' In the end Helen continued with her mathematics and in fact took a credit in it with her School Certificate. But even in such cases, the argument is one of speed and detail; there is seldom conflict over the ultimate destination or direction.

In the mixed catchment area the schools' response is more complex. In his work on streaming in *The Home and the School* (1964, Ch. 14) Douglas found that although teachers genuinely intended to stream children according to their measured ability, they none the less allowed these judgments to be influenced by the type of home the children came from. He reported that even where children of the *same level of ability* are considered, those from middle-class homes tended to be allocated to the upper streams and those from the manual working-class to the lower streams. Furthermore, children who were dirty or badly clothed, or who came from large families, also tended to be placed in lower streams, regardless of ability. He goes on to give evidence showing how children who are allocated to upper streams tend to improve their test scores, particularly if they are from middle-class homes, whilst those who go to lower streams deteriorate— particularly if they are from manual workers' homes. In consequence the school's selection, based on environmental differences, may lead to measurable differences in ability where they did not previously exist.

The work of Douglas has brought us to see that the community context of the school can not only influence pupils' response to the school; it can also influence the behaviour of teachers. A number of

American researches have indicated that teachers in schools in areas of high socio-economic status are different from those in schools in areas of low socio-economic status in such matters as professional competence, morale and innovation. An important account of work in this field is to be found in *Social Class and the Urban School* (Herriott and St John, 1966).

In Britain we have some evidence of the conflict which can arise between teachers and their pupils in the twilight areas. One such situation, where education is almost nullified, is well described by Webb (1962), who writes of the problems of teaching at 'Black School', where relationships between pupils and teachers are characterised by an ever present hostility—a continuing battle in which neither side can win, yet which is accepted by both sides as the inevitable and unchanging order of things. But not all schools in the culturally handicapped areas have accepted defeat when the conventional methods have failed. A whole new range of strategies for areas of this kind is being developed, based on curriculum activities that are linked with collective interests of the pupils which are immediate and relevant. Activity then becomes based, not on a denial of the community environment of the pupil and its values but on an understanding of them, which provides a basis on which effective wider education can develop. The Newsom Report has many examples of the way in which this is being done in mathematics, workshop activities and in science. But perhaps the most striking progress has been achieved in language. Examples of the achievement of many 'culturally handicapped' children when they are offered sensitive and imaginative teaching can be seen in Clegg's anthology *The Excitement of Writing* (1964). Work of this kind is not only important in the personal achievement it affords pupils who would not otherwise have had the experience, it may also be of significance in alleviating linguistic handicaps which may spring from the child's environment and which can impede his response to the whole of education (Bernstein, 1965).

Yet another series of developments lies in moves to link homes and school, whereby teachers reverse the state of affairs common in the suburban school and take the initiative in visiting pupils' homes. Associated with this are plans to give teachers special training and to equip some with a qualification to become 'teacher-social workers' so as to specially fit them to undertake this work in problem areas. A course for this purpose has been initiated at Edge Hill College of Education at Ormskirk. The integration of social work methods, particularly of casework techniques, into the practices of schools dealing with social problems seems overdue, and an advanced course at Leicester University is bringing professional social workers and teachers who plan to join staffs of colleges of education together for a year's study in an attempt to speed developments in this direction.

So far there have been no projects in Britain of the magnitude of the American schemes for the alleviation of cultural handicap. Such schemes include the St Louis 'Rooms of Twenty' in which small groups of pupils were assigned to specially competent teachers who were given a free hand to develop skills of literacy and numeracy. A large-scale attempt to raise levels of motivation was involved in the New York 'Higher Horizons' project. In the same city are situated the '600' schools designed to rehabilitate pupils from problem homes. All these schemes are marked by their dependence on audio-visual approaches to the culturally handicapped child. The new American 'Teaching Professions Act' is designed to implement a national scheme for a 'Teacher Corps' of teachers specially trained to work exclusively in city and country slums. The novelty of these arrangements lies not so much in their originality as in their urgency and magnitude. A case for special treatment of 'educational priority areas' in England has been made out in Chapter 5 of the *Plowden Report* (1967).

WISEMAN'S 'EDUCATION AND ENVIRONMENT'

The consequences of the school's response to its community environment both in Britain and the United States raises important educational issues. Wiseman (1964) illustrates some of the complexities which can arise from intensive work on basic attainment in the downtown schools which have a characteristically high proportion of backward children. He writes that this is a situation which

> presents such an obvious and fundamental problem to the teachers that immediate therapy is given first priority. The amount of time and effort given to basic arithmetic and to the teaching of reading becomes very much greater than that allocated to such subjects in the more fortunate suburban schools. By such devotion to these basic skills, the level of ability in them is raised above that which we might expect, having regard to the distribution of ability among the pupils. But this can only be done at the expense of other and more liberal studies (p. 157).

But this improvement in attainment, especially if, as Wiseman suggests, it is accompanied by a narrowing of the curriculum, may not have enhanced the pupils' occupational prospects substantially. It may not have brought them to the point where they can take part in the examination race. It may also have failed to offer the prospect of further full-time education which could have brought them to the point of 'take-off'. So the reward for substantial educational achievement may, in occupational terms, be negligible—the same unskilled work which could have been achieved without the higher attainment. This has led Bantock (1963) and some other writers to make the suggestion that some children might have derived greater benefit from a more liberal education, even at the expense of some degree of formal attainment; views which have aroused widespread debate.

At a time of rising educational standards there are certainly particular problems for the less successful pupils. Parsons (1961, p. 448) has warned us that

> as the acceptable minimum of educational qualifications rises, persons near or below the margin will tend to be pushed into an attitude of repudiation of these expectations. Thus the very improvement of educational standards in the society at large may well be a major factor in the failure of the educational process for a growing number at the lower end of the status and ability distribution.

COMMUNICATION AND IDENTITY

The solution to many of the problems of the culturally handicapped neighbourhood is frequently seen to lie, not just in the greater degree of *communication and understanding* between the school and its neighbourhood but in the greater *identity of interest* between the two. The confusion is understandable, but the difference is great. The latter presents dangers of perpetuation of a cultural handicap for the pupil who finds the school to be just an extension of home and community. A situation where the values of the school may have been unrelated to values of the community can be changed to one where the school seems to reinforce those of the community. In one downtown school visited by the author the old arithmetical problem 'In three months, how much more would a man earn if he was given a 10 per cent rise on his monthly salary of £40?' had been reworded. The new problem presented by a young and enthusiastic teacher, endeavouring to bring about 'social relevance', was: 'If unemployment payments were increased by 10 per cent how much extra benefit would a man originally drawing £10 a week receive in a twelve-week period of unemployment between jobs?' The calculations are the same but the values which the children learn whilst they are working them are very different.

Moreover, the school may only function imperfectly as an escape mechanism from handicapping community ties if it is itself part of the community. It is the task of the school not just to reflect the background the child knows but also to reflect wider ones. High prestige has always been attached to schools which are thought to be relatively free from local ties and restraints; this freedom is a condition of membership of the exclusive Headmasters' Conference group of schools. The problem is particularly important at a time when comprehensive education is being widely adopted, and when many of the schools are planned as neighbourhood schools. Indeed, the concept of the neighbourhood comprehensive school may often be a contradictory one for in many cases the neighbourhood catchment area is socially homogeneous and unlikely to offer a comprehensive range of pupils' social backgrounds. In consequence, the school is less likely to be able to present a challenge to any of the values of its community. But even the common school for widely divergent neighbourhoods may not allow children to escape from handicapping associations of their environment. Musgrove's study, reported in his *Migratory Elite* (1963), shows that even in a school where pupils from diverse communities appear to be fully integrated into the life of the school, this can be superficial and on investigation the underlying differences springing from diverse community backgrounds are likely to remain strong.

HOLLINGSHEAD'S 'ELMTOWN'S YOUTH'

So far, in the interests of clarity, we have generally made the assumption that schools have socially homogeneous catchment areas. For many schools these limitations do not apply, and the conflicts between the values of the teachers and the pupils which we have seen in the downtown schools are also acted out between the different groups of pupils. In Hollingshead's classic study of a mid-western community, *Elmtown's Youth* (1949), the social behaviour of the adolescent pupils is seen to be related functionally to the position their families occupy in the social structure of the community. For example, one of the 'class four' girls is reported as saying

That Country Club crowd really think they are somebody. They think they're way up. Now my dad's drove the Baker Oil Truck for ten years. We're as good as anybody, but a lot of people try to treat us like we weren't. I don't take anything off anybody. I've got spunk and if they don't like me they can go to the devil. Some of the girls who thought they were somebody used to snub me when I waited tables in high school. Mom wouldn't let me quit until I was sixteen, but you can bet your rights the day I was sixteen I walked out of that high school. They can't treat me that way and get away with it (p. 344).

THE COMMUNITY CONTEXT THESIS

Up to now we have used the concept of community as a convenient way of referring to the factors in the background of individual pupils which are general in some types of catchment area. It is a popular thesis, however, that distinctive values, attitudes and behaviours—in short a distinctive subculture—can arise in a modern community which can influence members over and above the influence of their individual socio-economic background. In particular such a sub-culture is often held to influence the educational aspirations of young people in the community. This *community context thesis* is perhaps most clearly stated by Rogoff (1961, pp. 243-4):

It follows that each of the social classes will be more heavily concentrated in some kinds of community environments than in others, and that communities will vary in the predominant or average social-class affiliation of their residents. Such structural differences may set in motion both formal arrangements—such as school, library and general cultural facilities in the community —and informal mechanisms, such as normative climates or modal levels of social aspiration, which are likely to affect *all* members of the community to some extent—parents and children, upper, middle and working classes.

In an attempt to explore Rogoff's thesis more fully, the writer analysed data from several school catchment areas in the Leicester-shire plan. In the plan, pupils have the opportunity to transfer at fourteen to the Upper School for an extended education or remain in the High School and leave at minimum leaving age. The only condition of transfer is that the pupil will remain until he is sixteen, a year after minimum school leaving age. Though in all areas the transfer rate of the non-manual workers' children was higher than that of the manual workers' children, the manual workers' rate was highest in the most middle-class community and lowest in the most working-class community. Fifty-nine per cent of manual workers' children transferred in the middle-class suburb, only 30 per cent in the working-class area. Conversely, only 77 per cent of non-manual workers' children transferred in the working-class area as against 89 per cent in the middle-class suburb (Eggleston, 1965).

The results suggest that the community context thesis has relevance for communities on this side of the Atlantic. The thesis is by no means proven by this evidence; however, it may be that the manual workers' families and their children in the middle-class suburb are fundamentally different from those in the working-class area and that their different area of residence is but a sign of these more fundamental differences. If this is the case, a careful examination of the individual children and their families may reveal some of these differences. An attempt to work on these lines has been made by Sewell and Armer (1966), who suggest that community context may not always be a *causal* factor in differences in student aspiration between different communities; the argument is by no means finally settled. What is unchallenged, however, is that the concept of community provides us with an illuminating guide to the expectations and requirements of the population of the school catchment area, as well as to the prevailing factors in the behaviour of its pupils and teachers. Moreover, it provides an important context for the detailed study of individual pupils.

REFERENCES

BANTOCK, G. H. (1963), *Education in an Industrial Society,* Faber.
BERNSTEIN, B. (1965), 'A socio-linguistic approach to social learning', *Penguin Survey of Social Sciences,* ed. J. Gould, Penguin Books.
BLYTH, W. A. L. (1965), *English Primary Education,* Routledge, 2 vols.
CENTRAL ADVISORY COUNCIL FOR EDUCATION (1963), *Half Our Future* (Newsom Report), H.M.S.O.
CENTRAL ADVISORY COUNCIL FOR EDUCATION (1967), *Children and their Primary Schools* (Plowden Report), H.M.S.O., 2 vols.
CLEGG, A. B. ed. (1964), *The Excitement of Writing,* Chatto & Windus.
CLEGG, A. B. (1966), 'The twilight children', *Where,* 24.
CONANT, J. (1961), *Slums and Suburbs,* New York, McGraw-Hill.
DOUGLAS, J. W. B. (1964), *The Home and the School,* MacGibbon & Kee.
EGGLESTON, S. J. (1965), 'How comprehensive is the Leicestershire Plan?' *New Society,* 5, no. 130, 17.
FRANKENBERG, R. (1966), *Communities in Britain,* Penguin Books.
GOLDTHORPE, J. H. and LOCKWOOD, D. (1963a), 'Affluence and the British class structure', *Sociological Review,* 11, 133–64.

GOLDTHORPE, J. H. and LOCKWOOD, D. (1963b), 'Not so bourgeois after all', *New Society,* 18 Oct. 1963.

HERRIOTT, R. E. and ST JOHN, N. H. (1966), *Social Class and the Urban School,* New York, Wiley.

HOLLINGSHEAD, A. B. (1949), *Elmtown's Youth,* New York, Wiley; paperback, New York, Science Editions, 1961.

JACKSON, B. and MARSDEN, D. (1962), *Education and the Working Class,* Routledge; paperback, Penguin Books, 1966.

MAYS, J. B. (1962), *Education and the Urban Child,* University of Liverpool Press.

MUSGROVE, F. (1963), *The Migratory Elite,* Heinemann.

NEWSOM REPORT (1963), *See* Central Advisory Council for Education.

PARSONS, T. (1961), 'The school class as a social system', *Education, Economy and Society,* eds., A. H. Halsey, J. Floud and C. A. Anderson, Glencoe, Ill., Free Press, pp. 434–55.

PLOWDEN REPORT (1967), *See* Central Advisory Council for Education.

ROGOFF, N. (1961), 'Local social structure and educational selection', *Education, Economy and Society,* eds. A. H. Halsey, J. Floud and C. A. Anderson, Glencoe, Ill., Free Press.

SEWELL, W. H. and ARMER, J. M. (1966), 'Neighbourhood context and college plans', *American Sociological Review,* 31, 159–68.

SWIFT, D. F. (1964), 'Who passes the 11-plus?' *New Society,* 5 March, 1964.

WEBB, J. (1962), 'The sociology of a school', *British Journal of Sociology,* 13, 264–72.

WISEMAN, S. (1964), *Education and Environment,* University of Manchester Press.

6

The subculture and the school*

John Barron Mays

Contextual studies form a bridge between the demographic and the subcultural approaches to the relationship of family, class and education, and as such they vary considerably. Some offer a strongly demographic treatment of responsiveness to education in a particular neighbourhood; others, like that of Professor Eggleston in Chapter 5 and of Professor Mays in this Chapter give greater importance to the neighbourhood's way of life, its pattern of norms and values. Following Professor Eggleston's review of the varying social climates in different kinds of urban locality and of the distinctive attitudes to education which are associated with them, Professor Mays considers the inner city district in more detail. This classic study was carried out as part of a wider research into urban redevelopment in central Liverpool, and this chapter is taken from Professor Mays's detailed report on the schools and their relationships with the various social groups in their catchment area.

Many facts that have emerged in preceding chapters [of *Education and the Urban Child*] have suggested that there are valid grounds for believing that the Crown Street schools are failing to fulfil their functions in certain respects and that they are producing many young people who are technically and intellectually ill-equipped to find a satisfactory niche for themselves in the economic and commercial life of the city. The existence of many related social problems within these areas, such as truancy, delinquency and mental backwardness, to select only those which have a close connection with education,

* Reprinted from *Education and the Urban Child*, Liverpool University Press, 1962, pp. 89–104, by kind permission of the author and the publisher.

indicated that pathological tendencies are not being entirely held in check and that there exists a more or less stabilised minority pattern of living which is, in some respects, in conflict with the norms of the community as a whole. What we are probably faced with in these inner city areas is not so much a well-integrated community whose standards and values are in sharp conflict with the wider society but a very loosely related population which as a whole is less intolerant of ways of behaving that would give offence in other areas, and where the mechanisms of social control are less rigidly applied. Illegitimacy, for example, is comparatively high in parts of the area and there are reports of households comprising four or five children all with the same mother but different fathers. On the whole, the fact of illegitimacy is accepted more casually and there is much less social stigma attached to it than elsewhere. Buried within this generally tolerant and unambitious mass are a number of smaller groups which are more closely knit together and which in many respects accept a deviant, even defiant way of life, and these smaller groups have a pervasive influence which to some extent infects the whole population to a sufficient degree to produce a pattern of life which is so unusual that it may be termed a subculture. Whether the term subculture should be applied to the whole inner urban area or whether it should be confined to the more closely-knit pockets of resistance where more dramatic deviation from the general norms may occur is a matter of considerable theoretical interest. At the moment, however, insufficient data are available and our conceptual categories are too blurred for us to resolve this question satisfactorily.

The standards that the schools of the district at their best are striving to uphold can be demonstrated most effectively by quoting from field notes written after attending one of the Crown Street schools' displays which was held on a week-day afternoon before an invited audience in the hall.

An impressive engagement. Several L.E.A. advisers and other guests present. Whole school and staff there and in their places before the visitors arrived. Girls very well behaved and quiet. The Head moving along the gangways in complete and serene control. Special guests received a 'rising' welcome.

All the girls seemed to be wearing the school uniform of white blouse with special tie, gym slip and ankle socks. Many looked exceedingly pleasing in this rig-out and the general impression was similar to any assembly of grammar school pupils. Most of the children were well controlled on the stage and exhibited considerable poise. The junior puppetry show was first item, followed by a verse-speaking choir which gave way to a pipe and percussion band which was well done. But the singing choruses later in the programme were below standard, with some evidence of straining and uneradicated local diction. A great many girls participated in the programme and seemed to derive considerable enjoyment from the singing and dancing and acting. The play, which consisted of a lengthy excerpt from *The Wind in the Willows*, was well cast: Mole was particularly effective and got many laughs. For a Scandinavian bridal dance the costumes were exceedingly bright and gay and a ballet-like effect was achieved. The whole programme passed off smoothly, effortlessly and was obviously the outcome of much rehearsing and good timing. It lasted for about two hours. The proceedings ended with speeches from the chairman of the school and the principal guest.

The same performance had recently been put on for the parents. One could not help wondering if it had appeared equally impressive before an audience of mams with attendant infants and babies howling in arms.

Such displays as the one described above tend to seem alien and out of context when the visitor passes from the controlled atmosphere of the school into the noise and confusion of the surrounding streets. How many of these older girls, dressed in their uniforms during the day, don tight-fitting skirts and go out jiving in the evening, and what do they think then of country dancing and songs about cuckoos and Linden Leas? How many indeed know what a Linden is and have seen one or have heard the call of the cuckoo in real life? The observer at such performances cannot help asking himself if some aspects of the syllabus as presented in such displays are not somewhat archaic, and, if that is so, whether they have much significance for the children and young people who have to live in the world of Liverpool 7? It is doubtless arguable that there is a real civilising and educative effect from bringing these children's minds into contact with selected aspects of the English tradition. Morris dancing and Robin Hood, Coeur de Lion and Treasure Island, Peter Pan and Christopher Robin no doubt are partial aspects of 'Englishness', but they are *partial* and in many ways sentimental and trivial aspects, mere pretty-pretty marginalia around the major texts of life as it is lived inside a ten-storey block of flats, which looks out, on a wet winter's night, over the smoky gloom of Paddington, across puddled streets and deserted rubble-strewn waste-sites, towards the coloured lights of Lime Street and the neon warmth of its restless, pleasure-seeking heart.

What the school teaches, according to a Ministry of Education report, 'should be connected with the environment. That is, the curriculum should be so designed as to interpret the environment to the boys and girls who are growing up in it'.[1] In urban areas this is interpreted as making reference to the essentially man-made and man-controlled environment and in arranging contact with such institutions as museums, art galleries and theatres to familiarise children with the complexity and variety of human artefacts from the arch to the beer barrel. 'A ship docking is as romantic today as ever it was; the chimneys of a power station, the furnaces and retorts of a great works, are monuments both to the knowledge amassed by man, to his physical capacity to dominate his environment, and a warning of the spiritual effort which is needed if the physical environment he creates is not to dominate him.'[2] Most teachers know the general theory well enough and are doubtless a little tired of being exhorted to remember the 'wider view' and 'to find points of interest which will arouse children's natural hunger for knowledge'. What they want in particular to know is how to get into communication in any way with their scholars if they show only a tepid interest in docking liners and are obviously bored by gas works and blast furnaces. They want to know more precisely how they are expected to interpret Liverpool 7 to the children of its streets and alleyways. They might well ask what they are to say by way of interpretation of the new blocks of flats for which incidentally no teacher or priest interviewed had a good word: 'The people of the tenements have no privacy. Everything is community life. If a mother comes here to see me, she brings a friend with her. One feels sometimes that the people don't want to be individuals. They go through life with arms linked, holding one another up.' 'They encourage ganging up of children and facilitate mass demonstrations.'

Liverpool has a famous power station on the waterfront with several massive chimneys which day and night belch smoke and other gases across the city, producing the most enchanting sunset touches as twilight falls. In sunlight enormous orange-coloured clouds, which at first sight might be mistaken for natural phenomena, billow and

1. *School and Life*, H.M.S.O., 1947, p. 31.
2. *Ibid.*

drift across the sky, and fill rooms and lungs with perpetual grit. How is this to be related to hygiene lessons and health education? How are teachers to interpret the racial confusion and hostility, the cries in the night of the outraged woman, beaten and insulted by her arrogant cohabitee? And the urge to get money quickly and easily? For not only do many of the girls earn a living as employees of football pool firms but the very schools in which many of the children are being taught have been partly erected on the proceeds of parochial gambling and lotteries. Where in all this do such infantile archetypal figures as Peter Pan and Toad and Hiawatha fit?

There is a rather sour joke current amongst teachers that the children are in reality bilingual, having one vocabulary and diction for school and an entirely different one for outside.

While the terms in which the essential problem stated above are no doubt somewhat exaggerated, since not the whole of the curriculum is devoted to the music of Handel or to story telling, country dancing and play acting, these have been chosen because they appear to typify the basic dichotomy of much educational work in many of our schools. We are still living in the long social twilight of the two nations; but the two nations of the present day are not the financially rich and the financially poor, the obviously privileged and the nakedly underprivileged classes of former times. They are certainly the outcome of earlier economic discrepancies and there is no doubt that the possession of affluence and the endurance of poverty have bitten into the cultural heritage of the present-day successors of the former deeply divided sections of the community. Old customs and habits die hard. The years of scarcity are for some a living memory. The days of full employment are still young, still uncertain. Suspicion of social discrimination and fear of possible unemployment even now activate the minds of many people. Between the ordinary teacher and the ordinary child in the downtown schools lies a cultural gulf. It is the same gulf that used to divide the elementary from the grammar school tradition. It is a gulf that has not yet been filled up, although a few pontoons have been strung over it and there is some cross traffic. Mr Edward Blishen[1] said in a wireless talk in which he followed a similar line of argument: 'For better or for worse, we worry now in the secondary modern school at the problem of providing a certain amount of common ground between our two nations. We are not happy that there should still be hostility and acute mis-

1. 'The task of the secondary modern school', *The Listener*, 21 February, 1957, pp. 303–5.

understanding when, in the persons of the young teacher and the secondary modern child, the two nations meet. And if I were asked to state very simply how I see the task of the secondary modern school, I should say that I see it as a struggle to reduce that misunderstanding.' Mr Blishen was speaking, of course, as a teacher who has several years' experience of work in such schools in urban areas. He went on to say that he was 'certain that the work of the secondary modern school must be directed towards closing, not inevitable gaps in ability and interests, but those gaps of habit across which our two nations have gazed at each other in fundamental incomprehension of each other's way of life'.

What then is the general way of life followed by Crown Street children and how far does it differ from other patterns? Any description of the typical Crown Street juvenile and adolescent culture leads inevitably into generalisation and to possible distortion. The deviant and pathological features tend to receive undue prominence, the less sensational and more ordinary to be overlooked. It must also be continually borne in mind that the survey area is far from being homogeneous and that there are wide divergencies of behaviour not only between members of individual households in each and every part of the area but particularly between the behaviour and attitudes of people in specific parts. Moving from the more disturbed and restless 'twilight zone' nearer the commercial centre to the more stable and solid lower middle-class streets on the periphery of the survey district we encounter a difference of outlook and mentality which distinguishes the true slum from the merely physically outworn and inadequate neighbourhood. The generalised picture that now follows is more true of the former than of the latter areas, though many factors are undoubtedly common features of both types of locality.

It is true of the working-class districts generally that life tends to be focused on two important centres—the home and the neighbourhood. Horizons are apt to be narrow, the sights aimed low, ambition and curiosity limited to the local and the concrete. Home is where the family lives and, while the closely-knit, emotionally jealous intimacy of the lower-middle-class household may not in every respect be emulated by the dwellers in Crown Street, there is still a firm distinction between the family and the neighbours.[1] Entertaining

1. For a good description of lower-middle-class family life and relationships at the beginning of the century see Richard Church's essay in autobiography, *Over the Bridge*, Heinemann, 1955.

in the way in which middle-class people understand that term is very rare. Relatives call regularly at one another's homes. They drop in for a cup of tea and they sometimes visit daily and share main meals together. Neighbours call in to borrow a pan or for the loan of a pound of flour. A good neighbour is one who is always ready to assist in such concrete ways, who stops for a chat and takes a lively interest in one's affairs without being 'nosey'. Standoffishness is not liked. As one housewife complained to one of the teachers, after returning to the district from a somewhat superior neighbourhood where she found life less friendly and not to her taste, 'Why, love, you can't even borrow a pan up there!' Life in such localities tends to be very social in the narrow sense, people dislike doing things on their own and seek the security and comfort of others both at work and for pleasure. They are characterised by closeness if not by a warmth of intimate relationship. In the parts nearest the city centre there is one big block of flats which houses families who were apparently moved *en bloc* from their old slum neighbourhood and where, according to parochial officials, there is much evidence of social cohesion and friendliness one to another. Only the mentally ill or the very old are isolated. The bulk of the people are closely connected with small groups of friends and relatives. If one of the women has cause to 'go up to the school' she takes a neighbour along with her for support. A girl always has at least one friend of her own sex with whom she 'knocks around'. Boys also are usually to be seen in clumps and clusters. Some of the youngsters so dislike the idea of leaving their pals that they have no desire to change schools at eleven-plus and have no wish to do well in the examinations. People of the district, except for the fringes of the area where the policy of keeping yourself to yourself is more the ideal, seem to have a fear of being alone and of being cut off from the warmth and cosiness of a close circle of regular associates. This ganging together may on the one hand make them less individually responsible but at the same time it fosters feelings of mutuality and solidarity. People who leave the locality to begin life in a new housing estate often return regularly to visit friends and relatives; many in fact still work in the Crown Street area. Similarly there are also a number of people who work in the new housing estates and who still live in the older central city areas. There is in fact a sort of daily shuttle service between Crown Street and the new estate at Kirkby, some five or six miles to the north-west. In this way it is seen how the new areas are closely linked to the life of the older areas and are organically related in a variety of ways which tend to mark them off from the better-off residential suburbs with which they do not seem to be in any way related.

Families tend to be larger in such areas than amongst other social groups, although they are still small by Victorian standards. Because the girls tend to marry young there are many young mothers in the population, girls in their late teens and early twenties with two or more children to tend. They are apt to seek help from their mothers in bearing the weight of this responsibility and when they marry and settle down they often live either with their own parents or fairly near so that married daughter and mother may not be cut off from each other during these vital years. Much valuable help must be received in this way, but 'there is always the danger', as one head teacher put it, 'that in spite of the work of the pre- and post-natal clinics, the voice of grandmother saying "Never mind what they said at the clinic" undoes everything a girl might have learned there'.[1] So too the advice of an older neighbour may eventually outweigh the expert instructions of the health visitor.

The work of the social services makes slow and difficult progress in such areas. The doctor who does not prescribe a bottle for an ailment is regarded with suspicion. Established principles of child training and dietetics are often brushed aside because the older folk disapprove of them or because the mothers are lazy or indifferent and let the children go their own way. Schools are places where children are taught and the teachers are paid to teach the children. It is not the parents' job to teach their children or to lay the foundations of literacy upon which the schools may more quickly and easily build. In better-off districts youngsters come to the infants' department already trained in simple manipulative skills, with some concept of number, with fair vocabularies and some interest in stories and a limited knowledge of words and letters. Thus they are already advanced by a year or more on the road to eleven-plus success before their slum counterparts have even begun their training. Some children in the worst areas, it is complained, come to school first at the age of five and a half having received no training whatever from their parents and with little idea of discipline and orderliness. Their homes are entirely bookless.[2] Day nurseries are also convenient places where toddlers can be deposited while the mothers go out to

1. Said another Head: 'The mothers run everything round here and the grandmas are very powerful, too.'
2. Said a local minister of religion: 'I can count the number of occasions on my hand when I have walked into anyone's house and found an adult reading anything other than a paper.'

work. Play centres and clubs too are welcomed because they ease the domestic problem and provide somewhere safe for the children to play. Knowledge of their existence and of their children's alleged membership does much to ease the parental conscience. Little effort is made to check up whether or not the children actually attend such places or to discover if the programmes offered there are suitable for them. All the services, voluntary and statutory, are accepted uncritically and made use of by hard-pressed parents. They are part and parcel of social living as they knew it in the late 1950s. Teachers at the schools in the inner parts of the survey area complain that they are expected to supervise pupils' visits to hospitals and clinics for the parents. A child may receive an injury during the dinner hour and will be sent back to school for attention because the mother is going out to work or has shopping to do. If a child has an accident in school it is often assumed to be the teacher's job to accompany it to the hospital, not the mother's. In the schools in the better parts of the district this would not be so and the parents themselves would come to school to take their child to the out-patient clinic. But there is a strongly held belief that teachers and other social workers can be expected to take over the parental function almost entirely. So a mother who was summoned before an attendance committee on account of her daughter's repeated absenteeism, when told she should bring her child to the gates, rejected the idea with some heat. 'What are the women in white coats[1] for then', she demanded, 'if the mother has to bring them to school herself?' So, too, when the time comes for children to go to work it is the responsibility of the Youth Employment Officer to find them suitable employment. At the appropriate time officials from the Y.E.B. visit the schools, interview leavers and suggest possible openings for them. Some of the Crown Street schools invite parents to attend these conferences and, while a minority do come, there is much obvious apathy. Only two children out of fifteen leaving one of the girls' departments at one of the superior schools attended the leavers' conference for instance. A similar function at a school in another neighbourhood might well secure one hundred per cent attendance. It would seem that many of the Crown Street parents have handed over to statutory officials (no doubt thankfully) as much of the responsibility for the care and training and launching into adult life of their offsprings as they possibly can. This is not to say that the children are necessarily

1. The reference is to the school crossing wardens provided by the civic authorities.

5

unwanted or are emotionally rejected and unloved. It is merely an indication of the trend of contemporary social organisation to which the statutory services themselves often unwittingly contribute.

Positive resistance to the work of the schools comes from a small but potent minority of households which are particularly located in the rooming-house district and in the less socially stable parts of the survey area. These are the families which in the main have given trouble to other welfare departments, whose adult members seem to be unable and unwilling to meet the demands made upon them by the wider society. School welfare and attendance officers of the local authority spend much time and energy on gingering up these defaulters and endeavouring to assist parents to do their job more effectively. Such households do not seem to value education at all or to be worried by the future results of missing school for the children. The regular series of broken weeks and half-days of unexplained absences from school seem to be characteristic of a definite way of life, embodying a fundamental inability to organise, to discipline or to plan affairs. The earliest years of childhood are probably deficient in routine and control. There is much spoiling due to laziness with the result that a substandard family life becomes endemic and well nigh ineradicable. Absenteeism runs in families and can be followed over the generations. Many specious excuses are offered to explain such a chronic state of irregularity away. The mother with the hard yet resigned face who sits before the enquiring committee will frequently give rein to her limited imagination to cloud the issue. 'There's something wrong with his stomach', she will say, or 'It's 'is stomach, sir. It's been bad since 'e was a baby.' A constantly defeated and defeatist, an inveterate ailing attitude to life, an almost automatic recoil from the probing question and avoidance of the problem which will make any demands on their own energy and will power, are characteristic of this minority of sub-standard families. There is the unemployed dealer with his hard luck story, whose wife goes out early to work and who allows the grandmother to call round to get the children's breakfast and send them off to school while he lies abed. There is the harassed, incompetent mother who keeps an older child at home to mind the house while she goes off to the clinic to have her varicose veins 'done' or who keeps a boy back to run errands or to wait for the 'clubman' or to pay the rent. Whatever their story or palaver of excuses, there runs beneath it the belief that school is not really very important, that education is something imposed on them from above, with which they are forced to comply to some extent however alien and almost unnecessary it may appear to be. It is the presence of the offspring of such families that makes teaching in some of the downtown schools so frustrating an experience for the keen and ambitious members of the profession that it tends to drive them away to work in more rewarding areas. In so far as this minority of families produce such a result they are a real menace to their more responsible and responsive neighbours.

The organisation of home life follows and reinforces the somewhat strict differentiation of male and female roles in the local community. Children are almost entirely the responsibility of the mother. The men, when employed, tend to work long hours. Some are on shift work, a minority are employed on the waterfront and some go away to sea. But wherever they work and, indeed, whether or not they are in employment, it is generally recognised that the children are the women's responsibility. Likewise with housework; this is traditionally shared by all the females in the household, the males confining their share to any tasks which require greater physical strength or manual skill such as shovelling coal or papering a room. In some families it is considered shameful for a man to be called on to undertake feminine chores, even in times of extremity. This was neatly epitomised by the mother who presented herself before the headmistress of one of the Crown Street schools to ask if her elder daughter, aged fourteen, could be excused so that she could stay at home for part of the day to do the shopping and prepare lunch while the mother herself went out to do part-time work. The father was a bedridden invalid and could do nothing to help. The headmistress was about to accede to this sympathetic appeal when she remembered that there were two teenage boys who might be available, for all the men of the family tended to follow a regular in-and-out-of-work routine. The Mam admitted that 'our Frank and our Ernest' were indeed at home at the moment, being temporarily 'on the dole', but she was clearly shocked by the suggestion that they should undertake any menial household duties. She threw her head stiffly back and folded her arms. 'I pray that as long as I've my strength, no man will ever be asked to cook in my house', she said. Clearly her daughter's schooling was of secondary account when it came to observing the social proprieties and the rigid traditions which governed male and female roles. Men go out to work and earn most, if not all, of the money. Men do manual jobs demanding muscular strength. Only cissies wash up. This somewhat rigid allocation of duties can be seen at work while children are still attending school. The older boys are often excused household chores, although they are permitted to work as errand boys and to earn money. Younger boys run messages and help in that way. But girls wash up and peel vegetables; they cook and sew and shop and identify themselves with the maternal role. This is nowhere more apparent than in the expectation that girls will look after younger siblings and stay at home to mind the house if and when the parents are away. Such baby-minding is looked down on by boys who are real boys, i.e. miniature men. A boy was sent to the headmaster of one school when the research worker was present for having hit another boy in the yard at playtime and bloodied his nose. The culprit pleaded mitigating circumstances. The attack, he claimed, was provoked by the other lad who had been taunting him. 'And what,' asked the headmaster, 'did he say to insult you?' 'He called me a baby-minder, sir,' came the prompt and apparently self-explanatory reply.

On another occasion the research worker had the opportunity to hold a general discussion with the girls of the top class of one of the unreorganised all-through schools. The notes of the discussion run as follows:

> The girls were painting and doing machining and obviously enjoying themselves. They went on with their work while I spoke to them, putting it down only when they were eager to answer a question or to supply information. I asked how many painted at home and how many possessed their own paints. Several hands shot up. I then asked how many would go on with this hobby when they left school. Instantly all hands dropped and the girls smiled. When asked why, one girl said her painting was not good enough. When I assured her that it was, she refused to believe it. The rest of the painters backed her up. I then asked about household chores. All the girls said they did them. I asked those with brothers how many of them gave a hand. They laughed at the idea and made remarks such as 'Too lazy' and 'Catch him'. I told them I often washed dishes and did the shopping and this greatly amused them. 'The boys all go out to play,' they said quite cheerfully, 'while we stay at home and do the work.'

The boys, on the other hand, claim to do a limited amount of housework, mostly of the errand-running variety. Few seem to do much before they are eight years old: the amount increases up to the thirteenth birthday and begins to tail off as school leaving age draws near. Clearly, however, the girls do very much more than the boys and for much longer periods. Roughly an hour a day seems to be spent by most fourteen-year-old girls on domestic chores, a factor which must very obviously have a bearing on school homework or private study. A further disadvantage of this arrangement is that the boys are much more free to take on out-of-school paid work, running paper rounds, for example, while the girls are expected to give their time and energy to the family without pay. In this way they are prepared for their future roles as wives and mothers, the body-servants of husbands and children. Going out to work as part-time cleaners or barmaids has the obvious advantage of securing a temporary release from this round of bondage and, apart from any financial gain, gives these women a measure of social life and contact with different people which they value. For the woman's life seems monotonously dreary, with few highlights apart from a weekend pint and probably no holidays whatsoever for the vast majority. There are the relatives to call on for a chat, a daily cup of tea or lunch with mother, an occasional visit for the younger wives to the local schools, where they themselves used to go, for a chin-wag with old teachers, perhaps Sunday morning mass, the occasional mêlée of a jumble sale, a trip to the flicks, almost certainly saddled with one or more toddlers. Such activities, together with the odd pint, the frequent cigarette, the regular TV shows and background music supplied almost throughout the day by the kindly B.B.C. make up the continuing fabric of their lives. The men enjoy more variety and greater freedom. They have their work, their work-mates, their evenings at the local with another set of cronies, perhaps their darts matches; and every Saturday afternoon of the winter, autumn and spring at one or another of the first class matches they watch the interminable football that supplies so much of the material for their conversation and a pleasant opportunity for a less demanding form of betting than putting your money on 'the gee-gees'. Young and old men are to be seen frequenting the cinemas; many even find their way to church, especially if they happen to be Roman Catholics.

Family life, then, is both intimate and impersonal. Members of households live, or rather sleep, in close proximity but take few pleasures together. Family meals are things of the past, except perhaps at weekends. Normally, as one head teacher put it, 'they'll just eat a couple of rounds of bread and something standing up and then out into the street to play, or they may eat while watching TV'. The grown-ups and children come in and out on different tides, stay long enough to satisfy their physical needs and then are away again in pursuit of their own interests which are often outside the home. Watching television undoubtedly occupies a large amount of free time for children of all ages. For this reason perhaps fewer are to be found roaming the streets than formerly, although a great many still do wander considerable distances in gangs looking for something exciting to attract their attention. They even penetrate to the city shopping centre after closing hours, and on Saturday mornings the open market places are powerful lures. There are television clubs attached to the schools. These are quite informal and are made up by the scholars themselves, those with sets available making dates with each other to watch specific programmes in one another's houses. Homes without TV sets are thought very poor indeed. I.T.A. programmes are, of course, immensely popular.

This is not the moment to undertake a general discussion of the place that televiewing has come to occupy in our national life and the way in which what was originally a high income group luxury has during the past few years become an all income group necessity. There is some evidence to show that this habit has had a detrimental effect on both cinema going and public house attendance and that reading and other sedentary hobbies have also tended to suffer because of it. What is of immense educational significance is the fact that many hours are spent by the children and adults watching television programmes with the result that the children tend to go to bed very late and turn up at school with dark rings round their eyes and other signs of tiredness.[1] Furthermore, the possession of a TV set must decrease the opportunity of reading and increase the general 'booklessness' of the homes. However, in fairness it must be stated that one primary school head teacher considered that television did more good than harm to the children. 'I'm amazed at the amount of useful information they assimilate from it,' she said, 'and it keeps them off the streets where they're liable to learn a great many more harmful things than they'll ever learn from TV.'

There is a fairly widely held and strong conviction, especially amongst the older teachers, many of whom have taught in the same sort of locality for a number of years, that children are, on the whole, pampered compared with their predecessors. It is not only that they are less inclined to settle down to hard work at school, nor is it merely

1. Extract from field notes: 'I asked the girls of a small backward class how many saw TV and nearly half did. One girl, the teacher said, always came to school tired and sleepy. They looked a dull crowd.'

that the academic standards achieved are well below those obtained by often needier children in former years.[1] It is much more a case of deliberate spoiling. As one very experienced headmaster said somewhat grimly: 'Children rule round here. The mothers bribe them; the fathers are not interested and the kids do very much what they like.' Large and very expensive presents are given at Christmas and birthday time, especially by the families occupying what were originally the poorer parts of the areas. Many parents in unskilled employment vie with one another in lavish gifts for their children—almost life-size walkie-talkie dolls for the girls and pedal motor cars and bicycles for the boys. The general philosophy seems to be to concentrate on having a good time while you can. 'Enjoy yourself, it's later than you think', as the once popular song goes, aptly summarises this attitude. Enjoyment demands money to spend. Both girls and boys want to have lots of clothes to wear. They want to be in the fashion, to have the latest hair styles and to keep up with the newest trends in dresses or suits. Boys no less than girls choose bright, even vivid, colours, various shades of purple—Mediterranean, Monaco and Neapolitan blue. With these glamorous suits and the streamer ties must go a personally selected haircut, the notorious D.A. or the Elvis Presley. Rock 'n' roll may be on the ebb tide as a cult but, whatever the mode, these young people want to hear the latest dance tunes and the current song-hits and are prepared to pay for the pleasure. They are great purchasers of gramophone records and 'just listening to records' is one of the major activities of most teenagers.

The girls know at a fairly early age exactly what they want to do with their lives. In the top classes of the mixed departments they are already going out with boy friends and seriously considering marriage. The boys of the same age group in the same school are beneath their contempt, mere kids with whom they can have nothing beyond fraternal relationships. These girls spend perhaps 5s per week on their hair and make-up. A well-intentioned teacher in charge of arrangements for a girls' Christmas party, asked her class what they wanted by way of programme. 'Oh, miss,' they cried with one voice, 'let's bring our records and have a jive and rock.' They did not want any of the traditional Christmas games, the carols and the paper hats and the crackers of infancy. The extra year, it is claimed, has tended

---

1. In the mid-1930s, for example, the boys in the top class of one parochial school were said to be taught Latin and Greek by a First Class Honours man from Oxford. Such a thing is quite unthinkable nowadays.

to make these top class girls more restless than ever, as they have to delay earning money for an additional twelve months which does not give them any further skill with which they can bargain economically. They are eager to get out to work so as to be able to earn more and save as much as they can (without curtailing pleasure, of course) before matrimony, round about their eighteenth or nineteenth birthday, truly has them in thrall. Thus a simple repetitive process job at a local factory, an opening at one of the big football pools firms or a chance to serve at one of the chain stores exactly meet their requirements, whatever 'the lady from the Youth Employment' may suggest. The boys, although in many ways much less sophisticated than the girls, have equally short-term objectives in view. They are willing to go for the manual and unskilled jobs until their turn comes to join the Forces.[1] After that they may perhaps think about settling down in earnest. Meanwhile they too want money and excitement and the more restless may try to get away to sea for a few years to 'have fun and see a bit of the world'. Marriage for the girl confers status. It is perhaps her only way of acquiring the outward signs of adulthood and a limited and temporary limelight. The engagement period is the golden age of her relationship with her future husband, for then she has a good time, spends money, has plenty of clothes, enjoys herself and stands high in the estimation of her peers and contemporaries. Consequently the actual marriage day, its costly ceremonial and ritual, is pre-eminently 'her day'—the glittering apex of her feminine career. It is this emotional and social concentration of interest that leads to what seems to those outside the culture a disproportionately expensive outlay. As a minister of religion put it somewhat tartly: 'First they order the cars—this being the most difficult matter to arrange. Then they plan the reception and the party . . . then they come to book the church and arrange the service—that being the easiest thing to organise!' A young couple had recently been to see him who had saved up two hundred pounds, all of which was to be spent on the wedding itself and nothing on decorations, fittings or furniture for their new home. Marriage is an occasion when you have 'a big blow out' and when the visitors expect to be able to 'get really tight'.

Young people's ambitions are limited; their economic goals short-term and bound up with immediate cash returns and this attitude tends to reduce the appeal of education. Very few young people, as

1. When this Report was written compulsory National Service was still in operation. (Ed.)

we have already seen, are in apprenticeships and an even smaller number are following any form of further education whatsoever.

Most of the Crown Street workers enter occupations which are at the bottom of the socio-economic scale and there they are likely to remain, with a few notable exceptions, for the rest of their working days. Their future toil will lie in the black-handed rather than in the black-coated battalion and, although financially they may be no worse off for this and, indeed, they may on balance in times of full employment earn quite high wages, they are unavoidably associated with a social tradition and a type of culture which is alien to the way of life characteristic of the professional, administrative and academic social groups. Blishen's 'fundamental incomprehension' will remain as a divisive legacy unless ways and means can be found in these downtown schools to make a breakthrough and establish a bridgehead of mutual respect and understanding.

This is a task which calls for immense courage, great imagination and extensive physical and financial provision. The children of exceptional merit from such areas will always have a chance to rise. The children of slightly lesser ability who could make use of equal opportunities should also be given the same chance to improve their lot in life. The remnant must not be written off as 'children of less ability' and offered a substandard education against which they will not protest and which probably they will passively accept. Here and now the problem must be faced of bridging the gap between conflicting cultures, between the teachers and their pupils, between the grammar and board school traditions. The board school tradition, which is a hangover from the day when society was much more deeply stratified and divided, must be eradicated entirely if the objective is ever to be achieved.

Clearly the answers to these immense problems do not rest exclusively on the shoulders of the teaching profession, nor even with the statutory authorities concerned with educational provision. Education is the responsibility of the whole community. It is intimately bound up with our total way of life—economic, political and social. Deficiencies in the commercial and industrial system such as unemployment cannot be met merely by the provision of unemployment insurance or National Assistance Board grants any more than the expected increase in the number of workless youths in five years' time can be treated, say, by giving them free admittance to billiards saloons. At best these are but palliatives and charitable gestures from the possessors to the disinherited.

5*

In the concluding chapter [of *Education and the Urban Child*] a number of things will be suggested which educational authorities and teachers together might do to assist the youngsters living in under-privileged areas to obtain a better start in life and to enable them to equip themselves more efficiently for the future struggle.

Further education generally and the Youth Service in particular exist to serve the same ends and through such provision much help and support can be given to the schools and the teachers. But the youth organisations which are striving to serve these particularly difficult areas are having a hard battle to survive, coping as they almost invariably are with too little money, too little manpower, inadequate premises and competition from commercialised amusements. Their plight is much worse than the plight of the schools while their task—that of catering wisely for the healthy recreation of thousands of boys and girls—is almost as gigantic. There is no space in this report for a full consideration of the problems facing youth organisations in the downtown areas. But there is no doubt that they could make a much greater contribution to the solution of many social and educational problems if they were to be given an opportunity and if their services were to be closely linked with those offered through the schools. Youth workers covering children's leisure, school teachers providing children's formal training are twin aspects of one basic service that should be offered to supplement parental effort and to fortify by a common purpose and an agreed policy the direction of home life and training upon which so many things depend.

7

Two subcultures*

This third example of the contextual approach to the relationship of family, class and education is taken from a study of a boys' secondary modern school in a northern industrial town where Hargreaves set out to analyse the social structure of the school by participant observation, concentrating on boys in their final year. A major conclusion was that by the fourth year, two predominant subcultures had emerged—'academic' and 'delinquescent'—and in this chapter they are described in detail. The particular significance of Hargreaves's study from the point of view of this volume is that it illustrates how the social context of the school may reinforce the values of the home. While there was no significant difference in social composition between the upper and lower fourth year streams, Hargreaves did identify significant differences in family size, house ownership, and parental attitudes, for example, which are probably indicative of the more 'activistic' (or middle-class) basic beliefs discussed in Chapter 1 and in more detail in Chapter 13.

David Hargreaves

The various chapters of [*Social Relations in a Secondary School*] combine to give us a (somewhat disjointed) picture of the differentiation of the values and behaviour of boys in different streams at Lumley Secondary Modern School. The boys are not distributed throughout the streams in a random way; rather, from our knowledge of a particular boy's stream we can within limits predict some of the main values he will tend to hold. We have seen that the higher the stream of a boy, the greater the tendency for him to be committed to the school's values.

* Reprinted from *Social Relations in a Secondary School*, Routledge, 1967, pp. 159–81, by kind permission of the author and the publisher.

His attendance at school is more regular and his participation in school activities is deeper. He likes school and the teachers, to whose expectations he conforms, whose values he supports and whose approval he seeks. This trend is particularly true of 4A boys, and as we move from the highest stream to the lowest, this trend tends to reverse itself, and the values held by low stream pupils are the opposite of those held by their peers in 4A.

Our examination of the normative structure of each form revealed a clear variation in the criteria on which boys assess one another and derive status or prestige in the informal group in different streams. We find that in the A stream informal status correlates positively with academic achievement and behaviour rating scores, whereas in the low streams informal status is a function of a negative orientation to the school's values. The A stream boys approve of the teacher's conception of his own role and define the pupil role in terms of conformity to the teacher expectations. In the low streams, the boys do not approve of the teacher's definition of his own role and disapprove of pupils who meet the teachers' definition of the pupil role.

This process of differentiation reveals itself, as we saw at the beginning, in the friendship choices made among the fourth year pupils. In each form the majority of boys choose their friends from their own form. This is hardly surprising, since it is with his classmates that each individual interacts most frequently during school hours, and often outside school as well. But we must also note that although between a quarter and a third of friends are chosen from other streams, these extra-form choices are not random. The process of selection of friends from other streams can be summarised in the generalisation that the greater the distance between streams, the lower the proportion of friendship ties.

In two cases, 4B and 4C, the form has two adjacent streams, one higher and one lower. Inspection of table I [in *Social Relations in a Secondary School*] shows that boys in 4B choose friends from 4A more often than they do from 4C; and boys in 4C choose friends from 4D more often than they do from 4B. Why should this be so? Several possible explanations suggest themselves. It may be a result of the school's policy of transferring boys from one stream to another on the basis of terminal examination results. This fact allows two possible explanations. The first is that if boys transferred *to* 4B originate more often from the A rather than the C stream, then these boys might tend to prefer boys from 4A rather than from 4C, since they are choosing boys with whom they formerly interacted more frequently. Table 7.1

shows this to be so: 38 per cent of 4B boys come from the A stream originally, whereas only 14 per cent came from the C stream. But this explanation does not hold for 4C's extra-form friendship choice tendency. 41 per cent of 4C were transferred from the B stream, and only 9 per cent from the D stream, which is the reverse of the prediction. The second possible explanation in terms of the transfer system is that if boys are transferred *from* the B stream to the A stream more often than to the C stream, then the boys who remain in the B stream are more likely to choose A boys than C boys as friends, since they will be choosing boys with whom they formerly had great opportunity for interaction. This is true for the C stream, where 26 per cent of C stream boys were transferred to the D stream, but only 14 per cent to the B stream. But it does not hold for 4B, since 41 per cent of the B stream boys were transferred to the C stream and 31 per cent to the A stream. The results of the friendship choice distribution cannot be explained by either of these two possibilities, unless they are combined.

TABLE 7.1. *Fourth-year forms by forms of origin.*

Fourth year form	Form of origin					N
	A	*B*	*C*	*D*	*E*	
4A	48	31	14	3	3	29
4B	38	48	14	—	—	29
4C	14	41	36	9	—	22
4D	—	9	26	39	26	23
4E	—	6	6	13	75	16

Figures are percentages.

It could be argued that these explanations are inadequate since they take no account of the *recency* of the transfers. Let us consider the transfers that took place at the end of the third year. If the differential choice process is the result of these transfers, then the newcomers— that is, those who have been transferred—should account for the tendency more than the core members, that is, those who have not been transferred. The relevant figures are given in Table 7.2. Whilst it is true that newcomers in 3B choose their friends from adjacent streams more often than do core members, they do not prefer A boys to C boys more often than core members. In 4C, we find that the newcomers choose 4D boys *less* often than core members. This explanation, then, does not account for the facts.

Although the above factors may play some part, we shall argue that the differential distribution of choices in the two central streams can be most adequately interpreted as an expression of a cultural dichotomy between the upper (A and B) streams and the lower (C and D) streams. In short, we are suggesting that the fourth year can be divided into two 'subcultures'. The upper stream subculture, embodied in the leadership of Adrian, is characterised by values which are positively orientated to the school and the teachers. The lower stream subculture, embodied in the leadership of Clint, is characterised by values which are negatively orientated to the school.

TABLE 7.2.   *Analysis of choices to adjacent forms.*

Choice donors	% of choices given to:		
4B	4A	4B	4C
All 4B	11	77	6
Newcomers	20	56	15
Core members	9	84	4
4C	4B	4C	4D
All 4C	7	70	17
Newcomers	18	63	9
Core members	3	72	20

The lower streams take the upper stream values and 'turn them upside down' and thus form an example of what Cohen terms a *negative polarity*.[1] The differentiation of values, though a continuum, is focused in two opposite poles of attraction which produce a gap in the friendship choices between the B and C streams.

We shall term these two suggested subcultures 'academic' and 'delinquescent'. 'Academic' indicates that the values are orientated to those of the school and the teachers; 'delinquescent' indicates that the values are negatively orientated towards school, and in the direction of delinquent values, though not of course being synonymous with delinquency. To posit the existence of such subcultures is to propose a model or 'ideal type' of the school's cultural structure. To what extent such an analysis 'fits' Lumley Secondary Modern School, that is to what extent it can serve as a meaningful and useful interpretative summary of our findings, has still to be justified. The 'ideal type' is presented pictorially in Diagram I. The dominant values of the A and B streams are academic, though this is less true for the B stream; delinquescent values in these forms are deviant.

1. Albert K. Cohen, *Delinquent Boys: the culture of the gang,* Glencoe, Ill., Free Press, 1955, p. 28.

In the C and D streams, the dominant values are delinquescent, though this is less true for the C stream, and academic values are deviant. Thus the A and D streams become the poles or extremes of the normative differentiation.

Representation of two subcultures

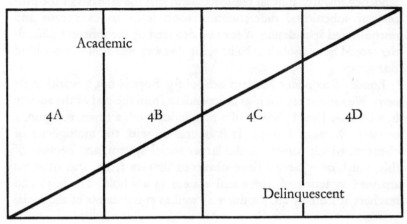

Academic

4A   4B   4C   4D

Delinquescent

Diagram I

Subcultural differentiation is a *process* which takes place over time, and if our analysis is to be valid, we must be able to elucidate its development from the first to the fourth years at Lumley. That much of the evidence presented in previous chapters makes sense in terms of this model is obvious, but a study of the fourth year alone gives us little information with which to explain its origin. We shall shortly present some comparative material from second year boys, but first we must attempt to outline in a more general way some of the factors which influence this subcultural development. Much of what is to follow will be speculative, based on theoretical elaborations and an eclectic review of some current literature, but wherever possible the speculation will be rooted in evidence from Lumley School.

Most attempts at explanation in social science are beset by the multiplicity and interconnections of the variables the researcher wishes to assess. Nor can one easily conduct experiments with human beings, although in recent years social scientists have devised many ingenious techniques for testing hypotheses about human behaviour. In studying the social process within a school, the researcher has to rely predominantly on observation and record and questionnaire data, rather than on experiments, to substantiate his hypotheses. The variables at work are almost infinite, and the assessment of the contribution of any one variable becomes exceedingly difficult. In this study many of the key variables have been totally neglected; those which have been treated have received superficial attention. They are interrelated in such a complex way, especially in their tendency towards mutual reinforcement, that the analysis of the process of subcultural differentiation soon leads to dangerous and unconfirmed speculation. Yet to be deterred by the inherent difficulties would be as foolish as to imagine that a simple solution is within our grasp.

Lumley Secondary Modern School for Boys is not a world of its own. We cannot regard it as independent from the rest of the society in which we live. It is part of a neighbourhood, a town, a region, a country, Western Europe. It is bound up with the multiplicity of elements which constitute the larger social system, and because of this, much of what we have observed derives from, and must be analysed in terms of, the social system as a whole. The boys and teachers at Lumley are products as well as components of the social system.

We cannot enter into the complexities of sociological theory, but it is essential that we take note of sociological analyses of society. For our purposes, we must consider that Western Europe and America are stratified societies, which means that human beings are differentially ranked as superior or inferior relative to one another in certain respects. Society ranks its members in terms of social hierarchy. This is a complex process, since the criteria by which we rank persons are really a set of interrelated variables such as social origin, occupation, education, wealth, residence, power, speech and so on. But ours is not a caste system: the boundaries between social groupings are fluid rather than fixed. Yet we may conveniently distinguish between these social groupings or classes and examine the variation and similarity of values between classes.

Many, especially American, sociologists have been concerned to show that our society's values are based on what has been termed the Protestant ethic. That is, the key value of our society is *achievement*: man is saved by his individual works and strivings. We exist on the myth of equality of opportunity to achieve—the beggar may become a millionaire. We are thus subjected as members of this society to pressures towards striving to achieve. Sociologists are interested in the degree to which people are orientated towards this goal, and in the differences between social classes. Merton has suggested that the orientations of particular persons or groups towards these goals, combined with their perception of and access to the means by which these goals can be attained, can contribute to our understanding of the values of different persons and groups.[1]

The basic division made by sociologists between social classes distinguishes the non-manual from the manual workers, or the middle class from the working class. Moreover, they have sought to show that the values which dominate, namely those stemming from the Protestant ethic, with its stress on personal achievement, are basically those of the middle class. The working class may not be able to attain these goals, due to their restricted access to the means, but many of them accept the validity of the values, even though they may sometimes appear to reject them.

This brief excursus into some sociological writings is not extrinsic to our purpose, for we are now better equipped to place the school in its social framework. If one of the key values of our society is achievement, then the school becomes a central focus and means by which individuals can achieve. Its stress on academic achievement, which is a major determinant of future occupation, represents an embodiment of these societal values. In England the influence of academic achievement is revealed in the distinction between the grammar schools and the secondary modern schools, for which children are selected on their 'success' in the competitive eleven-plus examination. That the nation has accurately perceived that entry to a grammar school offers greater opportunity for academic and therefore social advancement and success is evidenced by the growing amount of parental concern over the child's results in the eleven-plus examination, and by the predominantly middle-class opposition to the re-organisation of secondary education on comprehensive lines. The fact that the eleven-plus examination is seen in terms of 'success' and 'failure' indicates that academic and social aspirations have undermined the somewhat unrealistic concern in England to provide a variety of secondary schools appropriate to the abilities and aptitudes of their pupils and that such schools should have, in the eyes of the public, 'parity of esteem'. The educational system selects and differentiates its pupils in a further manner, for the vast majority of secondary schools, whether grammar, modern or comprehensive, stream pupils by their achievement relative to one another. Though

1. R. K. Merton, *Social Theory and Social Structure*, Glencoe, Ill., Free Press, 1967, Chapter 4.

there may be good educational grounds for so doing—a question which cannot be answered here—we cannot ignore that the effect of streaming is to separate children with relatively greater academic achievement into 'higher' streams; and to most of the public 'higher' is synonymous with 'better'. To succeed at school is to succeed in society. To divide our children in this way means that we must also have children who 'fail', by not obtaining entry either to a grammar school and/or to a high stream.

Concepts of 'success' or 'failure' in academic achievement thus form a reflection of societal values, which are most marked in the middle class, though sociologists maintain that such values are accepted as valid by many people of the working class, even when they do not adhere to them. The school is founded on, fosters and perpetuates those values which sociologists associate with the middle class, and the teachers themselves are mainly successful products of such schools, even though their social origin may be working class.

To what extent did the pupils at Lumley internalise and conform to middle-class values, even though the school catchment area is working class? Cohen lists the middle-class values as:

(i) Ambition is regarded as a virtue

In our study we have seen that, the higher the stream the greater the parental support for desiring a better job than father's, and the higher the occupational aspirations of the boys.

(ii) Individual responsibility, resourcefulness and self-reliance

No direct measures are available for these at Lumley, but we may note, for example, that high stream boys are more anxious than others to convince the teachers that they are able to work unsupervised, both in the class-room and at home, and they show greater interest in activities such as rock climbing and cycle tours.[1]

(iii) Cultivation and possession of skills

In our study the higher the stream, the more the boys prefer to work hard at school, approve boys who do likewise, and like teachers who make the pupils work hard and punish boys who misbehave.

(iv) Worldly asceticism, postponing immediate satisfaction in the interest of long-term achievement

1. This is not to say, of course, that members of the 'delinquent group' did not show considerable resourcefulness, especially in disrupting lessons and in the commission of theft. It is *positively* directed resourcefulness which is intended here.

This trend is most marked in the A stream at Lumley, where boys value academic achievement more than 'having fun'. In the low streams the reverse is true. This difference reveals itself particularly in the norms which govern copying.

(v) Rationality and planning

When the boys were asked to express their agreement or disagreement with the statement, 'Planning for the future is a waste of time', there was an association between disagreement and high stream (chi-square = $8·37$, D.f. = 3, P $< 0·05$).

(vi) Cultivation of manners, courtesy and personability

Members of the low stream approve cheekiness to the teachers significantly more often than high stream boys, and a direct measure of approval of good manners differentiated between the streams.

(vii) Control of physical aggression and violence

In the high streams, fighting ability is irrelevant to status, and fighting activity is deviant. In the low streams, physical powers and fighting ability form a major criterion of informal status.

(viii) Wholesome recreation

High stream boys tend to join youth clubs which organise activities for their members, whereas low stream boys tend to join clubs which do not organise specific activities and in which members may play very passive roles. Approval of boys with 'interesting hobbies' is associated with high streams.

(ix) Respect for property

Low stream boys, especially members of the delinquent group, are frequently involved in acts of theft and malicious damage, but this is not true for high stream boys.

In short, there is evidence in this study that the higher the stream the greater the degree of conformity to middle-class values. Moreover, there were indications in the meagre evidence produced in Chapter Seven [of *Social Relations in a Secondary School*] that high stream boys tend to come from homes which were more orientated to middle-class values than were the homes of low stream boys.

At this point, the interrelationship of home and school variables becomes complex. That the values acquired in the home and the held by the peer group reinforce each other seems a reasonable conclusion. The academic subculture thus predominantly consists of boys from homes which are more orientated to the middle class, and the pressures in the peer group are towards conformity to the middle-class expectations of the teachers. In the delinquescent subculture, a majority of boys comes from homes which are less orientated to middle-class values and the peer group exerts pressures towards non-conformity to the school's values. In cases at each extreme home and school are mutually reinforcing. When peer group and home influences are consistent, subcultural differentiation is considerably facilitated. When peer group and home conflict, the pupil is faced with a problem of adjustment.

We may consider the processes inherent in the school irrespective of home background. For boys in high streams life at school will be a pleasant and rewarding experience, since the school system confers status upon them. This status is derived from membership of a high stream, where boys are considered to be academically successful, and are granted privileges and responsibility in appointment as prefects and in their selection for school visits and holidays. The peer group values reflect the status bestowed on such boys by the school in being consonant with teachers' values. Conformity to peer group and school values is thus consistent and rewarding.

In the low streams, boys are deprived of status in that they are *double failures* by their lack of ability or motivation to obtain entry to a grammar school or to a high stream in the modern school. The school, as we have seen, accentuates this state of failure and deprivation. The boys have achieved virtually nothing. For boys in low streams, conformity to teacher expectations gives little status. We can thus regard the low stream boys as subject to status frustration, for not only are they unable to gain any sense of equality of worth in the eyes of the school, but their occupational aspirations for their future lives in society are seriously reduced to scope.[1]

The allocation and attitudes of teachers increase this divergence between the upper and lower streams. Whilst the fact that lower stream pupils are not entered for external examinations must inevitably lead to a reduction in motivation to achieve, the tendency to assign teachers with poorer qualifications and weaker discipline to

1. We suggest that this in part explains the widely reported high correlation between delinquency and low academic attainment. T. Ferguson, *The Young Delinquent in his Social Setting*, O.U.P., 1952, p. 119, found that a low level of attainment was probably the most powerful single factor associated with high incidence of delinquency.

these forms reduces even further the pressure exerted on such boys towards academic goals. Once teachers remove the incentive of examinations from these pupils, provide greater opportunities for indiscipline, and begin to expect little from them, it is hardly surprising that they become progressively retarded and alienated from the school's values.

Lumley school is selective in its educative process; there is a constant movement of boys between streams. Those with positive orientations towards the values of the school will tend over the four years to converge on the higher streams; and those with negative orientations will tend to converge on the low streams. On every occasion that a boy is 'promoted' or 'demoted' on the basis of school examinations, the greater becomes the concentration of the two opposing subcultures. As boys with similar values and attitudes are drawn together by this selective process, the more we would expect these values to persist and the greater will become the domination of subcultural values, leading to an increase in pressure towards conformity to the peer group. Demotion to the delinquescent subculture is unlikely to encourage a boy to strive towards academic goals, since the pressures within the peer group will confirm and reinforce the anti-academic attitudes which led to demotion, and the climate within the low streams will be far from conducive to academic striving. In order to obtain promotion from a low stream, a boy must deviate from the dominant anti-academic values and overcome the obstacle of pressures towards 'messing'.

This concentration of boys with similar orientations, which may well be a continuation of a process already established in the primary school, not only increases the vulnerability of the individual to group pressures, but it also tends to insulate members of different streams from interaction and from mutual influence. Individuals become increasingly exposed to their own subculture and increasingly insulated from the values of the other. All these mutually reinforcing factors thus lead, by the fourth year, to a polarisation of values.

At Lumley several aspects of the school organisation, whilst intended purely as a convenience for the construction of the timetable, serve to reinforce this divergence between subcultures. If we examine the timetable we discover that all the boys in fourth year go to the games field on one particular morning of the week. The playing fields are several miles distant from the school, entailing a journey by bus. During the first two periods of the day members of 4A and 4B travel and play games together. After the mid-morning break, 4C and 4D do likewise. The same is true for Handicraft. The boys are asked to select woodwork or metalwork. Two-thirds of the boys do woodwork in two workshops and the remaining third does metalwork. The boys are systematically rotated between woodwork and metalwork and between workshops. The significant point is that 4A and 4B take Handicraft simultaneously, as do 4C and 4D. Thus at any one stage we will find boys from *either* both the upper streams *or* both the lower streams taking Handicraft at the same time, but never upper and lower streams together.

The effect of this separation of the upper from the lower streams for Handicraft and Games is that they have differential opportunities for interaction. A boy of either the two upper or the two lower streams will, in these two subjects which enjoy six periods a week, be brought into immediate contact with the members of the other stream in his subculture, but not with members of the other subculture. In this way the structure of the timetable divides the streams into two halves and helps to account for the division in the friendship choices we observed at the beginning of the chapter, and for the normative differentiation, since this differential opportunity for interaction creates an artificial barrier to communication.

When we add to this the fact that members of upper streams have common teachers, common homework, and common school visits, we can see that these organisational elements may have far-reaching effects on the pupils.

When we consider these differential opportunities for interaction and the convergence of boys with similar motives in upper and lower streams, it is hardly surprising that attitudes between streams should be so hostile, as we saw in Chapter Three [of *Social Relations* . . .]. As Newcomb has pointed out,[1] barriers to communication are likely to lead to the formation of stereotypes, especially where a status-differential is involved; and as long as the barriers remain, the hostile attitudes will persist and perhaps be reinforced. By the fourth year the values and attitudes of members of upper and lower streams have diverged, and there is evidence of deep hostility between the A and the D streams. The barriers existing between the upper and lower halves reinforce the perceived differences and elevate them into irreconcilable and totally opposed stereotypes.

The teacher, whilst he is usually aware that anti-academic boys in

1. T. M. Newcomb, 'Autistic hostility and social reality', *Human Relations,* 1 (1947), 69–86.

high streams are deviant from the group norms, often fails to take adequate account of the fact that academically orientated boys in lower streams are also deviant from group norms. Deviance and conformity are defined in terms of the teacher's own definition of the pupil role, not in terms of peer group values. Because academic low stream boys conform to his expectations, he does not recognise their deviance from the group. To the teacher, it is the high status boys in the low streams who are deviant, yet it is in fact these very boys who are most integrated on a peer group level.

When the teacher rewards boys in high streams for good work or behaviour, he is confirming the dominant values amongst the boys. But when he does this to boys in lower streams, he is confirming the minority norms. In other words, teacher rewards demonstrate the *unification* of teacher and peer group values in high streams; but the same teacher rewards in low streams reveal the *disjunction* between teacher and pupil values. Teacher rewards thus confirm both subcultures, but in the lower streams this is the reverse of what the teacher intends, for by rewarding the deviant academically orientated boy he reinforces the dominant group values.[1] Teacher rewards cannot have their intended effect in low streams at Lumley until the boys as a whole accept the validity of his definition of teacher and pupil roles.

In the academic subculture, because the boys behave in conformity to teacher expectations, and because the two sets of values are consistent, the teacher is able to exert considerable control over the peer group. In the delinquescent subculture, the teachers have little power of social control, because of the conflict which exists between teacher and pupil values. Attempts to change the culture of low streams must thus begin with the conversion of the leaders or high status boys. When teachers regard the high status low stream boys as 'worthless louts' with whom they cannot afford to 'waste time', they are in fact discarding not only these few boys, but also their only means by which group change might be effected.

The members of the delinquescent subculture, if our contention that they are status-deprived is just, reject the system which confers this status and the values on which the status-system is based. Such boys are thus forced to seek a substitute system which can confer

1. Willard Waller, in his classic *The Sociology of Teaching* (1932), Science Editions, Wiley, 1965, p. 335, also points out that when a relationship of hostility exists between the teacher and the student, unfavourable recognition by the teacher acts as a positive identification mechanism.

prestige in proportion to the degree of rejection of the school's values. It is through the anti-academic rejection of the school's values that informal status within the delinquescent group is achieved. They reject the pupil role and replace it with an autonomous and independent peer culture. Conformity thus becomes more important than in the academic subculture, where the boys are united through *individual* effort in academic competition. In the delinquescent sub-culture self-esteem is a *collective* product, since it can be obtained only in relation to the group as a whole, that is, through conformity to anti-academic group pressures, whereas in the academic subculture boys can develop self-esteem on the more individualistic basis of academic competence.

The members of the delinquescent subculture, then, seek alterna-tives to the pupil role as defined by the teachers. Their rejection of the pupil role is supported by the evidence in earlier chapters [of *Social Relations* . . .] and need not be repeated here. The important point is that in redefining the pupil role, such boys aspire to roles outside the terms of the school. Although the low stream pupil is legally forced to come to school, his status as a schoolboy is resented. One solution is to redefine the pupil role in terms of *adult* roles, as well as behaving in ways opposed to teacher definitions. The rejection of the pupil role and the associated status system leads to admiration and premature imi-tation of adult roles beyond the school. This aspiration towards adult roles is a measure of the rejection of the pupil role, for these boys anticipate their adult socialisation before they take up the appropriate work-role outside the school. This premature and anticipatory adult socialisation expresses itself in the exaggerated display of selected aspects of behaviour associated with adult status.[1] Members of the delinquescent subculture thus exhibit behaviour which symbolises adult status, for example, smoking and drinking. The delinquent group smoked more cigarettes per day than any other group at Lumley and they frequently drank bottles of cheap wine or sherry in secret. To consume nicotine and alcohol, and to be seen to consume them,

1. The obsessive concern with masculinity of delinquents is thought by many to be a compulsive reaction formation which is the result of cross-sex primary identifications. See A. K. Cohen, *op. cit.*, W. B. Miller, 'Lower-class culture as a generating milieu of gang delinquency', *Journal of Social Issues*, 14 (1958), 5–19; J. McCord, W. McCord and E. Thurber, 'Some effects of paternal absence on male children', *Journal of Abnormal and Social Psychology*, 64 (1962), 361–9. We feel that the exaggerated masculine behaviour may be more simply explained in terms of the importance of fighting ability and 'threat displays' for status in the delinquent group, combined with the premature imitation of adult male roles.

compensates for their lack of satisfaction in the pupil role.[1] One of the reasons why many members of the delinquescent subculture were so anxious to leave school was because they wanted to have their status at *home* changed from being a 'school boy' into a 'worker', for as workers they would be allowed to smoke openly at home and would no longer have to run errands for the family. As Derek replied when I asked him what would be the nicest thing about starting work: 'Walking in the house at night with a fag in my gob.' We need no longer wonder why the billiard hall was such an attraction to low stream boys.

The implication of much of this analysis is that there is a real sense in which the school can be regarded as a generating factor of delinquency.[2] Although the aims and efforts of the teachers are directed towards deleting such tendencies, the organisation of the school and its influence on subcultural development unintentionally foster delinquent values. The influence of the school on the delinquent group cannot be discussed unless we have a framework in which to set our ideas. Albert Cohen, to whose ideas the present writer is indebted, has suggested a theory to account for the existence of delinquency as almost entirely a working class, male phenomenon.[3] His argument, which cannot be adequately treated here, states that the working-class boy is handicapped in his achievement in the middle-class system and that this differential access to the means for this achievement produces a status-frustration, especially since the working-class boy is constantly surrounded by middle-class agents who emphasise his lack of status. Such boys are thus faced with a problem of adjustment to which delinquency is one of several possible solutions.

Miller, however, believes that gang delinquency is primarily generated through a lower-class culture;[4] that is to say, working-class boys can learn certain values and behaviour patterns which are already normative within the working-class culture, with its 'focal concerns' of law violation, physical prowess, freedom from restraint,

1. It is significant that the 'cock of the school' in the previous year smoked a cigarette in the middle of the school playground in open defiance of the teachers on his last afternoon in the school.
2. The importance of the school in the generation of delinquency has been inadequately treated in the literature. Some discussion is devoted to the role of the school in A. K. Cohen, *op. cit.*, and in D. J. Bordua, 'Delinquent subcultures: sociological interpretations of gang delinquency', *Annals of the American Academy of Political and Social Science*, 338 (1961), 119–36.
3. A. K. Cohen, *op. cit.*
4. W. B. Miller, *op. cit.*

shrewdness, desire for 'thrills' and concept of fate. For Miller, delinquency is a form of integration into working-class culture, whereas for Cohen the delinquent cannot be really integrated into working-class culture because he is frustrated by his inability to succeed in terms of the 'middle-class measuring rod'. If Cohen's argument is to stand, it needs to show that the working-class delinquent is indeed surrounded by middle-class agents by which his lack of status may be induced. Such boys are indeed exposed to middle-class values through the mass media, especially television; but their main exposure will be through the school, where they spend a considerable proportion of their youth and where they are subjected to the middle-class values of the teachers. The teacher thus becomes the principal *direct* agent by which the working-class boy is exposed to middle-class values. High stream boys can internalise and abide by such values, since it is in the acquisition of such values that their hopes of future success are contained. For low stream boys, however, the school simultaneously exposes them to these values and deprives them of status in these terms.[1] It is at this point that they may begin to reject the values because they cannot succeed in them. More than this, the school provides a mechanism through the streaming system whereby their failure is effected and institutionalised, and also provides a situation in which they can congregate together in low streams.

It is at this point that a group solution becomes both more urgent and more possible. As Cohen points out: '. . . it is a hallmark of subcultural delinquency that it is acquired and practised in groups rather than independently contrived by the individual as a solution to his private problems.'[2] In other words, the crucial condition for the emergence of the subculture is the existence of a *group* of persons with the same problem of adjustment, and Cohen points out the paucity of research which has investigated the factors influencing the creation and selection of solutions. It is our contention that the school is an influence both in the determination of the status deprivation and in

1. In his article in the *Journal of Social Issues*, 14 (1958), 20–37, Cohen accepts that the delinquent, whilst committed to the deviant system, recognises the moral validity of the dominant normative structure. M. and C. W. Sherif, *Reference Groups*, New York, Harper and Row, 1964, emphasise that youths from *all* social backgrounds are influenced by the American 'success' ideology and desire the same tangible symbols of that success (p. 199). Even boys in lower-class areas accurately perceive the value of education for future occupational success (p. 200). They differ from middle-class youth only in their lower probability of attaining these goals (p. 219). This restriction of opportunity for lower-class boys is central to the thesis of R. A. Cloward and L. E. Ohlin, *Delinquency and Opportunity*, Routledge, 1961.
2. A. K. Cohen, *op. cit.*, p. 43.

the creation of conditions in which the subculture can form and define itself.[1]

Cohen goes on to suggest some of the mechanisms by which a group solution can occur, especially in his discussion of 'exploratory gestures'. By this he means that persons with the same problem of adjustment, which cannot be solved legitimately in terms of the dominant culture, will initiate solutions in a tentative way by probing gestures of mutual exploration. By a process of joint acceptance and elaboration of the exploratory gestures a solution is arrived at. Those elements which are most rewarding to the group and which most facilitate a solution form the basis of group culture. This study cannot, of course, offer a systematic body of evidence to substantiate this hypothesis, but some of the material, such as the early history of Clint and Clem, is by no means inconsistent with the theory.

Before we continue, let us summarise our theoretical, 'ideal type' analysis. We suggest that subcultural development is a function of a number of mutually reinforcing variables. The first of these is the home, which predisposes the child to an acceptance or rejection of the school values and which affects the child's career in school and the way in which he will be integrated into or isolated from his peer group values. The second important factor is the organisation of the school. At Lumley, the structure of the timetable led to differential opportunities for interaction for boys in upper and lower streams and the consequent segregation favoured the development of common values within each half and of negative stereotypes between halves. This factor also includes the allocation of teachers. The system of transfers between streams leads to a convergence of boys with similar orientations in the same stream. Thirdly, the pressures towards conformity to the informal norms of the stream increase the pressures towards uniformity of values, even when these are inconsistent with those of teachers or parents. The fourth factor concerns the tendency of teachers to favour and reward high stream boys at the expense of their peers in low streams.

All these factors mutually reinforce one another—what engineers call 'positive feedback'. When the school system is viewed in the setting of societal values, the upper stream members are 'successful' and their efforts and values are rewarded by the status they derive. The low stream boys are 'failures'; they are status deprived both in

1. The function of the school in providing the delinquent with a tangible enemy is emphasised by J. Webb, 'The sociology of a school', *British Journal of Sociology*, 13 (1962), 264–72.

the school and in society; their efforts meet with little success. Their problem of adjustment is solved by a rejection of societal and teacher values, which are substituted with a set of peer group values, and status is derived from conformity to a reversal of societal and teacher values.

To show that this is indeed a process which occurs over time now becomes essential to our analysis of subcultural differentiation and of the influence of the school in generating delinquency. The difficulty is that intensive study of fourth year boys at Lumley tells us very little about the influence of the previous three years in the school. Ideally, we would like to have the same measures on the same group of boys over a period of four years; on this basis we could assess the changes that had taken place during the time interval. In this study we have made mere speculation about the process, based on inferences from evidence about fourth year boys. There is no adequate way in which our analysis can be verified in the terms of this study, but we can offer some comparative material on *second* year boys which may be regarded as slight evidence for the suggested analysis. (We have, of course, to remember that we are now comparing two groups of different boys at different stages of their school careers, which is a method considerably inferior to one in which the same group of boys is tested at different stages.) From these second year pupils, who were also streamed into five forms, three sorts of evidence have been collected, for which three hypotheses can be erected.

Firstly, the Sentence Completion Test was administered to them. If our analysis of the process of normative and subcultural differentiation is correct we should expect that these items should fail to differentiate between streams, or differentiate between them at a much lower level of statistical significance.

Secondly, these pupils completed seven selected items from the multiple choice Orientation Test. The prediction is similar to that for the Sentence Completion Test.

Thirdly, behavioural ratings by teachers on each boy were collected and correlations between informal status and behaviour, and between informal status and academic position, were calculated. Three predictions follow from this.

(*a*) It should be untrue, or less true than in the fourth year, that the higher the stream, the higher the average behavioural score.
(*b*) The correlations between informal status and academic position should be similar for all streams, and should be positive rather than negative.

(*c*) The correlations between informal status and behavioural scores should be similar for all streams, and should be positive rather than negative.

The results are given in Tables 7.3 and 7.4. On the Sentence Completion Test, three out of the six items which differentiate between fourth year streams also differentiate between second year streams. Since three out of the six items do not differentiate between second year forms, and one differentiates at a lower level of significance than for the fourth year, there is some evidence for the prediction. In the

TABLE 7.3. *Comparison between second and fourth year streams* (*A*)

	Second year		Fourth year	
Dimensions	*Chi-square*	*P-value*	*Chi-square*	*P-value*
Boys in the A stream are . . .	15·44	<0·005	17·17	<0·001
Boys in the D stream are . . .	31·39	<0·001	13·51	<0·005
Teachers are . . .	4·51	Not sig.	14·48	<0·005
Teachers think of me as . . .	2·56	Not sig.	16·50	<0·001
When lessons are boring I . . .	7·41	Not sig.	9·62	<0·025
When teacher says my work is bad . . .	10·69	<0·025	7·82	<0·05
Teachers who control the class	8·39	<0·05	8·43	<0·05
Teachers who make boys work	5·08	Not sig.	18·69	<0·001
Boy who pays attention	2·56	Not sig.	19·16	<0·001
Boy who obeys	2·01	Not sig.	14·45	<0·005
Boy who works hard	2·24	Not sig.	23·16	<0·001
Boy who lets you copy	3·80	Not sig.	13·05	<0·005
Boy you have fun with in lessons	0·85	Not sig.	8·94	<0·05

For each chi-square test, 3 degrees of freedom.

TABLE 7.4. *Comparisons between second and fourth year streams* (B)

Dimension	*Year*	*A stream*	*B stream*	*C stream*	*D stream*
Informal status and	Second	+0·10	−0·06	+0·16	−0·17
academic position	Fourth	+0·50*	+0·16	−0·15	−0·15
Informal status and	Second	−0·37*	−0·52*	−0·13	−0·37*
behaviour	Fourth	+0·30*	−0·12	−0·58*	−0·57*
Form average behaviour	Second	3·44	3·33	3·35	3·49
score	Fourth	3·92	3·57	3·56	3·24

* Statistically significant.

results to the items of Orientation Test, only one of the seven items differentiates between second year streams at a statistically significant level. We can thus regard the prediction as verified.[1]

The average behaviour scores for each second year stream do in fact cluster together, the largest differences between forms being 0·16, whereas the fourth year figure is 0·68. Moreover, the average scores do not decline as we descend the streams; 2D has the highest average. We may thus conclude that behavioural scores are not stream-related in the second year, though they are in the fourth year. None of the correlations between informal status and academic position in second year forms reaches significance level; they are all close to nought. Moreover, the decline from positive to negative correlations with stream which was found for the fourth year forms does not hold in the second year. The correlations between informal status and behaviour are all negative in the second year and do not follow the progression from significantly positive in the A stream to significantly negative in the D stream which we found for fourth year boys. This finding is in line with the prediction in that the correlations tend to be similar, but it is difficult to explain why three of them should be significantly negative. (An *ad hoc* hypothesis might be that in the second year, when pressures towards academic achievement are not strong, it is the boys who tend to misbehave who acquire high status in all streams; after the second year, when academic pressures are exerted on high streams, criteria of status change in high and especially the A streams, but continue in the same direction in low streams.)[1]

We may conclude that there is no evidence of normative or sub-cultural differentiation between streams in the second year.[2] This

1. When we compare the distribution of responses to these seven items of boys in the A and D streams in the second and fourth years, we find that 4A shows more pro-school responses than 2A in six cases out of seven, and fewer anti-school responses in five cases out of seven. 4D shows fewer pro-school responses than 2D in four cases out of seven, but more anti-school responses in only two cases out of seven. This may indicate that in the third and fourth years at school the A stream makes greater movement towards an academic orientation than does the D stream towards an anti-academic, delinquescent orientation. Such an inference is supported by the fact that 2A and 2D show the same negative correlation of −0·37 between informal status and behaviour (see Table 7.4).
2. The earlier development of a delinquescent subculture could be facilitated by primary differentiation in the junior school. This would be most likely when the junior school contains several streams, which was not the case in the junior schools which 'fed' Lumley Secondary Modern School. Subject to future research findings, we suggest, for reasons to be elaborated in the main text, that the formation of a delinquescent subculture is improbable before adolescence, though the roots may be laid many years before its appearance.

supports our contention that this differentiation is a process which takes place during the four years at school, and also confirms the claims of the teachers that the low streams become 'difficult' only in the third and fourth years. It may of course, be that either or both the second and fourth years are atypical; certainly it would be preferable if we had evidence on one year group tested in the second and fourth years. Our conclusion about the process of normative and subcultural differentiation must be regarded as tentative and subject to more detailed testing—but there is no evidence in this study *against* the analysis.

If it is true that normative differentiation and subcultural development do not become marked until the third and fourth years, then it is possible that status deprivation does not constitute, or is not perceived as, a problem for the younger boys. This is consistent with our analysis in that the mutual reinforcement of the key factors we have suggested will take time to be effective. Moreover, the perception of status deprivation in low stream boys will be in part a function of their realisation of their societal as well as their scholastic failure. That is, the relation between stream and external examinations, and between academic success and the occupational structure, does not become a reality until the later years of life at school.

The subcultures persist year after year because the school system persists unchanged and unchallenged. The same problems produce the same solutions, especially when we consider the function of senior boys in providing role-models for younger boys.[1] Thus younger, low stream boys learn that fighting ability and delinquescent orientations are the bases of informal status to their elders. The subcultures are perpetuated over the years.

It is now time to put our feet back on the ground; speculation is a seductive and dangerous path. Our distinction between the academic and the delinquescent subcultures is a considerable over-simplification of the facts. Although the extremes can be clearly distinguished, there remains a large proportion of boys who, whilst tending towards one of the poles, cannot easily be contained in either. This is particularly true of 4B boys, who are often closer to the D stream's orientation than to the A stream's, as an examination of some of the tables will confirm. 4B is an intermediate form in conflict between the two poles. It may be true that in other years the B stream will be drawn more

1. As Waller, *op. cit.*, p. 179, points out, pupils tend to heroify children who are a few years older than themselves, especially those who are in the next higher age group.

towards A stream values, especially when we remember that in the fourth year considered here the most academically orientated members of the B stream were assigned to the A stream for C.S.E. purposes and replaced by the least academically orientated members of the A stream, a fact which has led to a somewhat artificial increase in the difference between the two. This may well have produced a dominance of non-academic values as we observed in Chapter Two, where we pointed out that 4B members tended to perceive themselves as 'leavers', by which the morale and prestige of the B stream was lowered from its traditional near-equality with the A stream.

Perhaps our major unsolved problem is to explain the existence of deviants in each subculture. Why do boys persist in nonconformity to peer group norms? It is possible that for deviants in either subculture home background plays a powerful role. For example, low status low stream boys deviate from the peer group because they are sufficiently gratified by the teacher rewards they derive from hard work and acceptance of school values to be able to reject peer group pressures. Values internalised in the home may provide a reservoir of resistance against informal norms, so that they continue to resist even when they are unable, through lack of ability, to ascend into the higher streams to which they aspire. Why these low status low stream boys deviate in the face of powerful pressures from the dominant group is a fundamental question; they either have a different problem of adjustment or they find a different solution. In this study we have insufficient knowledge of the effect of our variables on *individuals* to be able to proffer an answer. This is particularly true of the deviants in the academic subculture, who make such an interesting compromise between the two poles. It is at this point that other variables, such as personality, which have been excluded from this study, may play such a critical part.

It may be that our analysis of the subcultural differentiation raises more problems than it solves. Certainly it has been speculative; and it is based on empirical data from one single school. Both these facts are serious weaknesses, and underline the dangers of making generalisations from this study. It is possible that the structure of social relations in Lumley Secondary Modern School for Boys is typical of many similar schools in Britain. Only when we treat this analysis of Lumley as a set of hypotheses for testing on a wider basis will the generality of our conclusions be known.

PART FOUR Subcultural studies I

8

Parental encouragement*

J. W. B. Douglas

The demographic studies of Part Two illustrated ways in which the social-class gradient in educational opportunity and performance may be identified and measured; the contextual studies of Part Three suggested the importance of neighbourhood and school influences; Part Four demonstrates attempts to analyse in more detail the determinants of educability. This chapter is part of Dr Douglas's major report on the primary school experience of a cohort of five thousand children whose progress has been followed since birth. In this study he singles out the crucial importance of the class-linked predictor 'parental interest', and this is pursued further in Chapters 9 and 10.

Social class, as defined in the last chapter [of *The Home and the School*], summarises many different aspects of the home environment. We now look at the extent to which parents take an interest in their children's work at school and encourage them to succeed. The aim of this chapter is to see how the performance of children in the tests and in the secondary selection examinations is influenced by the attitudes of their parents, and the encouragement they receive at home.

A rough measure of the mothers' educational aspirations was given in Chapter III [of *The Home and the School*] by separating those who wished their children to go to grammar schools and stay there until they were more than sixteen years old, from those who were educationally less ambitious. The mothers' attitudes, even when measured in this rough way, have an important influence on their children's chances of getting grammar school places. But parents may give support and encouragement to their children even though they

---

* Reprinted from *The Home and the School,* MacGibbon & Kee, 1964, pp. 52–9, by kind permission of the author and the publisher.

realise that they are not clever enough to stand a chance of getting a place in a grammar school. A more generally applicable measure of educational interest is needed, which, moreover, takes account of the attitudes of both parents and not of the mother alone.

The middle-class parents take more interest in their children's progress at school than the manual working-class parents do, and they become relatively more interested as their children grow older. They visit the schools more frequently to find out how their children are getting on with their work, and when they do so are more likely to ask to see the Head as well as the class teacher, whereas the manual working-class parents are usually content to see the class teacher only. But the most striking difference is that many middle-class fathers visit the schools to discuss their children's progress, whereas manual working-class fathers seldom do so. (Thirty-two per cent of middle-class fathers visit the schools, but only 12 per cent of manual working-class fathers.) The teachers' contacts with the working-class families are largely through the mothers, and this may explain why they become relatively less frequent as the children get older, whereas with the middle classes they become more frequent. The working-class mothers have a particular interest in seeing how their children settle in when they first go to school, but may feel diffident about discussing their educational progress with the teachers at a later stage; and it seems either that their husbands are not prepared to take on this responsibility, or that they are unable to do so owing to the difficulty of taking time off work to visit the schools.

The parents who make frequent visits to the schools and are seen by the teachers as very interested in their children's education are also outstanding in the use they make of the available medical services. They seldom fail to bring their children to the child welfare centres or have them immunised against diphtheria and other diseases and they are regarded by the health visitors as giving a high standard of care to their children and homes. Their children benefit not only from the support and encouragement they get in their school work but also from the excellent personal and medical care they enjoy at home.

In contrast, the parents who seldom visit the schools and seem to the teachers to be uninterested in their children's progress make little use of the available medical services, often fail to take their children to the welfare centres or to have them immunised and, according to the health visitors, often neglect their homes and give their children low standards of care. There is a greater amount of illness and school absence among their children, whose work suffers to some extent from this as well as from their parents' lack of interest in their educational progress. Perhaps this extra burden of illness explains why these parents worry about their children's health and behaviour more than the other parents. These worries may be partly justified, but one carries away a picture of a group of mothers who are worrying about their children without taking the steps necessary to put things right.

In this study, the level of the parents' interest in their children's work was partly based on comments made by the class teachers at the end of the first and at the end of the fourth primary school year, and partly on the records of the number of times each parent visited the schools to discuss their child's progress with the Head or class teacher. Parents are said to show a 'high level of interest' if the teachers regarded them throughout the primary school period as very interested in their children's work and if they had also taken the opportunity to visit the primary schools at least once a year to discuss their children's progress. They show a 'fair level of interest' if they fall short on one of these counts, and a 'low level of interest' if they fall short on more than one.

These three groups of parents differ sharply in their educational aspirations—for example, in their views on school leaving and their hopes that their children will get grammar school places. On the average, the children in these three groups are also of widely different ability and, as will be shown in the next chapter, have very different attitudes to their studies; moreover they are numerous enough for satisfactory statistical comparisons to be made among the four social classes. Although this grading gives only a crude picture of the level of the parents' interest, it has been a great aid to understanding the part played in primary school education by the support and encouragement children receive from their homes.

The parents who are most interested in their children's education come predominantly from the middle classes, and those who are least interested from the manual working classes. Within each social class, however, the parents who give their children the most encouragement in their school work also give them the best care in infancy. The manual working-class parents show this more strongly[1]

1. The correlation coefficient showing the relation between the parents' interest score and the maternal care score is $+0.17$ in the middle classes and $+0.48$ in the manual working classes. (For these correlations more detailed scores running from o to 50 were used.)

than the middle-class parents; if they show a high level of interest in their children's school work, then their standards of care and their use of the services are also high, and they have middle-class standards too in their views on the school leaving age and in their expectations of grammar school awards.

An eight-year-old child will be greatly influenced, one would imagine, by the attitude of his parents to his school work. His own attitude to his work will be moulded by theirs and, if they are ambitious for his success, he will have the further advantage of home tuition in reading and probably other subjects.[1] Even in the early years at the primary school his test performance will show the effects of these pressures which, as he grows older and the eleven-plus examination approaches, are likely to increase in intensity. It is expected, then, that the parents' attitudes will have a considerable effect on the performance of children at eight years and an even greater effect on the performance of the eleven-year-olds. This is borne out by the results of this survey.

At both eight and eleven years, but particularly at eleven, the highest average scores in the tests are made by the children whose parents are the most interested in their education and the lowest by those whose parents are the least interested. This is partly a social-class effect stemming from the large proportion of upper middle-class children among the former and of manual working-class children among the latter. But the relation between the children's scores and their parents' attitudes persists within each social class. It is less marked in the middle classes than in the manual working classes, but is substantial in both and cannot be explained away in terms of social selection alone. In the upper middle class, for instance, the children of very interested parents make scores that are 3·7 points higher on the average than those made by the children of uninterested parents. In the lower manual working class they make scores that are 9·2 points higher.

The children who are encouraged in their studies by their parents do better in each type of test, in picture intelligence tests as well as in those of reading, vocabulary and arithmetic. Their advantage is, however, less in the tests which are given pictorially or in diagram matic form. Those with very interested parents make higher scores

1. In both the middle and manual working classes, for example, the proportion of children who were given reading lessons before they went to their primary schools is twice as high among those whose parents were later classified as showing a high level of interest, as among those showing a low level.

at both eight and eleven years in the tests of school subjects than they do in the picture or non-verbal intelligence tests. At each age they may be considered as being on the average 'over-achievers', and by the same criterion, the children of uninterested parents may be considered 'under-achievers'.

The children whose parents show a high level of interest not only make higher average scores in the tests at eight and eleven years, but also improve the level of their performance between these ages so that they pull ahead. After allowing for the influence of social class, the children whose parents show a high level of interest improve their scores by an average of 1·06 points, those whose parents show an average interest improve by 0·29 points, and those whose parents show little interest deteriorate by 0·18 points. The increasing advantage of the children with interested parents cannot be explained by the changes that were made in the types of test used at eight and eleven because it is as marked in the reading and vocabulary tests[1] as in the combined test scores.

The children with interested parents pull ahead of the rest whatever their initial starting ability, as is seen in Table 8.1.

TABLE 8.1. *Lower manual working-class children.*

| | Level of parents' interest | | |
| | High | Average | Low |
Level of measured ability at eight	Change in score 8–11 years	Change in score 8–11 years	Change in score 8–11 years
40 or less	*	+2·07	+0·58
41–45	*	+0·79	−0·42
46–50	*	+2·17	−0·71
51–55	+0.60	−0·63	−0·96
56–60	+1·50	−1·65	−3·16
61 and over	−1·36	−4·00	−5·71

* Fewer than 10 children in these groups. (+ = improved. − = deteriorated.)

The children who are encouraged in their work by their parents are, it seems, at an advantage both in the relatively high scores they make in the tests and in the way they improve their scores between eight and eleven years. How far is this because these children are stimulated by their parents? Could it not equally well be explained by saying that the interested parents are themselves likely to be

1. These were given in exactly the same form at eleven years as at eight.

relatively successful in life and so in a position to live in good homes and to send their children to the best schools ? May not the advantages enjoyed by their children stem mainly from the better teaching they get in school and from the generally good environment in which they live ? A firm answer to these questions is given in the analysis made by H. R. Simpson,[1] where the overlapping effects of standard of home, size of family and academic record of the school, on test performance are removed, leaving a series of adjusted average test scores which show the residual influence of parents' interest on measured ability. After these adjustments, the advantage of the children with interested parents is somewhat reduced but still considerable.

In each social class, children have a considerable advantage in the eight-year tests if their parents take an interest in their school work, and an even greater advantage at eleven. The influence of the level of the parents' interest on test performance is greater[2] than that of any of the other three factors—size of family, standard of home, and academic record of the school—which are included in this analysis, and it becomes increasingly important as the children grow older. It is among the girls especially that this effect is seen. Among the working-class boys, parents' interest is only slightly more important at eleven than at eight, whereas among the middle-class boys it even shows a relative decline: the test performance at eleven is then correspondingly more affected by the type of school they attend and the number of brothers and sisters they have.

As one would expect from their test scores, children do relatively well in the secondary selection examinations if their parents take much interest in their work and relatively badly if they take little interest. This difference is most marked in the manual working classes, where 40 per cent of the former and only 10 per cent of the latter go to grammar schools. The teachers, though more optimistic than the results of the eleven-plus examinations justify, take a similar view and consider that 59 per cent of the manual working-class children are suitable for grammar schools if their parents are interested, and only 15 per cent if they are uninterested. In the middle classes also the teachers' views show a similar agreement with the results of secondary school selection and the level of the parents' interest.

The children with parents who are interested in their work do well in the secondary selection examinations and are favourably rated by

1. Appendix II of *The Home and the School*.
2. Greater as judged by the level of the statistical significance of its effect.

their teachers largely because they are of superior measured ability at eleven. Once this factor is allowed for, they still have a slight additional advantage in the examinations; those with very interested parents get 10 per cent more places than we would expect, whereas those with uninterested parents get 7 per cent fewer. It is however the children at the borderline of the level of ability needed for grammar school entrance, who get substantially more grammar school places if their parents are interested in their work; they get 19 per cent more places than expected, whereas those with un-interested parents get 14 per cent fewer.

The influence of the parents on their children's chances in the secondary selection examinations is better shown when the children are grouped by the wishes their parents expressed when they were ten years old, wishes for the type of school they should go to, and how long they should stay there.[1] This is hardly surprising, for the school interest score is an attempt to measure the level of support and encouragement which will help children of widely different ability to take an interest in their studies and use their capabilities as far as they can, whereas the wishes parents expressed for the type of school their children should go to are likely to indicate the pressures that may have been used to stimulate children of above average ability to get a valued prize.

We have seen in this chapter that children, when their parents take an interest in their work and encourage them, improve their scores in tests of school performance and mental ability between the ages of eight and eleven years and have a slight advantage in the eleven-plus selection examinations. On the other hand, when parents take little interest, their children lose ground in the tests and gain rather fewer places in the selection examinations than would be expected from their measured ability. The influence of the parents' attitudes on their children's behaviour in school is described in the next chapter [of *The Home and the School*].

1. Among children of measured ability between 55 and 60, i.e. those who are at the borderline for grammar school entry, those whose mothers wish them to go to grammar school and stay there till seventeen at least get 23 per cent more places than expected, those whose mothers are doubtful get 24 per cent fewer places and those who expect to go to a secondary modern school and leave before seventeen get 69 per cent fewer places than expected.

9

The survey of parental attitudes and circumstances, 1964*

Roma Morton-Williams

Following Dr Douglas's examination of the importance of parental interest in the achievement of primary school children, Miss Morton-Williams reports on the Plowden Committee's national survey. This major investigation based on over three thousand interviews offers a fuller exploration of the involvement of parents in the primary education of their children, and adds to our knowledge of social-class differences in the way the educational system is perceived and utilised. In its concern to map the dimensions of belief as well as of behaviour the focus of the study may be regarded as subcultural, and this is carried further in Chapter 10 by Professor Musgrove.

The Education Act of 1944 created two Central Advisory Councils for Education (one for England, the other for Wales) whose functions were to advise the Minister for Education upon such matters connected with educational theory and practice as they thought fit, and upon any questions referred to them by him. In 1963 the C.A.C.E. (England), under the chairmanship of Lady Plowden, were asked by the Minister 'to consider primary education in all its aspects, and the transition to secondary education'. To assist them in this task the Council commissioned, through the Department of Education and Science, a number of research and information-collecting projects of which one was an interview survey among parents of primary school children conducted by the Government Social Survey.

This survey had two main purposes. One was to obtain *parents'* views on the education their children were receiving, on their

* Based on Appendix 3 to vol. 2 of the Central Advisory Council for Education (England) Report, *Children and their Primary Schools,* H.M.S.O., 1967, by kind permission of the author and the publisher.

relationships with the teaching staff of their children's schools and on certain aspects of primary school organisation about which the Plowden Committee might wish to recommend changes (school starting age is an instance of this). The other purpose was to collect information about parental attitudes and home backgrounds of children. This was to be related to their school circumstances and educational achievement in a study of the interrelationships between home and school environment and educational progress. The overall plan of the project for studying the association between home and school circumstances and achievement, of which the parents' survey formed a part, was by Gilbert F. Peaker, c.b.e., and Stella M. Duncan, h.m.i. This chapter discusses only the parents' survey itself which was designed and carried out by the Government Social Survey. Other aspects of the project are described in *Children and their Primary Schools*, vol. 2, Appendices 4 and 5.

THE DESIGN AND METHOD OF ENQUIRY OF THE SURVEY

The parents' survey was based on a two-stage sampling procedure. First a random sample of schools was taken from all types of maintained primary schools in England, with the exception only of special schools. (In the case of separate junior and infants schools the junior school was randomly selected and drew into the sample the infants school which mainly supplied its intake.) In all, 173 schools were selected. Within them a random sample was taken of children from three classes, top and bottom juniors and top infants. The parents of these children formed the interview sample. The sample was designed to give each child in a maintained primary school in England an equal chance of being selected, regardless of the size of family to which he or she belonged. Parents' chances of coming into the sample were related therefore to the number of children they had in primary schools. 3237 parents were selected and interviews were successfully carried out with 3092 (95 per cent) of them.

Although this chapter talks about *parents'* attitudes, in fact the very great majority of interviews were with *mothers*, and it is important to bear this in mind in considering the information presented here. The reason for interviewing mothers was, in the first place, that it is extremely difficult to carry out a standardised form of interview with two people together and within the time available for the enquiry it was not feasible to see both parents separately. The question then was 'Which parent should we interview'? It was considered important to aim always to interview the same parent, either all mothers or all fathers; the mother was decided upon because it was thought that in the majority of families she would be the one having most direct contact with the school, at least when the child was at the primary stage of education.

Mothers were interviewed in their homes by Government Social Survey interviewers over the period 22 June to 31 July 1964. The interviews were structured, that is interviewers asked precisely defined questions in a specified way. The questionnaire used is printed in full in Appendix 3 of *Children and their Primary Schools*, vol. 2.

The preliminary stages in the development of the questionnaires included an examination of previous research in this area, discussions with people working in schools and homes—heads and other teachers in primary schools, child welfare officers, care committee workers— and also with groups of parents. Great help was given by Stella M. Duncan, H.M.I. Freely-ranging interviews were carried out with a quota sample of approximately fifty parents, contacted by asking schools to provide names of specified numbers of parents who appeared to be more and less interested in their children's school progress, with brighter and duller children, and mothers working and not working. On the basis of this exploratory work questionnaires were devised which were then tried out in interviews with approximately 200 mothers of a random sample of children from twenty randomly chosen schools. The majority of the main survey interviews lasted between three-quarters of an hour and an hour and a half. Parents generally showed great interest in the enquiry and were very ready to give their views.

THE HOME BACKGROUNDS OF PRIMARY SCHOOL CHILDREN

Parents' attitudes towards the education their children are receiving, the sort of relationship they have with the schools and the role they expect or wish schools to take in the upbringing of their children are of course likely to be related to characteristics of the parents themselves, such as their own level of education, and to home circumstances such as the financial position of the family. In presenting the findings of this survey it was obviously not enough to show, for example, that a certain percentage of all parents were happy with the arrangements for visiting the schools. It was important to know whether some groups of parents were more or less satisfied with the arrangements because it then became possible to consider what produced differences between parents and whether any steps could be taken to alter the situation if desirable. The question was what would be the most useful ways of grouping parents for this particular enquiry. It was decided that, of the many possible alternatives, the Registrar General's social class grouping (1960), based on occupation, had the most advantages and fewest disadvantages for our purpose. It has the merit of being widely used and so enabling data from many different sources to be compared. Furthermore it was thought that teachers studying information from this survey would find it easier to think of their pupils' home backgrounds in terms of fathers' occupations—professional, clerical, skilled trades, etc.—than, say, their incomes or education, although, of course, occupational levels are associated with these.

The social class of the family was determined by the occupation of the father or father substitute. If there was no father or father substitute in the household at the time of the interview then the classification was based on the occupation of the father or father substitute when last in the household. If the father was unemployed, then his last occupation was used. Only one per cent of families could not be classified by paternal occupation. The proportions of the sample falling into each social-class group are shown in Table 9.1. For comparison is given the social-class distribution of married males aged twenty to sixty-four in the general population at the time of the 1961 census.

TABLE 9.1.   *Comparison between the social-class distribution of the survey families and married males in the general population.*

Group		Fathers of primary school children	Married males aged 20 to 64 in the general population
I	Professional	4	4
II	Managerial, includes self-employed	14	16
III	Non-manual: clerical workers, sales staff	11 } 59	51
III	Skilled manual trades: includes foremen	48	
IV	Semiskilled manual workers	16	19
V	Unskilled labourers	6	7
	Unclassified	1	3
	Number interviewed (100%)	3092	

A summary of the main findings of the survey begins with a description of the home backgrounds of children in different social-class groups. Three areas are singled out, each of which is likely to have some bearing on a child's reactions to school: parents' education and reading habits, the educational support and encouragement given to children at home, and some material circumstances of the family. This information provides a necessary background against which to consider the findings presented in the next section—parents' views on various aspects of primary school organisation, their contacts and relationships with the staff of the schools and the kind of anxieties they had about their children's education.

Parents' education and reading habits

Parents'
educ^nal
experience

Clearly the type of education which parents themselves have had is likely to colour their attitudes in one way or another towards the value of education in general and to affect their aspirations for their children. Parents' own educational experience may well also affect their understanding of what the schools are trying to achieve and may limit the extent to which they are able to follow what their children are doing, irrespective of how interested they are or how anxious to encourage their children in their school work. Table 9.2 summarises information, from this survey, about parents' education and reading habits. For brevity we show only the percentages of families in each social class who were in a relatively unfavourable position in terms of these characteristics. Detailed tables are given in the full report.

Over half these children's parents had completed their continuous full-time formal education by the age of fourteen; 63 per cent of the fathers and 81 per cent of the mothers had had no further education after leaving school. (Further education is defined here as professional, academic, trade or vocational courses taken full or part-time or by correspondence but lasting for at least a session; completion of full apprenticeship or qualification as state registered nurse is included.) It follows from the nature of the occupational classification used that there was a very close association between level of parents' education, particularly father's, and the occupation of the father. Only a very small proportion of fathers who were doing semiskilled or unskilled work had stayed at school beyond the age of fourteen or taken any further education. In the large skilled manual occupational category further education of fathers had mainly taken the form of apprenticeships. The majority of mothers in this group had had no further education after leaving school.

Further information is gained about a family's educational experience by considering whether any member, that is father, mother,

TABLE 9.2. *Parents' education and reading habits, by social class.*

Parents' education and reading habits	I Professional	II Managerial	III Non-manual	III Skilled manual	IV Semi-skilled	V Unskilled	Unclassified	Total
				Percentages of parents				
Education								
Father completed full-time education at age 14 or younger	6	38	44	73	79	85	30	64
Mother completed full-time educataion at age 14 or younger	13	43	50	64	69	76	48	59
Neither parents nor child's brothers/sisters had attended a selective secondary school	5	24	24	56	66	71	28	48
Reading habits								
Neither parent had belonged to a lending library during the previous ten years	10	21	15	35	46	47	32	32
Father rarely did any reading	3	14	12	22	27	24	—	20
Mother rarely did any reading	6	17	17	30	31	41	25	27
Parents possessed fewer than six books, apart from children's books	5	11	15	33	39	56	45	29
Number of parents interviewed (100%)	110	430	338	1486	499	189	40	3092

brother or sister of the selected child, had attended a selective secondary school. A selective secondary school is taken as one in which there is some selection of entrants by ability. Included here are state grammar and technical schools, private grammar schools, and pre-1947 secondary, central, intermediate and higher grade schools. Comprehensive schools have also been included as they provide a wide range of courses. The proportion of families who, in this sense, had had no experience of selective secondary education ranged from only 5 per cent in social class I to 71 per cent in social class V.

The probability is that if parents have firm habits of reading their children will be more likely to develop similar interests. The proportions who rarely did any reading at all in their spare time ranged from virtually none of the professional-class parents to approximately a quarter of those in manual occupations. In each social class fewer mothers than fathers read in their spare time. If we take more concrete indications of reading habits, number of books owned and library membership, we find the same marked social class trend with the proportions rising to over half of unskilled occupation parents owning fewer than six books and approaching half having made no use of lending libraries within the previous ten years. Not surprisingly, then, the proportions of children who were read to regularly, or who read to themselves on most evenings, increased consistently with social class.

The educational support and encouragement given to children in their homes

The first issue in considering the educational support and encouragement given to children in their homes is the extent to which parents were in fact available to spend time with their children. One or both natural parents was missing from at least 8 per cent of the homes in which interviews were conducted (interviews were not attempted for the 0·3 per cent of children in the sample who were living in institutions). In 5 per cent of homes there was no natural father or other male person who could have adopted the father's role in the child's upbringing and in 1 per cent there was no mother or mother substitute. There were no social-class differences in the proportions of broken homes or in the lack of a father or mother figure, but in the majority of families in the 'unclassified' category there was no father.

Over a third of the mothers were in paid employment. For 17 per cent their work took them away from home for five hours or more a day. The lowest proportion of working mothers was in social class

I, 18 per cent, while in the other social-class groups the proportions of working mothers varied only from 34 per cent in class II to 44 per cent in class IV. A third of the mothers of children in the top infants' forms worked and the proportion rose to almost half of those with children in the top juniors. Over a quarter of fathers in skilled and semiskilled manual occupations were on shift work or permanent night work or were regularly working away from home for at least two nights each week.

It is noteworthy that not many more than half the mothers in any social-class group said that they were free to spend time with their children on most weekday evenings. Social class V mothers were the only group noticeably less likely than others to be able to spend time with their children in the evenings. Mothers were more generally available to their children on weekday evenings the lower the child was in primary school. Whether mothers were working or not and the hours they worked seemed to make little difference to their being able to give time to their children in the evenings. A quarter of the fathers were unable to join in activities with their children on weekday evenings and almost a third were only available occasionally if at all at weekends. In families in which the father was a manual worker there was a slight tendency for him to be less often available to spend time with his children than in other families.

Going for outings together as a family was very much associated with social class, with non-manual occupation families being much more likely than manual to go on outings together and also to have had their last outing more recently.

The social-class groups showed very different patterns in the responsibility taken by fathers over the educational progress of their children at the primary stage. These are summarised in Table 9.3. The proportion of mothers who said that their husbands had taken an interest in which school their children went to increased consistently with social class. Over 40 per cent of the fathers in manual occupations had left the starting of their children at the sampled school entirely to their wives, almost half of these fathers had not been to the child's present school at all and less than a quarter of them had talked to the heads. The majority of mothers in all social classes said that their husbands took an interest in how their children were getting on at school, but again rather more of the manual occupation fathers left this responsibility to their wives. Control of the children, however, appeared to be carried out as much by fathers as mothers in all social classes.

TABLE 9.3. *Interest taken by father in child's education and upbringing, by social class.*

Interest taken by father in child's education	Social class						
	I Profes- sional	II Mana- gerial	III Non- manual	III Skilled manual	IV Semi- skilled	V Un- skilled	Total
	Percentages of fathers						
Left interest in school child went to to the mother	15	22	27	43	48	56	38
Had not been to child's school	19	23	26	45	48	65	40
Left interest in child's school progress to the mother	3	9	10	19	19	28	16
Husband took small or no part in control of children	20	19	15	24	22	23	22
Total number (100%)	110	430	338	1486	499	189	3052

Note. The 40 families 'unclassified' by social class are omitted as in the majority there were no fathers.

In Table 9.4 are shown parents' views on whether children should be given school work to do at home at the primary stage of their education and the extent to which they themselves tried to help their children with school work.

Over the school years covered in this sample there were marked increases both in the proportions of children already doing some school work at home and of parents approving of their doing so. In the top juniors 61 per cent of children were already given work to do at home and as many as 75 per cent of parents wanted homework for their children. Among the top infants 26 per cent already had homework and 46 per cent approved of the idea. It is of interest that the children of manual workers were rather less likely than other children to be given any school work to do at home but that there was little social-class difference in the proportions of parents wanting their children to be given some homework.

Whether children received help at home with school work was related both to their social class and to the stage they had reached at school. The higher up children were in primary school the less likely they were to be helped with school work at home. This dropping off, as children moved up the school, in the help given may well be related to the difficulties that many parents said that they had in helping their

TABLE 9.4. *School work done at home, by social class.*

				Social class				
Whether school work done at home and help given	I Professional	II Managerial	III Non-manual	III Skilled manual	IV Semi-skilled	V Un-skilled	Unclassified	Total
				Percentages of homes				
Child given school work to do at home	52	47	47	41	35	39	38	42
Mother liked child to have school work to do at home	63	63	59	60	60	54	58	60
Parents had asked school for work for child to do at home, or how they could help child with school work at home	40	37	34	28	27	23	18	30
Child received help with school work at home	76	72	68	66	64	57	62	67
Parents had bought copies of school textbooks for child to use at home	57	49	50	36	29	19	20	38
Total number (100%)	110	430	338	1486	499	189	40	3092

children because methods of teaching had changed so much since they themselves were at school.

Almost a third of the parents had taken the initiative in seeking for their children to be given some school work to do at home, or had asked teachers to show them how they themselves could help their children with school work, and just over a third had bought copies to have at home of some of the textbooks their children were using in school. These actions again were associated with social class. It may be arguable whether they would in fact be helpful to a child educationally or were merely symptoms of parents' anxieties about the eleven-plus examination which was still generally in existence in England when the interviews were carried out. Nevertheless, they demonstrate social-class differences in positive steps which were taken by parents arising from the importance they attached to their child's educational progress.

At the time of this inquiry approximately half the pupils in maintained secondary schools stayed on beyond the statutory leaving age and the trend was for this proportion to increase. Three-quarters of the parents in this sample had positive hopes at that stage in their children's lives that they would stay at school longer than the minimum leaving age. Only 7 per cent definitely wanted their children to leave as soon as possible. While parents may become less keen, for financial or other reasons, for their children to stay on at school as they approach the permitted age of leaving, there have been steady increases in the proportions of pupils staying on at school voluntarily and staying on right into the sixth forms. It seems likely, therefore, that parents' attitudes towards the value of a longer school life are changing and, if this is so, these younger parents might be expected to be in the forefront of any general change in this area.

There were considerable social-class differences in parents' attitudes towards their children staying on at school as is shown in Table 9.5. Virtually none of the non-manual occupation parents wanted their children to leave as soon as possible and over half hoped that they would stay until eighteen or over. Among the manual workers the proportions of parents definitely wanting their children to leave at the minimum age possible ranged from 8 per cent of the skilled manual to 15 per cent of the unskilled, but a fifth of these parents were not prepared to say whether they wished their children to leave early or to stay on. It is encouraging, however, that over a third of the social class V parents hoped that their children would stay at school till seventeen or over.

TABLE 9.5. *Parents' attitudes towards their children staying on at school, by social class.*

Parents' attitudes towards child staying on at school	Social class							
	I Professional	II Managerial	III Non-manual	III Skilled manual	IV Semi-skilled	V Unskilled	Unclassified	Total
	%	%	%	%	%	%	%	%
Wanted child to stay on:								
to 18 or over	68	59	54	37	32	25	45	42
to 17	13	12	14	16	14	11	12	14
to 16	3	6	9	12	16	17	8	11
beyond statutory minimum but exact age not known	7	8	9	10	7	11	5	9
Could not say either way at that stage	9	13	12	17	20	21	25	17
Wanted child to leave as soon as possible	—	2	2	8	11	15	5	7
Total number (100%)	110	430	338	1486	499	189	40	3092

There was little difference between the attitudes towards age of leaving school of parents with children in the different forms included in the sample, or towards the leaving age thought appropriate for boys compared with girls.

Material and physical circumstances of the homes

Social-class differences in material circumstances are well documented but it is nevertheless worth looking briefly at some of the physical aspects of the home backgrounds of these primary school children as a reminder of the kind of implications they may have for a child's schooling. Table 9.6 summarises this information.

Although there was a wide spread of incomes within each social-class group, there was nevertheless a very steep increase from class I to class V in the proportions of families where the father's net income (or if no father, the head of the household's) was only £15 a week or less. Income level obviously has important corollaries. The lower the father's income the more likely it was that the mother would go out to work while she had at least one child in primary school and the more likely also that her work would entail her being away from home for five hours a day or longer.

Obviously associated with income level is the type of accommodation that can be afforded. Manual workers were unlikely to be buying their own homes whereas, in the main, professional, managerial and other non-manual workers owned or were buying their own accommodation. The advantages accruing to children in the higher social-class groups in terms of space, privacy and other amenities do not need stressing. Overcrowded homes are clearly a strain on both parents and children and when really bad, children are likely to arrive at school tired out and unable to listen or concentrate. A useful index for examining standards of accommodation is based on the numbers of people in the household of different ages and sexes related to the number of bedrooms they have. This index, as one would expect, showed a steady deterioration in standards by social class; among professional families only 3 per cent had one or more bedrooms less than the standard considered satisfactory, while approaching half of the unskilled workers had too few bedrooms. Although, overall, the proportion of houses with no running hot water and no fixed bath or shower is now low, again the lack of these valuable amenities for families was associated with social class: 17 per cent of unskilled workers' families had no running hot water and 19 per cent no fixed bath or shower.

TABLE 9.6. *Material and physical circumstances of children's home backgrounds, by social class.*

Material and physical circumstances of children's homes	Social class							
	I Professional	II Managerial	III Non-manual	III Skilled manual	IV Semi-skilled	V Un-skilled	Unclassified	Total
	Percentages of homes							
Father's (or head of household's) net income was £15 or less per week	3	12	26	46	69	79	95	44
Family was in rented accommodation	10	26	31	60	65	85	68	53
Accommodation was at least one bedroom short of the number needed by the family	3	11	16	28	33	43	43	25
Accommodation had no fixed bath or shower	—	4	3	12	12	19	17	10
Accommodation had no hot water tap	—	1	2	9	9	17	15	7
Family did not own or have use of a car	7	16	37	45	57	83	82	44
Number of parents interviewed (100%)	110	430	338	1486	499	189	40	3092

Owning or having the use of a car has considerable implications for the way of life of a family with young children, both in connection with the various activities involved in running a home, and by making a variety of outings with the whole family more feasible: 93 per cent of the professional-class parents had a car compared with only 17 per cent of the unskilled workers—a striking difference.

PARENTAL ATTITUDES TO PRIMARY EDUCATION

Parents were asked to give their views on various aspects of the organisation of primary schools. Considered first are their opinions on the most suitable ages for their children to start school and whether they thought it better for them to attend for a full or half day in the first instance.

School starting age

Just over half these children had started attending school, either nursery or primary, for a full day before the age of five. Only 2 per cent had not started until they were five-and-a-half or older; 16 per cent had attended a nursery school or nursery class. It is of some interest that the highest proportions of children who had been to nursery school were in the professional and the unskilled social-class families. Undoubtedly the reasons for this would be very different for the two groups. Rather smaller proportions of children of professional and managerial than of other parents had started full-time school before four-and-a-half.

A common tendency found in surveys is for people to be contented with their circumstances rather than to express a wish for something different. It is therefore striking to find that as many as a third of parents would have preferred their children to have started school at an earlier age than in fact they did and only 5 per cent thought a later start would have been better. The proportions preferring their children to have started earlier were closely related to the actual ages of starting and ranged from 5 per cent among parents whose children started at three-and-a-half to almost half of those whose children started at five or older. There was little variation between the social classes in the proportions who would have liked their children to have started school earlier or later than they did but the considerations behind their preferences may well have been very different. In all, over two-thirds of parents would have liked their children to have started full-time school before the age of five.

Hardly any of these children had started school by going for only half a day in the first instance and the majority of parents in fact were in favour of their children attending both mornings and afternoons from the beginning. Over this issue there were substantial social-class differences with as many as 42 per cent of the professional family parents preferring a half-day start compared with only 15 per cent in the unskilled worker groups. These differences are very understandable in view of the social-class variations in material circumstances of the homes already discussed.

Parental contacts with the primary schools

There is considerable evidence pionting to the importance, for children's school progress, of parents' interest in their education. The amount of parental contact with the schools is a positive indication of this interest. Now examined are the extent to which parents visited the schools and discussed their children's progress with the staff, the variety of opportunities provided for parents to see what the schools were doing and whether parents took advantage of them and, finally, parental satisfaction with arrangements for seeing school staff.

First, what happened when these children started at the schools they were attending at the time of the survey? Just over half the parents said that they had made inquiries about the sampled school or visited it *before* sending the first of their children there. If parents had themselves been at the school, they were asked whether they had taken steps to find out what it was like when their children were ready to start there. The proportions who had made inquiries or visited the schools increased with social class from 50 per cent of parents in class V to 80 per cent of those in class I. It is of interest here that almost three-quarters of the children had had other relatives attending the sampled schools either at the time of the survey or previously. Sixty-two per cent had, or had had, brothers or sisters there and as many as 20 per cent of the selected children's fathers or mothers had been at the same schools. In manual-worker families children were rather more likely to have had parents, siblings or other relatives at the same school than in non-manual-worker homes and there might therefore have been less need for these parents to make specific inquiries when they first sent any of their own children to the school.

More than a third of the parents had had no actual talk with the head when the selected child first started in the school which he or she was attending at the time of the survey. By a talk is meant something more than the minimum communication necessary for the child's enrolment. The proportions of parents who had talked to heads when their child started at school was higher among those with children in the infants than in the junior forms. Again there were differences between the social-class groups with the proportions varying from 78 per cent of parents in class I having had an initial talk with the head to 60 per cent of those in class V.

As would be expected the frequency with which parents had discussed their children with heads or class teachers in their children's schools was related to the length of time the child had been at the school. In all 8 per cent of parents had had no talks at any time about their children with heads or class teachers; 45 per cent had had four talks or more. The frequency with which parents had discussed their children with school staff was unrelated to whether mothers were working or not but was markedly associated with social class as shown in Table 9.7. There was little variation by social class in the lengths of time that children had been at these schools.

This tendency for the amount of contact with school staff to increase with social class is found again when we compare the proportions of parents in the different groups who had had a talk about the selected child specifically with any of the child's own class teachers. Only 6 per cent of parents in class I had not talked with the child's class teacher, but the proportions rose steadily to 27 per cent of those in class V.

It may be assumed that the provision of opportunities for parents to visit schools has three main purposes: first, to facilitate meetings between parents and teachers so that both come to know each other better; second, to enable parents to see for themselves what the schools are doing and how their children are progressing; and third, so that children feel that their parents are interested in and know what happens at school and that home and school are not separate worlds. It seems likely that in these respects some types of school activities to which parents are invited will be more valuable than others. Comparison is now made between the extent to which various opportunities for parents to visit the schools were provided and were taken advantage of by parents. Table 9.8 shows the proportions of parents in each social class who said that they had been invited to various school functions and the proportions who attended.

Open days and evenings in general provide opportunities both for parents to see children's work and to talk to class teachers. The majority of parents had received invitations to open days and three-quarters had, in fact, attended them. There was no social-class

TABLE 9.7.   *Number of talks parents had had with school staff, by social class.*

Number of talks parents had with heads or class teachers	Social class							
	I Profes-sional	II Mana-gerial	III Non-manual	III Skilled manual	IV Semi-skilled	V Un-skilled	Unclassi-fied	Total
	%	%	%	%	%	%	%	%
No talks with head or teacher	2	5	7	8	11	15	8	8
One talk	8	11	12	14	15	16	20	13
Two talks	9	13	15	17	15	16	12	15
Three talks	17	17	18	18	18	16	20	18
Four to six talks	29	23	24	21	21	18	20	22
More than six talks	35	31	24	22	20	18	20	23
Total number (100%)	110	430	338	1486	499	189	40	3092

TABLE 9.8.   *Opportunities provided for parents to visit the schools and advantage taken of them by parents, by social class.*

School activities to which parents were invited		I Profes-sional	II Mana-gerial	III Non-manual	III Skilled manual	IV Semi-skilled	V Un-skilled	Unclassi-fied	Total
Open days and evenings	Provided	78	81	82	81	82	82	85	81
	Attended	77	76	76	70	70	65	62	72
Prize days	Provided	12	16	17	13	16	16	8	14
	Attended	11	13	12	9	9	11	8	10
Sports days, swimming galas	Provided	51	56	56	54	58	51	42	55
	Attended	42	39	43	39	42	28	33	39
School plays, shows, concerts, school carol and other services	Provided	81	80	77	74	72	71	72	75
	Attended	74	73	68	62	61	55	55	64
Parent/teacher association meet-ings or other activities	Provided	24	28	26	26	23	16	28	25
	Attended	20	19	15	12	11	5	8	13
School outings	Provided	12	17	14	14	13	12	15	14
	Attended	4	7	5	4	4	3	8	4
Jumble sales, bazaars, social evenings to raise money for the school	Provided	72	70	68	64	61	62	62	65
	Attended	54	50	55	49	39	44	35	49
Medical or dental examinations	Provided	88	89	87	88	88	89	92	88
	Attended	75	77	75	76	71	75	57	75
Total number (100%)		110	430	338	1486	499	189	40	3092

Note. The percentages who said that the activities were provided and the percentages who attended are both out of the total sample.

differènce in the provision of open days but the manual occupation parents were not quite so likely to attend them as the non-manual.

A quarter of these parents said that there was a parent–teacher association attached to their children's schools. Here there was a marked rèlationship between attendance and social class: 20 per cent of social class I had been to P.T.A. meetings or activities but only 5 per cent of class V. During the preliminary stages of the inquiry working-class mothers who had attended P.T.A. meetings had several times said that they did not care for them as the more fluent and confident parents dominated the meetings and they themselves were not able to express their views.

The great majority of parents had been invited to school medical or dental examinations of their children and most had been to them. There were no social-class differences either in the proportions who had received invitations to or who had attended these examinations. School events open to parents, such as plays, concerts, sports days, carol and other services, were fairly generally organised and attended.

Heads or other teachers had talked to just over a quarter of the parents about the teaching methods which were used in the sampled schools. Rather more of the non-manual than manual occupation parents had had such a talk.

In general these parents were satisfied with the arrangements at their children's schools for seeing heads or class teachers and with the reception they had when they visited the schools. The proportions making any criticisms of contacts between themselves and the staff were small. Only 11 per cent were not completely satisfied about the arrangements for seeing the head or class teacher; 9 per cent felt that it was not easy to see the teachers whenever they wanted to, 7 per cent did not feel that the teachers seemed very pleased when they went to the schools, and 11 per cent considered that teachers would prefer to keep parents out of the school.

Social-class differences found here were that parents in the professional and managerial classes tended to be slightly more critical of the school's arrangements for seeing the head or class teacher. As we have already seen, these particular parents were more likely to want to visit the schools. On the other hand, parents in the manual occupational categories were the more inclined than non-manual to consider that teachers had favourites among the parents which suggests that they may have felt less at ease in their relationship with school staff.

It was clear throughout this inquiry that many parents were reluctant to go to the schools unless they were invited to some school function or were specifically asked by the heads in order to discuss their children. The impression gained from talking to these parents was not that they were uninterested in their children's schooling but that they were confident that the heads would let them know when they needed to visit the school for any reason. Approximately a quarter of the parents said that they felt that they were interfering if they went to the school uninvited. This attitude was not related to social class. Twenty-nine per cent considered that teachers had enough to do already without having to talk to parents. There were indications that a number of parents took the initiative in going to see school staff only when they wished to make some specific complaint and that this was particularly the case among social class V parents. The points discussed here strongly suggest that, if close contacts and good relationships are to be established and maintained between parents and teachers, positive initiative has to come from the school side in encouraging parents to visit the schools.

While the first step in establishing relations between parents and teachers is for parents to visit their children's schools, the important issue then is that the contact established should be helpful to both groups. Information from this survey gives some indication of the value of contacts between parents and teachers. Approximately half the parents said that they would have liked to be told more about how their children were getting on at school. Almost a third thought that the teachers should have asked them more about their children. A fifth considered that if they went up to the school teachers only told them what they knew already. Each of these points tended to be made more frequently by parents in the manual than non-manual occupations, suggesting that satisfactory communication between parent and teacher is considerably easier for the latter category of parents. We have already drawn attention to the limited educational experience of the majority of manual occupation families. An encouraging finding of this inquiry is that, within the social-class groups, parents were *less* likely to say that they wanted to be told more about how their children were getting on or that they thought teachers should ask them, the parents, more about their children if open days were arranged by the school or if parents had had several talks with the heads or class teachers.

Parents' views on some aspects of school organisation and teaching methods

This section deals with parents' preferences for combined and separate schools for infants and juniors, their views on the advantages and disadvantages of streamed and mixed ability classes in the primary schools and their satisfaction generally with the methods of teaching and the progress of their children at school.

Slightly more children were in separate than in combined junior and infants' schools. The most common preference among parents was for whichever type of situation their child happened to be in. This suggests that, from a parent's point of view, there are advantages and disadvantages about both separate and combined schools but that the disadvantages are rarely so overwhelming as to make either arrangement very unsatisfactory.

The ways in which parents thought that their children were allocated to classes, that is whether they were in streamed or mixed ability groups, were related to the stage they were at in the primary school: 53 per cent of parents of children in the top juniors said that their children were in streamed classes compared with 16 per cent of those with children in the top infants. There was a clear preference among the majority of parents for their children, at whatever age they were at the time of the survey, to be taught with other children of the same capacity, that is for the quicker and slower children to be allocated to separate classes rather than mixed together. Separate ability groups were preferred by as many as 59 per cent of the parents with children in the top infants class and by 70 per cent of those whose children were in the top juniors form. One needs to bear in mind here that this survey was carried out while the eleven-plus examination and the tripartite system of secondary education were still general in most parts of England. It would be interesting to know whether the widespread introduction of a comprehensive school system affects parents' attitudes on this issue.

There were no marked social-class differences either in the ways in which these children appeared to be allocated to their classes or in parental preferences for stream or mixed ability classes. However, a greater proportion of the manual occupation parents were concerned about the advantages of streaming for the teaching of slower children whereas more of the non-manual groups mentioned the help to the brighter child.

Parents were asked whether they were quite happy with the methods of teaching used at their children's schools and with the way the children were progressing in their work. No attempt was made to separate parents' views on methods of teaching from concern about school progress because it was found in the preliminary interviews that, in general, parents saw these as aspects of one issue and could not assess them separately. A third had some worries about their children's progress or the teaching methods. The proportion was the same for each of the forms included in the survey. Non-manual occupation parents were somewhat more inclined to be anxious about these matters than manual.

The anxieties most frequently expressed by parents were that they thought that their children were not being brought on fast enough or were not up to standard for their ages. Next came mention of too little individual attention being given to pupils, that classes were too large or that teachers were not interested in children's progress. Points falling in this category were made more frequently by parents with children in the higher classes. Criticisms or anxiety about new methods of teaching were expressed by a number of parents, particularly by those of younger children. Parents with children in the infants' class were also more inclined to say that too much time was spent on play and other activities which they considered did not help a child's school progress.

Anxiety about methods of teaching and their children's progress was to a certain extent related to parents' educational aspirations for their children. Among parents whose children had not at the time of the inquiry been allocated to their secondary schools, those who hoped that their children would go to a type of school other than secondary modern were slightly more inclined to worry about their children's progress than those who considered that secondary modern schools would suit their children. This relationship was not found, however, among parents of top junior children who had already been allocated to their secondary schools. Higher proportions of parents who were worried about their children's progress or the teaching methods had bought copies of the school textbooks to have at home.

On the whole parents thought that the control exercised by the schools over the children was about right, but practically all of those who would have preferred it to be different in any way would have liked teachers to be firmer and not less firm with the pupils. As children progressed up the schools parents were rather more inclined to want firmer discipline than the school provided. Parents who themselves found their children difficult to control were more likely to want the schools to be firmer with the children. There were no clear social-class differences in parents' attitudes towards teachers' control of the children.

After parents had answered specific questions about various aspects of the school they were given the opportunity to mention any other matters which worried them about their children's schools. The proportion who wished to make additional comments varied markedly with social class and ranged from two-thirds of class I parents to less than one-third of class V. The most frequently made complaints, and particularly by professional and managerial-class parents, were, firstly, of poor, old-fashioned school buildings, lack of facilities or inadequate equipment in their children's schools and, secondly, about the size of classes, shortage of teachers and general overcrowding. Next came comments about the discipline, control and general behaviour of the children and about teachers' relations with the pupils. Equally frequently mentioned were worries about the standard of teaching, the progress made by their child, and about various aspects of the curriculum. Criticism of the liaison between home and school were made more frequently by professional and managerial than other parents.

CONCLUSIONS

An attempt is now made to draw together and add emphasis to some of the findings of this survey by relating them to just three of the recommendations made by the Plowden Committee:

Recommendation 8. As a matter of national policy 'positive discrimination' should favour schools in neighbourhoods where children are most severely handicapped by home conditions.

Taking father's occupation as the index of social class we have noted that, coming down the social-class scale, income levels naturally dropped. At lower income levels mothers were more likely to go out to work while they had children in primary schools and to work longer hours. The homes of semiskilled and unskilled workers were much more likely to be overcrowded with increased likelihood of parents and children suffering from fatigue, strain, lack of privacy and a general lowering of the quality of their lives. These families were less likely to own or be buying their own homes or to have the type of amenities such as a car, running hot water, or a fixed bath which make life so much easier, particularly in families where there are young children.

Among manual-worker families parents were unlikely to have continued their education beyond the age of fourteen. They were much less likely than non-manual occupation parents to read in their

7

leisure time, to own books or to use libraries. They were also less likely to help their children with school work at home or to think that they should do so. The tradition is much more general among manual-worker homes for responsibility for children's education to be left to mothers with fathers taking little active part.

This survey was able to look at only a very few of the aspects of home circumstances which have implications for a child's educational progress. These circumstances are, of course, closely interrelated and a high proportion of families at the lower end of the social-class hierarchy may be handicapped in most of these ways, while at the other extreme many are favoured on all counts. Furthermore, the tendency is for educationally handicapped families to congregate in poor neighbourhoods and the issue of the educational priority areas arises from the problem of assisting schools to cope with high proportions of children from families which are handicapped in many ways.

Recommendation 43.   There should be a large expansion of nursery education and a start should be made as soon as possible.

Increased provision of nursery education may also do much to compensate for inadequacies in home backgrounds; as we have seen the majority of parents were in favour of their children starting school before the age of five. The proportions wishing their children to attend for *both* mornings and afternoons in the first instance were highest among manual workers and particularly those in unskilled employment.

Recommendation 1.   All schools should have a programme for contact with children's homes to include . . . [then follows a list of six specific points of action aimed at increasing parent–teacher contact].

There were consistent social-class differences in parental contacts with the schools—over starting their children in school, in the frequency with which they discussed their progress with school staff and in attendance at school functions. The indications in this survey were not that manual-occupation parents lacked interest in their children's educational progress but that they less generally saw the importance of showing this in positive ways and more commonly left the responsibility entirely to the schools. Many of these parents clearly felt that there was a lack of communication between teachers and themselves. The Plowden Committee attached great importance to increasing the interest and understanding of parents in their children's education through a closer partnership between parents and teachers and they made specific proposals for action aimed at ensuring that there was contact between homes and schools.

IO

The 'good home' *

Frank Musgrove

In this paper, Professor Musgrove summarises some of the essential elements raised in earlier chapters, but at the same time he introduces a level of analysis which is further developed in Part Five. He begins with a review of several demographic aspects of the relationship of family, class and education, and then sets out to clarify what is meant by 'parental interest'. This leads to a consideration of the structure of the home motivational environment in terms of child-rearing practices and the concept of achievement motivation (or 'need achievement'), and of social-class variations.

The 'Good home' is an aid to success in our school system. It is small; the parents are ambitious for their children; the father is at least a skilled manual worker; and if it is a working-class home, the mother has preferably 'married down'. The father is somewhat ineffectual, perhaps rather feckless; but one or both parents are demanding, even ruthless in their expectations of achievement. Relationships in the home are emotionally bleak. The family is unstable and has moved often; the mother goes to work. The children grow up to be rather withdrawn and solitary, conscientious and given to self-blame. They are 'good grammar school material'.

BIRTH-ORDER AND FAMILY SIZE

The feature of the 'good home' which is least in doubt is its size. In general the small family produces the most intelligent children as measured by intelligence tests, presumably because 'intelligence' is

* Reprinted from *The Family, Education and Society*, Routledge, 1966, pp. 72–93, by kind permission of the author and the publisher.

to a considerable extent inherited, and intelligent parents show their intelligence by limiting the size of their families.

It is also possible that in the small family the child is in closer touch with its parents and habitually uses more grown-up language and ideas than he would if he were lost in a cloud of siblings. He may therefore appear to have a higher level of intelligence than he 'really' has, particularly on tests which are wholly or mainly verbal. The trend to smaller families may thus, conceivably, mask a real decline in innate intelligence by giving a boost to the environmental component.

The negative correlation of approximately point three between intelligence and family size has been established in numerous surveys, such as the Scottish Mental Survey of 1947. A correlation of this magnitude means, roughly, that in a random sample of a hundred families, sixty would demonstrate this relationship; but in twenty there would be high average intelligence in large families, and in the remaining twenty low average intelligence in small families.

If intelligent parents are not directed by their intelligence to limit their families, then their families may be large and their children of high intelligence. There does not appear to be the same connection between family size and intelligence among Catholic as among Protestant families (and presumably in the past, before the advent of modern birth control methods, there was no connection in the population at large). In one fairly recent survey in Middlesbrough only 6 per cent of children from families of four or more children gained grammar school places, but 18 per cent of Catholic children from families of this size did so. Catholic children from small families showed no such superiority.[1]

It sems that even children of good intelligence will not use their intelligence as effectively as they might if they are members of large families, particularly when their fathers are manual workers. In her inquiries in boys' grammar schools in 1951 Himmelweit found that working-class boys from small families (one or two children) had a better chance of gaining a grammar school place than working-class boys from large families. 'Since no such differences were found in the non-manual groups they require an explanation over and above that of the known negative correlation between I.Q. and family size.'[2]

1. J. E. Floud, A. H. Halsey and F. M. Martin, *Social Class and Educational Opportunity*, Heinemann, 1956, p. 137.
2. H. T. Himmelweit, 'Social status and secondary education since the 1944 Act: some data for London', in D. V. Glass, ed., *Social Mobility in Britain*, Routledge, 1954.

More recently, in his research on a national sample of primary school children, Douglas found that middle-class boys (but not girls) were also less likely to succeed in the eleven-plus selection tests if they came from large families. However, in the middle class it was only families of four or more children that had a depressing effect; among working-class children the prospects became progressively worse as the family increased in size above one or two.[1]

In working-class families of three children, 14·1 per cent were expected to gain grammar school places judging by their measured abilities, but only 13·2 per cent did so; in middle-class families of the same size 33·9 per cent were expected to gain places, and a still higher percentage (38·6) in fact did so. The explanation appears to lie very largely in the attitudes, expectations and assumptions of parents with large families. If the school is very good, and if the parents' attitudes are favourable, the handicap for working-class children from large families can almost, though not entirely, be eliminated.

The significance of birth-order is also reasonably well established, although the interpretation of the facts is neither easy nor certain. In his nineteenth-century studies of eminent scientists Galton found that it was an advantage to be an eldest or an only son. Subsequent research in the general population both here and in America has amply confirmed this judgement.

Social-class differences have been found in this connection too. It matters much more to be an eldest son or daughter in a working-class than a middle-class family, at least as far as eleven-plus selection is concerned. One investigation demonstrated that 'a working-class boy, whatever the size of his family, is more likely to attend a grammar school if he is an eldest child, and . . . this again does not apply in the case of a middle-class boy . . .'.[2]

Douglas's findings were similar. The eldest child tended, in the eleven-plus examinations, to exceed the expectations based on his measured ability. This was found to be the case among both middle-class and working-class children, but to a more marked extent among the latter.

Douglas did not find that only children did any better than 'expected', and attributed this principally to lack of sibling rivalry. Other investigators have found both 'onlys' and 'eldests' more

1. J. W. B. Douglas, *The Home and the School*, MacGibbon & Kee, 1964, p. 170.
2. A. H. Halsey and L. Gardner, 'Selection for secondary education and achievement in four grammar schools', *British Journal of Sociology*, 4 (1953).

scholastically able than intermediates and youngests. There is no evidence that they are more intelligent; they are more disposed to use their intelligence with effect in the school setting.

Lees and Stewart established in two Midland cities in 1955 that both eldests and onlys were found in grammar schools significantly more often than in modern schools. Thus onlys were 18·3 per cent of the grammar school population in one city, but only 11·7 per cent of the modern school population. The advantage of being an eldest girl diminished in families of four or more.[1]

The interpretation of these findings is not easy. In earlier research into the background of a group of adult students Lees, like Douglas, attributed the superiority of eldests principally to sibling rivalry, particularly when younger brothers and sisters were getting on well and so seriously threatening the eldest's status.[2] Clearly this cannot account for the success of onlys; and in their later work Lees and Stewart advance an explanation which might apply to any first-born child—his rather lonely position of eminence and perhaps responsibility in the family which provides him with an early training for handling 'situations demanding individual initiative, and, incidentally, of coping with such situations as those presented by intelligence tests and examinations at eleven-plus years'.

This explanation is diametrically opposed to that offered by Stanley Schachter to account for the superiority in some situations of first-born Americans. Lees and Stewart say the first-born is successful because he has a capacity for loneliness; Schachter says he is successful because he has not.

First-born children, argues Schachter, are less rather than more able to cope on their own with their problems and anxieties. Far from being highly 'individualistic', they will seek solutions to their problems in groups. First-borns undergoing group therapy have been observed to continue their treatment longer than necessary; later-borns drop out before they should. There is a greater tendency for later-borns to become alcoholics, handling their anxieties in non-social ways. The first-born, as an infant, has enjoyed a concerned and attentive mother, fussing over her first child: she has come to his side whenever he faced discomfort or fear. Later-born children have a mother who is probably more blasé; they will more often be left to

1. J. P. Lees and A. H. Stewart, 'Family or sibship position and scholastic ability', *Sociological Review*, 5 (1957).
2. J. P. Lees, 'The social mobility of a group of eldest-born and intermediate adult males', *British Journal of Psychology*, 43 (1952).

deal with their problems alone and will grow up accustomed to handling their anxieties in solitude.[1]

The significance of birth order has attracted a great deal of attention. Much has been written about it and psychologists have conducted a variety of experiments to check their theories. Recent experiments by Sampson in America indicate that first-born males, at least, are inclined to greater social conformity: they fall into line more readily when rewards are offered and are more susceptible to social pressures. (They also have a stronger need for achievement than later-borns.) First-born girls, on the other hand, showed a greater independence than later-borns.[2] It is not easy to reconcile these findings, particularly with regard to sex differences, with other research, although in a general sense they are in line with Schachter. But it seems reasonable to suggest that first-born boys at any rate may be successful in our school system not because they are individualistic, but because they are not: because they need the approval of adults and conform closely to the expectations of teachers.

'FAVOURABLE PARENTAL ATTITUDES'

The importance of parental attitudes to a child's progress at school seems to be firmly established. Yet the concept of 'favourable parental attitude' is perhaps one of the most ambiguous and misleading in the contemporary discussion of educational achievement. The measurement of this attitude has been crude in the extreme; and precisely what has been measured is open to very serious doubt. It would be very dangerous indeed to equate parental interest and concern with kindly, beneficient and understanding encouragement. The usual measures of parental interest might equally signify ruthless, unreasoning, inexorable and even quite unrealistic demands.

The most common and apparently objective measure of parental interest is the frequency of visits to school. Middle-class parents score high here, and working-class mothers higher than working-class fathers. But while the frequency of school visits undoubtedly provides some indication of the level of parental interest, it also measures the level of parents' social competence and assurance.

Other factors which have usually been taken into account are the age at which parents wish their children's education to end; and the

1. *The Psychology of Affiliation* (1959).
2. E. E. Sampson, 'Birth order, need achievement, and conformity', *Journal of Abnormal and Social Psychology*, 64 (1962).

type of school or institution of further education they wish them to attend. (One inquiry, for example, obtained favourable–unfavourable attitude scores according to (1) the frequency of parents' school visits, (2) their preference for selective secondary education, (3) the intention to keep the child at school until at least sixteen, and (4) their preference for further education after school.[1]) The longer the period of education envisaged and the more selective and academic the type of institution preferred, the more favourable is parental attitude judged to be.

Attempts have been made to take into account more intangible aspects of parents' attitudes, but these are often difficult to incorporate into attitude scales. Teachers' judgments of parental interest have also been taken into account (by Douglas), and cultural interests have been estimated in the light of the Sunday newspapers they take, their membership of public libraries and cultural organisations. The emotional atmosphere of the home has been estimated, the degree of harmony prevailing, and the emotional security afforded the child. The level of material well-being in the home is easier to establish; and it has been shown (in Middlesbrough) that below a certain level, low material standards may nullify the advantages of favourable parental attitudes as conventionally judged by visits to the school and ambitions for the child.

There is no doubt that parents who visit the school often and wish their children to enjoy a selective and protracted education in general give a boost to their children's educational progress. At all social levels, and in socially contrasted areas, children tend to be more successful in the eleven-plus examinations if they have parents who have discussed their future with the primary school teacher and would prefer them to stay at school till eighteen.[2] There are clear signs in recent research that parental interest (measured by similar crude means) is more important with children of borderline ability, and from working-class rather than middle-class homes.

This is the conclusion of Douglas's report on his national sample of primary school children. Children of borderline ability obtained 23 per cent more places in grammar schools than had been expected in the light of their measured ability, if their parents were educationally ambitious for them; but they gained 69 per cent fewer places if their parents were unambitious. Children with ambitious parents tended to be 'over-achievers'. When the school's academic standard, the material standards of the home, and parental ambitions were

1. J. E. Floud *et al.*, *op. cit.*, p. 93.
2. *Ibid.*, p. 102.
    7*

analysed for their relative importance, parental encouragement was shown to have the greatest effect.

'Parental encouragement' is not necessarily the same thing as humane consideration and kindly, understanding interest. It may be a ruthless and inflexible demand for achievement. When 'family dynamics' have been investigated by clinical psychologists for their bearing on achievement, unambitious parents have obviously been of little help to their children; but neither have 'normal' parents, setting reasonable and realistic goals. The most effective parents are, it is true, ambitious for their children; but it is not a particularly attractive characteristic, ruthless and demanding.

This is the picture that emerges from the research of Kent and Davis in Cambridgeshire, and is amply supported by inquiries in America. Kent and Davis investigated the relationship between 'discipline in the home' and intellectual development among a sample of primary school children (as well as a group of juvenile offenders and children referred to a psychiatric outpatients' clinic). The homes of the children were investigated and classified as 'normal', 'unconcerned', 'over-anxious' and 'demanding'.

'Normal' parents were tolerant, patient, but firm, making reasonable demands on the child, realistically related to his abilities, interests and needs. The unconcerned were indifferent to the child's progress, without ambition for his success, content if he kept out of trouble and made few demands upon them. But the effective home was the 'demanding' home: the parents set high standards from an early age; they were ambitious for their child; they 'reward infrequently and without generosity'; approval and affection are conditional upon achievement. But within the general framework of high demands and expectations the child is free to learn and good opportunities are afforded for him to do so. In the light of other research on achievement which is reviewed in the next section, it is perhaps the conjunction of demands and opportunity which is important.

Such homes were not confined to middle-class social levels. Whatever their social position, they tended more than other types of home to produce children of high ability. 'One may argue therefore that the cause of the high development of verbal and academic abilities lies in their demanding discipline, and that the poor development of these abilities in the children of the unconcerned class is due to the lack of encouragement given them by their parents.'[1]

1. N. Kent and D. R. Davis, 'Discipline in the home and intellectual development', *British Journal of Medical Psychology*, 30 (1957).

There seem to be few rewards in our educational system (and perhaps in our society generally) for 'normality' or even for humanity. The driving, demanding home, with exacting standards and expectations and remorseless pressure on the children, appears to be the 'good home'. The kindly, reasonable, understanding, tolerant and helpful home pays less handsome dividends. This may be why frequent moves, working mothers, and wives who have married beneath themselves are valuable ingredients in the good home: they are symptoms or causes of the striving and straining which seems so invaluable.

Research in America into the family background of able schoolchildren and university students lends support to the view that family relationships which are demanding and lacking in warmth are associated with high intellectual capacity. In their studies of adolescents who were of high intelligence but comparatively low in 'creativity' on the one hand, and of others who were of rather lower intelligence but high in creativity on the other, Getzels and Jackson found that the former more often had mothers who were 'vigilant', 'critical' and 'less accepting'. Mothers of the children of high I.Q. both observed more about their children and observed a greater number of objectionable qualities. The mothers of the children who did best in tests of creativity apparently subjected their children to a less intensive and censorious scrutiny; and they were more at ease with themselves and with the world.[1] (We are given no information about fathers.)

American studies of university students are in general congruent with these findings. Very thorough investigations have been made of the academic performance, personality development, family background and subsequent careers of the women graduates of Vassar College. The early family life of 'under-achievers' at college had been happy and secure. 'Fathers are seen as having been competent, loving, lots of fun . . . Mothers were warm, sociable, happy and accepting.' Over-achievers, on the other hand, tended to have mothers with high social aspirations and fathers who were selfmade men. 'On the whole there is close conformity with strict parental demands.'

Those graduates who achieved distinction in their subsequent careers (typically by middle life they had not married or had few children if they had) did well in their studies at Vassar. They had been lonely at college and 'In their early life and adolescence they have experienced conflict arising from domineering and talented mothers, against whom there is considerable repressed hostility associated with strong guilt. As a group their early lives tended not to be free from

1. J. W. Getzels and P. W. Jackson, *Creativity and Intelligence*, Wiley, 1962.

upsetting events such as deaths, moves, economic crises and the like, nor were their childhoods outstandingly happy.'[1]

A more impressionistic picture is given by Jackson and Marsden, in their study of 'Marburton', of the home circumstances of successful grammar school pupils. Sixth-formers in 'Marburton' came mainly from driving and ambitious homes with frustrated parents who belonged to the 'sunken middle class' and fathers who were foremen without hope of rising to managerial rank. Some of the children, successful at the grammar school, in the end failed their degrees. For one girl this failure brought a great sense of release: 'I decided then and there that I'd go and do what I wanted. I'd been doing what other people wanted for so long and now it was time that I did what I wanted. I went to the employment exchange and they offered me all kinds of academic things—but I decided definitely that I was going nursing.'[2]

Kent and Davis found frequent moves of home closely related to the highly productive demanding discipline. 'An especially large proportion of the children of the "demanding" class had experienced three or more moves' compared with the normal class. Douglas found a similar situation: 'When the average test performance of children of families which have never moved is compared with the performance of those in families that have moved, it is found that the former make lower average scores in the tests than the latter. . . .' But there were slight indications that the disadvantages of a stable home-background were less marked for preschool children.

Investigations in an American university have isolated early geographical mobility as a common factor in the background of students of high ability who, when subjected to a battery of personality and attitude tests, undervalued themselves, felt insecure and lonely, and were strongly inclined towards guilt feelings and self-punishment. These able students had one significant early experience in common: geographical instability. 'In all of their histories are accounts of moving from one town to another. One of the girls probably expressed the feelings of the group when she wrote in her autobiography, "Several times I was dead sure that my whole life was being torn completely asunder. . . ." '[3]

1. D. R. Brown, 'Personality, college environment and academic productivity', in Nevitt Sanford, ed., *The American College*, Wiley, 1962, pp. 536–62.
2. *Education and the Working Class*, Routledge, 1962, pp. 151–2.
3. E. Paul Torrance, 'Personality dynamics of under-self-evaluation among intellectually gifted freshmen', in E. P. Torrance, ed., *Talent and Education*, Univ. of Minnesota Press, 1960.

Of course such a history of family instability is not a necessary condition of academic excellence. And it would be a mistake to ascribe the intellectual development associated with it to the stimulus of changing environments. The migrant home is often the striving home, and it is the attitudes of migrant parents rather than the migration itself which probably accounts for these findings. The value to working-class children of a mother who has 'married down'[1] perhaps has a similar explanation: she strives to make up for her social decline through the achievements of her children.

The fact that mothers go to work is also more commonly a symptom of parental striving and ambition than of selfishness and negligence, and for this reason assists rather than impedes the child's educational progress. During research in Aberdeen, Fraser found no evidence that children were handicapped at the secondary stage by having a mother at work: 'if there is any difference at all, it appears to be very slightly in favour of the children whose mothers go out to work, especially in the middle ranges of intelligence'.[2]

In America there is more positive evidence that working mothers may foster educational ambitions and promote higher attainment. The greater tendency for urban as opposed to rural wives to take up paid employment outside the home has been held to account for the backwardness of rural children. 'A mother who works at least part-time in a small town or larger city is likely to be exposed to the fact that a college education is required for most high status jobs, whereas the mother who is submerged in the home-making problems of a farm family is unlikely to be impressed with this reality.'[3]

PERMISSION AND PUNISHMENT

One of the most interesting but as yet rather inconclusive ways of examining the influence of family background has been to compare social groups which differ significantly in their general level of occupational and educational achievement. Urban children are generally superior to rural children; middle-class children to working-class children; the children of Jewish immigrants to the United States to Italian immigrants. Can broad differences in attainment between these groups (of course there is a great deal of overlap too) find an explanation in differences in child-care practices and family dynamics?

1. J. E. Floud *et al.*, *op. cit.*, p. 88.
2. E. Fraser, *Home Environment and the School*, University of London Press, 1959, p. 66.
3. G. H. Elder, 'Achievement orientations of rural youth', *Sociology of Education*, 37 (1963).

The general tendency for middle-class children to do better in the school system in both England and America has been attributed not only to differences in parental encouragement but to social-class differences in early child rearing practices. The training of middle-class infants, it is argued, makes them particularly able to succeed later on in scholastic pursuits and perhaps in the activities involved in professional work. Working-class children of good intelligence may be defective in other attributes which ensure academic success. Whatever the long term consequences of social class differences in infant care, there can be no doubt that these differences are still with us. As the Newsons observe after their recent exhaustive investigations in Nottingham: 'The classless society in Britain is still a long way off. Men may be born equal; but, within its first month in the world, the baby will be adapting to a climate of experience that varies according to its family's social class.'[1]

Scholastically able people are not only intelligent, they also tend to be conscientious, capable of long-term effort and planning, able to forgo many immediate satisfactions for more distant gains. Often, too, they are orderly, careful, meticulous, and punctual. Some or all of these attributes have been ascribed to the stricter methods of infant care which are perhaps characteristically middle-class: early and severe toilet training; early punishment of aggression; feeding by rigid schedule, and early weaning; early independence training; and control through 'love-oriented' techniques of discipline. It has also been claimed that middle-class upbringing induces 'adaptive, socialised anxiety' which deters the child from incurring the disapproval of his parents and teachers.[2] Working-class upbringing, though not unproductive of anxieties too, was supposed to be more permissive and indulgent, less likely to produce far-sighted, controlled and conscientious personalities.

These views are currently under heavy fire. The relevance of early toilet training to a controlled and orderly adult personality has been seriously questioned.[3] Hallworth has shown that the academically successful are not generally more anxious, at least at the secondary school stage, than the less academically gifted.[4] But most startling of all has been the apparent demonstration both in England and America

1. J. and E. Newson, *op. cit.*, p. 217.
2. Allison Davis, *Social Class Influences upon Learning,* Harvard Univ. Press, 1948.
3. I. L. Child, 'Socialization', in Gardner Lindzey, ed., *Handbook of Social Psychology,* Addison-Wesleys, 1954, vol. 2.
4. H. J. Hallworth, 'Anxiety in secondary modern and grammar school children', *British Journal of Educational Psychology,* 31 (1961).

that the middle classes are more permissive and less punitive in their child-care practices than the working classes. These claims need very careful scrutiny for the limits of their validity.

Recent research with mothers in Devonshire seemed to show that, with reference to five-year-old children, 'In England, as in the U.S.A., middle-class mothers are less punitive than working-class mothers,' and that 'English middle-class mothers are also like American middle-class mothers in being more permissive of aggressive behaviour.'[1] And indeed there seems little doubt that with regard to 'immodesty' and aggression the middle-class mother of today is more permissive than twenty or thirty years ago. She has been lectured by the psychologists, and she has taken heed. This was clear too in the Newsons' study of mothers of one-year-old babies in Nottingham. Middle-class mothers breast-fed their babies more often than working-class mothers, and were no less inclined than the latter to 'demand feeding'. They checked the child's inclination to play with its genitals less often than working-class mothers, and less often smacked the child for 'naughtiness'.

But all this does not add up to a revolution in middle-class child-care methods to an unprecedented general permissiveness. Over many areas of behaviour, and in essence, middle-class child training remains ruthless. The Newsons found that in some respects middle-class mothers had high and inflexible expectations of their children: toilet training began earlier and was less casual; they were less inclined to soothe the baby to sleep ('there seems to be a strong middle-class feeling that babies should learn early to go to sleep at a "reasonable" hour without help and without making a fuss'); and while they are now much given to breast feeding, the dummy ('secondary oral gratification') finds little approval.

The working class seems to be less permissive principally in the sense that it is more inclined to resort to physical punishment. Middle-class discipline is more subtle, unflinching and effective; working-class discipline is simply more desperate.

The most authoritative review of recent research in this field concluded that 'the most consistent finding . . . is the more frequent use of physical punishment by working-class parents. The middle class, in contrast, resort to reasoning, isolation, and . . . "love-oriented" discipline techniques.' 'Yet . . . it would be a mistake to

1. R. Lynn and I. E. Gordon, 'Maternal attitudes to child socialization: some social and national differences', *British Journal of Social and Clinical Psychology*, 1 (1962).

conclude that the middle-class parent is exerting less pressure on his children.' 'Though more tolerant of expressed impulses and desires, the middle-class parent . . . has higher expectations for the child. The middle-class youngster is expected to take care of himself earlier, to accept responsibilities about the home, and—above all—to progress further at school.'[1]

The 'love-oriented' technique of discipline would be repugnant to many working-class parents; for in essence it is a tacit bargain between child and parents, love and affection given in return for good behaviour, withdrawn for misdeeds. Love is offered on strictly limited, contract terms. This appears from the cross-cultural surveys of anthropologists to be the most effective way of producing conscientious people prone to high guilt feelings and self-blame[2]— the very stuff of high academic promise.

Within the fringe of middle-class permissiveness exists a hard core of inflexible demand. Over many areas of behaviour there is simply no question that things should be otherwise than parents decree or just quietly, tacitly assume. This applies not least to the age of school leaving and the type of school attended. When the author investigated the attitudes to education of parents in Leicester in 1960, working-class parents were inclined to say with regard to the choice of secondary school: 'Wherever he'll be happy.' Middle-class parents were quite clear on this issue, there was really no choice—the grammar school (or in some cases a public school) was the obvious place. 'Happiness' was an irrelevance.[3]

NEED-ACHIEVEMENT

The will to achieve—indeed the need to achieve—has its roots in family circumstances. Of particular importance are the child's relationships with its parents. If these are close, warm, and affectionate, he is likely to be handicapped for life.

Moralists in the past, Freudian psychologists today, and our own common sense, suggest that the young boy needs an adequate example and model in his father. The latter should be an effective human being with whom the boy can 'identify'. The evidence seems

1. U. Bronfenbrenner, 'Socialization and social class through time and space', in E. E. Maccoby, T. M. Newcomb and L. Hartley, eds., *Readings in Social Psychology*, Methuen, 1958.
2. J. W. M. Whiting and I. L. Child, *Child Training and Personality*, Yale U.P., 1953.
3. F. Musgrove, 'Parents' expectations of the junior school', *Sociological Review*, 9 (1961).

to be—in spite of Betty Spinley's *The Deprived and the Privileged* (Routledge, 1953) and Madeline Kerr's *The People of Ship Street* (Routledge, 1958)—that the moralists, Freudian psychologists, and common sense are wrong. The boy's long-term interests are best served by an inadequate and feckless (if 'demanding') father.

Family relationships ('interaction patterns') have only quite recently been subjected to direct study and analysis for their bearing on children's development and achievement. There has long been a great deal of clinical evidence on family life, but this is of an indirect nature, drawn from patients' recollections of the often quite distant past. Of particular interest have been attempts to measure the strength of an individual's need for achievement (nAch) and to relate it to his family background. These attempts have not yet given a consistent and reliable picture and a great deal more work remains to be done. There is the further complication that high 'need achievement' may not necessarily, for a wide variety of reasons, lead to actual achievement, at least in any specific field of endeavour.

Need-achievement has been measured by projective tests. Subjects write stories about pictures which are shown to them, and the stories are scored for their achievement imagery. The subjects, who have been aroused and put on their mettle by impressing on them the significance of the tests as indicators of their organisational abilities, will put their own hopes for success and fears of failure into their stories. But of course people hope for different kinds of success; and perhaps success for women is more typically in terms of getting on well with people, while for men it is getting on well in a career. Some individuals with high need-achievement scores may be indifferent to scholastic success, but hope for it in the sphere of athletics or the conquest of women. As one American investigator has pointed out: 'Motives have both force and direction. Present measures of need-achievement consider only the former while neglecting the latter.'[1] It is perhaps for this reason that general need-achievement scores have not been shown to relate very closely to success or failure at school.

Families of Jewish and Italian immigrants in America have been closely studied in an attempt to discover why children of the former tend to succeed at school and in their subsequent careers while children of the latter in general make poor progress.[2] It has been

1. M. C. Shaw, 'Need achievement scales as predictors of academic success', *Journal of Educational Psychology* (1961).
2. F. L. Strodtbeck, 'Family interaction, values and achievement', in D. C. McClelland *et al.*, *Talent and Society*, Van Nostrand, 1958.

supposed that the subordination of the Italian child to the interests of the family might induce a sense of resignation and undermine the will to achieve. But Italian and Jewish fathers of similar occupational standing did not differ in the extent to which they expected children to be tied to their families. The investigators suggested—although the evidence is not really very firm—that very capable fathers produce a sense of helplessness in their sons, who feel they can never be masters of their own fate.

When family interaction processes were analysed, Italian fathers were found to give more support to their sons than Jewish fathers to theirs. The helpfulness of fathers seemed at best a mixed blessing: the fact that help is necessary tends to underline or suggest the son's incompetence. In line with this is the quite firm finding among American university students that people with high need-achievement scores perceive their parents as unfriendly and unhelpful. (Much may depend on the age of the person who is offered help. American high school pupils who are high in need-achievement do *not* see their parents as unhelpful.)[1]

The friendliness or unfriendliness of parents to their children of whatever age, their authoritarian or non-authoritarian attitudes, are perhaps an irrelevance. What matters is the independence they accord. The unhelpful parents, the non-authoritarian parent, the negligent parent, the ineffectual parent—all tend to be alike in this respect, that for no doubt quite different reasons they leave their children alone. But it is perhaps a help if, while leaving them alone, they also expect them in a general sense to do well.

Farmers in America make considerable demands on their children. Their expectations are detailed and specific; their control and guidance close. Perhaps for this reason farm families produce comparatively few successful children for non-farming careers. Farm boys have heavy demands made upon them for various kinds of achievement at a very early age; but the tasks are quite specific. In caring for livestock, milking and the like, they may have close guidance, help and instruction; but they have no freedom to explore, to shape their lives in their own way, to experiment with some degree of freedom in their growth towards independence.[2] Theirs is the opposite of the 'negative education' which Rousseau recommended before puberty. They need a good dose of neglect. As they then discovered for

1. D. C. McClelland *et al., The Achievement Motive,* Appleton-Century-Crofts 1953, p. 283.
2. G. H. Elder, 'Achievement orientations and career patterns of rural youth , *loc. cit.*

themselves a mastery of problematic situations, the confidence and will for achievement might be born.

To be left alone is perhaps one of the most urgent needs of children in a child- and home-centred society. (Studies of the careers of successful American scientists and scholars indicate that at some stage of their education their teachers have had enough sense to leave them alone. They have often suffered prolonged 'neglect', but in a general context of high expectation.) It is not only the kindly and tolerant parent who might, as a conscious decision, grant a child such freedom. 'The contrast should not be thought of too simply in terms of the autocratic–democratic dimensions, currently so popular in psychological literature.'[1] The important thing is that, for whatever reason, there is scope for 'the independent development of the individual'.

This may account for the high achievement, both scholastically and in professional careers, of men whose family relationships in youth were anything but warm and supportive. The men who have risen through education and their own efforts to the top of American business life perceive their early relationships with their fathers as at best detached, reserved, cool.[2] Fathers were often weak, inadequate and unreliable (although mothers were often strong and competent).

Perhaps such a childhood was a good preparation for the somewhat impersonal relationships of modern large-scale bureaucracy. The essential characteristic of these men in adult life was their independence. Similar rather detached and vague relationships with their parents seem to characterise the childhood of men who succeed in the physical sciences. Often in childhood they have had the experience of bereavement. Eminent social scientists have usually had a more stormy involvement with their parents, though scarcely more satisfactory from the point of view of psychology, humanity or common sense.[3] Neither humanity nor common sense seems to pay the highest dividends in the educational system and social order which we have devised.

A QUESTION OF CLASS

It is possible that our notion of the 'good home' needs to be redefined, or at least less naïvely defined. But there can be no doubt about the

1. D. C. McClelland *et al.*, *op. cit.*, p. 329.
2. W. L. Warner and J. C. Abegglen, *Big Business Leaders in America*, Univ. of Minnesota Press, 1955, pp. 59 ff.
3. Anne Roe, 'A psychological study of eminent psychologists and anthropologists, and a comparison with biological and physical scientists', *Psychological Monographs*, 67 (1953).

continuing influence of home background on educational and vocational advancement. In our contemporary democracy the influence of birth remains great and shows signs of increasing. Modern sociology and psychology are invoked to justify and promote enhanced parental power. Social science is used to support a position which social philosophy has discredited.

In less crude and direct ways than formerly, but no less effectively, parents have a powerful influence on the life-chances of their children. Their influence is particularly great in the intermediate ranges of ability, among borderline cases for selection and promotion. The outstandingly able will often make their own way whatever their family circumstances; and the outstandingly dull will have difficulty whatever backing they receive. But the great majority are neither outstandingly able nor dull; for them parents are often decisive.

The relationship between educational opportunity and attainment and 'social class' has been demonstrated often enough during the past decade. When middle-class children make use of the state system, they tend to get more grammar school places in proportion to their numbers than working-class children, to stay longer when they get to the grammar school, to be more involved in its extra-curricular activities, to have better examination results, to pass more often into the sixth form, and still more often to the university. Indeed, the further through the system we look, the more are children from white-collar and professional homes 'over-represented' in our grammar schools and institutions of higher learning.

There is no doubt that the children of skilled manual workers have benefited greatly from the 'scholarship system', particularly since 1944; but in the Ministry of Education's inquiry into early leaving in the nineteen-fifties they were somewhat underrepresented in the grammar school intake at twelve, and more markedly underrepresented in the sixth-form entry. (The children of skilled workers were 51 per cent of all children, 43·7 per cent of the grammar school entry at twelve, 37 per cent of the sixth-form entry. In contrast children of professional and managerial families were 15 per cent of all children, 25 per cent of the grammar school intake, 43·7 per cent of those entering the sixth form. Children of unskilled labourers were strikingly underrepresented in the sixth form: they were only 1·5 per cent of the entry, but constituted 12 per cent of the age group.)

Although the general tendency is for children from the homes of manual labourers to deteriorate even when they enter the grammar schools, some do very well and exceed their initial promise. The Ministry's inquiry found that 12 per cent of these children who began in bottom streams had risen to top streams over five years. Although these children are, in general a bad risk, it is a risk that must be taken: there is no way of telling which individuals will in fact do better than expected, and which will do worse.

The influence of family background operates today in more subtle ways than in the past—there is undoubtedly far less flagrant nepotism and patronage; but it is still very pervasive. The open competitive examination is the great social invention of the past century which has done most to eliminate it; and those who would abolish such examinations must face the certainty that the advantages of birth and family circumstances would be greatly enhanced.

With all its limitations and unfortunate side-effects, the open competitive examination for entrance into schools, universities and the public services is the main safeguard of the interests of people of humble origins, and our main guarantee of a measure of social justice. Only the lottery would remove altogether the advantages and disadvantages of birth. The open competitive examination remains the most effective instrument we have yet devised for the elimination of parents.

But they remain astonishingly potent. This is reflected in the high degree of self-recruitment still to be found in the major professions —and, indeed, in humbler employment, such as dockwork, where there may be special encouragement and opportunity for sons to follow in their fathers' footsteps. The sons of lawyers, doctors, parsons and teachers themselves become lawyers, doctors, parsons and teachers to a quite remarkable degree. In some professions this tendency to follow in father's footsteps has actually increased in a quite dramatic manner over the past century.

Only 6 per cent of Cambridge graduates who became teachers in the second half of the nineteenth century were the sons of teachers; in 1937–8, 14 per cent were teachers' sons. At both dates about a third of those who became doctors or parsons were the sons of doctors or parsons. Fifteen per cent of those entering law at the earlier date had lawyer fathers; in 1937–8, 26 per cent had lawyer fathers.[1] If we take a longer time span, over some two hundred years, the most remarkable change among Cambridge graduates is the extent to which the Church has become self-recruiting. In the eighteenth century the extent to which the sons of parsons became parsons barely exceeded

1. R. K. Kelsall, 'Self-recruitment in four professions', in D. V. Glass, *op. cit.*

what might happen by chance; by the nineteen-thirties they became parsons five times the chance expectation.[1]

Even in the academic world of twentieth-century Cambridge, where examinations and other objective tests of merit might be expected to have eliminated family influence, it is still a marked advantage in securing senior, or even junior, appointments to be a Macaulay, a Butler, a Trevelyan, a Huxley, or a member of the Wedgwood-Darwin connection, for example. The Provost of King's College, Cambridge, has analysed these intricate family alliances and has shown how once again, even at this level, the importance of having chosen the right father comes out at the borderline of ability (a very high borderline, of course, in this particular case).

> Clearly certain families produce a disproportionately large number of eminent men and women. But equally clearly the study shows that men of natural but not outstanding ability can reach the front ranks of science and scholarship and the foremost positions in the cultural hierarchy of the country if they have been bred to a tradition of intellectual achievement and have been taught to turn their environment to account. Schools and universities can so train young men, but such a training has a far stronger command over the personality when it is transmitted through a family tradition.[2]

It is the task of schools in the second half of the twentieth century to achieve a similar command over the personalities entrusted to them even when the family has not done more than half their job for them.

1. C. A. Anderson and M. Schnaper, *School and Society in England*, 1952, Tables 2 and 6.
2. Noel Annan, 'The intellectual aristocracy', in J. H. Plumb, ed., *Studies in Social History*, Longmans, 1955.

PART FIVE Subcultural studies II

11

Parental factors in educational mobility*

Having considered the demographic mapping of social-class variations in educational opportunity and school success in Part Two, the contextual influence of neighbourhood and of school in Part Three, and the subcultural studies of Part Four which focused attention on the motivational environment of individual families, we carry these subcultural investigations a stage further in Part Five. This contribution by Professor Cohen involved the study of two groups of working-class American high-school boys, matched on intelligence and on school, only one of which was aiming to proceed to college. An analysis of some of the demographic characteristics of the parents showed significant differences between the two groups; the sons of foremen, for example, were more likely to have college aspirations. But more important, when such demographic features were interpreted as part of a social process, the interaction of the home with the occupational and social structure, and were analysed in terms of expressed attitudes and behaviour, more revealing differences between the two groups emerged. This study of the distinctive 'parental ideology' in the homes of ambitious schoolboys is a starting point in the more probing analysis of the home motivational environment which is attempted in Part Five.

Elizabeth Cohen

INTRODUCTION

Researchers who have studied the process of upward social mobility through education have often pointed to the parents of the upward

* Adapted from 'Parental factors in educational mobility', *Sociology of Education*, 38, no. 5 (1965), 404–25, by kind permission of the author and the publisher.

aspiring boy as the source of his ambition. It is the aim of this study[1] to test the general hypothesis that working-class parents are a major source of college aspirations in high-school boys. If previous research, observation and speculation are correct, parents of upward mobile working-class boys should give clear evidence of having provided a socialisation favourable to good school performance and the aspiration to attend college. These parents should be distinguishable from parents of non-mobile boys in their attitudes toward a college education, in their encouragement of high aspiration and good school performance, and in certain background characteristics leading to a high degree of parental ambition.

Motivation to mobility is here viewed as a process which starts with a parent who has conscious or unconscious ambitions for a son, moves on through socialisation techniques used on the young child and terminates in the child's favourable attitude toward school and school performance. We are by no means implying that the probability of college entry is completely determined by the early elementary school period; certain school influences may be necessary to reinforce motivation, or peer-group influences may interfere with parental efforts. However, if our premise that parental influence is a sufficient condition for the formation of college aspiration is untenable, the results of our research should be clearly negative.

The findings of Stouffer, Cleveland and Kahl[2] are basic to the design and conceptualisation of this research:

1. I.Q. is a powerful predictor of college attendance within each social level.
2. Social status is a predictor of college attendance within each I.Q. level.
3. The degree of ambition in the parents is related to college aspirations in the son among the 'common man' families studied in Kahl's intensive exploratory interviews.

In order to investigate the correlation between parental factors and a son's mobility it is necessary to control strictly for social class and I.Q. the two other factors with the above-demonstrated relationship to mobility. Therefore, this study used a matched pair design; a group of parents of clearly upward mobile boys was compared with a group of parents of clearly non-mobile boys. All fathers had working-class

1. The study was financed by the American Association of University Women Fellowship.
2. J. A. Kahl, 'Educational and occupational aspirations of "common man" boys', *Harvard Educational Review*, **23** (1953), 186–203.

occupations and the mobile son had the same I.Q. score as his non-mobile opposite number in each matched pair. Therefore, each comparison between parental groups made in the data analysis has the advantage of strict control on the I.Q. and status variables. Specific predictions centred on three types of differences we expected to find between parents. The first type concerns background characteristics of the parents which are seen as potential sources of their desire for a 'successful' son. The other two types concern the nature of the socialisation of the upward mobile boy. Parents of upward mobile boys should be distinguished by their general *attitudes* toward a college education and by their direct encouragement (*behaviour*) of good school performance and college aspirations.

SOURCES OF PARENTAL AMBITION: HYPOTHESES

Hypotheses concern three principal sources of parental aspiration: (1) closeness to middle-class position on socio-economic variables, (2) paternal job dissatisfaction, and (3) maternal downward mobility. In the first place, families selected for study by the criterion of a father holding a manual job will encompass a broad range of income, job type, and maternal employment. Because of the solid economic gains of the semiskilled and skilled worker, many families in this occupational group maintain a style of life quite indistinguishable from that of middle-class families. It should not be surprising to find that such families, able to afford a middle-class style of life, should develop middle-class aspirations for their children. Past research in the area of subjective social-class identification indicates that many people with a working-class occupation consider themselves to be 'middle class'; thus an obvious source of parental ambition in manual-worker families of this general character is the taking on of the middle-class emphasis on good school performance and the importance of a college education. We hypothesised that working-class families who are closest to the middle-class boundary, that is, the father is at the top of the manual job hierarchy, the mother holds a white-collar job, and either or both of the parents identify themselves as 'middle class', will be more likely to produce a mobile son than parents without these characteristics.

The second hypothesised source of parental aspiration is paternal job dissatisfaction. A common pattern emerging from interviewing during the course of the Harvard Mobility Project and in Kahl's work was a father, frustrated and unhappy in his work, feeling that his lack of education was a major barrier between him and job satisfaction. This father became convinced of the necessity of college education for his son in order that the boy might find a secure, satisfying job. Within the framework of a controlled design and with a standardised measure of job dissatisfaction we wished to test the hypothesis of paternal job dissatisfaction as a predictor of a son's college aspiration.

The third source of parental aspiration stems from the mother who has married downward from a white-collar background. There has been a fair amount of speculation on the downward mobile mother who desires to recover her lost status through her son both in the Mobility Project and in the sociological literature in general. However, this idea had not been put to a systematic test; and we proposed to examine maternal family background as a predictor of upward mobility in working-class sons.

PARENTAL ATTITUDES AND BEHAVIOUR: HYPOTHESES

1. *Parental attitudes towards college*

The specific hypothesis to be tested is that parents of mobile sons will exhibit an unambivalent and favourable abstract evaluation of a college education in comparison with parents of non-mobile sons. Evaluation of college as an abstract, generalised attitude may include both positive and negative feelings; for example, the belief that college is the only path to success may coexist with the belief that college involves estrangement from the family for a working-class boy. Although the cultural bias towards college is positive, a substantial ambivalence on the part of the parents may easily account for a boy's lack of interest in college attendance. A favourable outcome of parental pressure for college would seem to require a basically favourable and unambivalent evaluation of the importance and worthwhileness of a college education.

2. *Parental pressure and encouragement*

What is the concrete behavioural evidence of long-standing parental influence on a son's aspiration? The specific predictions are that parents of mobile sons will exhibit more frequently than parents of non-mobile sons the following types of behaviour:

(*a*) Deliberate encouragement of going to college from an early point in the boy's life and active pushing toward this goal.

(*b*) Concern with school performance.

(*c*) Aspiration for a middle-class job for their son.

A major source of these predictions is Kahl's finding that parents who believed in the value of 'getting ahead' started to apply pressure from the beginning of the school career, stressed that good performance was necessary for occupational success, and even suggested various occupations. These predictions are also based on the observation that the parent–son alliance in these working-class families with upward mobile sons is particularly strong.

STUDY DESIGN

The major requirement of this design was that it have a clearly upwardly mobile and a clearly non-mobile group of working-class boys whose parents could be compared on the above variables. Stringent controls of I.Q. and type of community were also necessary if we wished to isolate the relation of parental characteristics to mobility.

Therefore a matched-pair design was selected in which a junior or senior high-school boy of working-class background who was definitely planning on a four-year college was *matched*[1] *on I.Q. and community* with a boy of working-class background who was definitely *not* planning on college.[2] The group who were planning on college were called 'mobile' and the group who had decided against college were 'non-mobile'.

Previous work also suggested that care be taken that certain ethnic groups (Jews, for example) not be overrepresented in the mobile as opposed to the non-mobile group. Although there was no precision matching on this variable, these ethnics were approximately equally represented in the two groups.

The precision matching on the I.Q. variable resulted in a limitation of our subjects to the 60th to 90th percentile range of I.Q. scores

1. The definition of a 'match' on I.Q. was that both boys scored within the same decile provided by the normative population of the intelligence test used. Both came from the *same* community.
2. The question used to select mobile and non-mobile subjects was:
   Do you plan to go to college? (A four-year college, leading to a regular college degree, like Bachelor of Arts or Bachelor of Science.)
   Definitely will go.
   Almost sure to go.
   Very likely to go.
   Unlikely to go.
   Definitely will not go.
   If you are likely to go to college, what are some of the colleges you have in mind? (An alternative but similar question was used for some subjects.)
   Boys who chose 'Definitely' were considered mobile; boys who chose 'Definitely Not' or 'Unlikely' were considered non-mobile.

because in 1957 no non-mobile match could be found for the mobile boys with very high I.Q.s. Also, the few sons of unskilled labourers who were in school could rarely be matched on I.Q. Much of the school drop-out comes from among sons of unskilled labourers, so that there were comparatively few junior and senior boys from this background. They are also the group least likely to aspire to college or to have an I.Q. score suitable for college work. Thus we could not find many clearly mobile sons of unskilled workers to include in our sample. Any boy who had not made a definite decision for or against college, or who did not have both parents alive and living at home, was omitted from our study. Thus the sample consisted of 100 moderately intelligent boys who are by no means representative of the sons of all manual workers. Occupationally, their fathers are more likely to be semiskilled or skilled than unskilled. The boys were white; and they came from relatively stable homes where both parents were present. The overwhelming impression received from interview visits to these homes was one of 'bourgeois' respectability. Everything was clean and neat and by no means poverty-stricken. Children were carefully controlled; religious symbols were much in evidence; care was taken to avoid profanity. In other words, these boys came from what is known as the 'respectable working class'.

The boys were selected by means of a written questionnaire. Next, a standardised interview was administered in their home to the mother and father of each of the boys who made up the mobile and non-mobile group.

MEASUREMENT OF PARENTAL BACKGROUND CHARACTERISTICS

The interviewer obtained detailed information on father's occupation so that the job could be classified as skilled, semiskilled, or unskilled according to *The Dictionary of Occupational Titles.*

Subjective status was measured by (1) the question: 'If you were asked to use one of these four names for your social group, which would you say you belonged in—middle class, lower class, working class, or upper class?', (2) response to a Guttman scale made up of public opinion questions which have been known to produce middle-class and working-class differences, and (3) political preference. The prediction was that parents who thought of themselves as belonging in the middle class, or had a middle-class response to the scale, or tended to vote Republican, would be more likely than others to have a mobile son.

In addition, father's job satisfaction was measured by three questions taken from the work of Elizabeth Lyman[1] on social-class differences in valuation of various aspects of the job. These questions do not measure satisfaction with the particular job the father now holds, but represent a more general satisfaction with place in the occupational status structure.

MEASUREMENT OF PARENTAL INFLUENCE

1. The most difficult measurement problem concerned the attitude towards a college education. Not only did we conceive of this attitude as multidimensional, but it was necessary to tap hidden fears of the consequences of a son's college attendance. An example of a common source of ambivalence in a working-class family is the fear of a boy's growing away from and looking down on his parents after he has gone to college. A typical item used is 'When a boy goes to college, he no longer admires those who do honest hard work. Agree, slightly agree, slightly disagree, disagree.'

Five dimensions were conceptualised for the purpose of constructing Guttman scales; and suitable items were composed for each topic. These dimensions were:

1. College as a way of mobility.
2. College as a financial sacrifice.
3. College and the family.
4. College as a means to job security.
5. Value of time spent in college.

The Guttman scales were pre-tested. In addition, to correct for differences between pre-test and experimental samples, five new scales were constructed on half the experimental sample; these replicated satisfactorily on the other half of the sample.

2. Measuring the hypothesis of a higher level of encouragement and ambition on the part of the parents of the mobile boys presented great dangers of interviewer effect. Since the interviewer was sponsored by an educational institution, and the crucial decision to go to college on the part of the boys was undoubtedly known to the parents, the chance of a glowing report of parental encouragement from the parents of the mobile sons seemed rather likely, whether or not it was an accurate reflection of their behaviour.

1. Elizabeth L. Lyman, 'Occupational differences in the value attached to work', *American Journal of Sociology*, 61 (September, 1955), 138–44.

Three precautions were taken to avoid this type of error:

1. The study was presented as an investigation of how boys select the jobs they do rather than how they make educational plans.
2. The instrument measuring parental attitude toward college was self-administered and was placed at the very end of the interview.
3. No mention was made of college in the oral section of the interview until the end of a funnel series designed to elicit spontaneous reports of occupational and educational plans the parents had held since the boy's childhood.

The hypothesis of specific occupational aspiration of these parents for their sons was measured by two methods. One was a direct question on their choice of job for their son when he was forty years old. This was not felt to be adequate since the answer would probably be a partial reflection of the boy's current aspiration. Therefore, subjects were asked to sort out a series of fourteen index cards with jobs written on them into two piles. In one pile they were to put those jobs which they would be happy to see any of their sons have when he was forty years old as well as those jobs which they wouldn't feel one way or another about. In the other pile, they were to put those which they would be unhappy to see their sons have. These jobs were selected from the North-Hatt listing[1] and represented different positions on the prestige continuum. Parents of mobile sons were expected to find fewer clearly working-class jobs acceptable than parents of non-mobile sons.

RESULTS

Response rate

The design of this study called for an unlimited number of call-backs; refusal of one individual could mean the loss of not only that family but its match in the other experimental group. By persistent call-backs, the refusal rate was reduced to 8 per cent.

Sources of parental ambition: closeness to the middle class

The general hypothesis of a closeness to the middle class among families of upward mobile working-class sons yields several specific predictions as to the relationship between parental socio-economic characteristics and the probability of upward mobility.

1. National Opinion Research Center, 'Jobs and occupations: a popular evaluation', in R. Bendix and S. M. Lipset, eds., *Class, Status and Power*, Glencoe, Ill.: Free Press, 1953, pp. 411–26.

Prediction 1.   The higher the status of the particular type of factory job held by the father, the higher the probability of his having a mobile son.

Examination of Table 11.1 shows that the sons of foremen were significantly more likely to have college aspirations than the sons of semiskilled and skilled workers. There is no significant difference between the probability of mobility for the sons of skilled as compared to the sons of semiskilled workers.

If income were the major explanation of the differential probability of mobility of sons of various manual occupations, we would definitely see the skilled worker's son having a higher probability of mobility than the semiskilled worker's son.[1]

TABLE 11.1.   *Three types of paternal working-class jobs and the probability of a son planning college.*

Father's job	Number of cases	% Fathers with sons planning college
Foremen	37	65
Other skilled	22	36
Less than skilled	39	44

Foremen *v.* Other skilled and Less than skilled: P<0·05.
Foremen and Other skilled *v.* Less than skilled: P>0·05.

Prediction 2.   If the mother is employed, the higher the status of her job, the greater the probability of her having a mobile son.

About half the women in the sample were employed in full or part-time work. The fact of employment alone is not related to a son's decision about college, but the nature of the work is. If the mother holds a white-collar job, her son is much more likely to plan on college than if she holds a manual job. This result can be seen in Table 11.2.

Prediction 3.   The more closely the parents identify themselves with the middle class, in name and values, the higher the probability of having a mobile son.

1. Previous studies have failed to find any relationship between type of paternal working-class occupation and a son's mobility. Our results suggest that the failure to separate foremen from other skilled workers may obscure differences in the probability of upward mobility.

Using three different indices of parental perception of social-class membership and the holding of class-related attitudes, we find no significant differences between the parents of mobile and non-mobile sons, although fathers show non-significant differences in the predicted direction in two of the three indices (see Tables 11.3, 11.4, and 11.5).

TABLE 11.2.   *Mother's occupation and probability of a son planning college.*

Mother's occupation[1]	Number of cases	% Mothers with sons planning college
Manual	26	38
White-collar	23	74
	P<0·01	

1. Of the fifty-four unemployed mothers, 48 per cent had sons planning college.

TABLE 11.3.   *Subjective social-class identification and probability of a son's planning college.*

Identification	Number of cases	% Parents with sons planning college
Fathers		
Middle or upper class	30	60
Working class	68	46
Mothers		
Middle or upper class	41	51
Working class	56	50

In contrast, the percentages of mothers showing a middle-class response are very similar for the two comparison groups. Here is the first evidence of the different pattern of mobility orientation of mothers and fathers which emerges from this study.

SOURCES OF PARENTAL AMBITION: DOWNWARD MOBILITY OF THE MOTHER

Prediction 4.   Mothers who have married downward from a white-collar background have a higher probability of having an upward mobile son than mothers who come from a manual-worker background.

Support for the prediction of a relationship between maternal social-class origin and mobility arises from an examination of the occupation of the maternal grandfathers. The figures in Table 11.6

show that 80 per cent of the downwardly mobile mothers had sons planning on college, while only 42 per cent of the mothers from a working-class family of orientation had sons planning on college.

TABLE 11.4. *Parental 'class-related public opinion scale' score and probability of a son's planning college.*

Scale score	Number of cases	% Parents with sons planning college
Fathers		
Low[1]	55	56
High	43	42
Mothers		
Low	56	50
High	47	53

1. The lower the score, the more likely the subject is to be described as having attitudes similar to those of the middle class.

TABLE 11.5. *Political preference and probability of a son's planning college.*

Political preference	Number of cases	% Parents with sons planning college
Fathers		
Democratic	68	51
Republican or Independent	30	47
Mothers		
Democratic	60	52
Republican or Independent	39	49

In contrast to this finding, there was no significant relationship between father's social-class origin and the mobility of his son. Again we have an indication, and a strong one, in this analysis, of a pattern of inspiration to mobility on the part of mothers which is different from that of fathers.

SOURCES OF PARENTAL AMBITION: FATHER'S JOB DISSATISFACTION

Prediction 5. Fathers who are dissatisfied with their jobs are more likely to have an upward mobile son than fathers who are relatively satisfied with their jobs.

The three questions which made up the index of job satisfaction were as follows:

1. If you had it to do all over again, and you were just graduating from high school, would you go into the same kind of work again, or what work would you like to do?

2. How would you feel about a son of yours going into your kind of work?

TABLE 11.6.   *Maternal grandfather's occupation and probability of a grandson planning college.*

Maternal grandfather's occupation	Number of cases	% with grandsons planning college
Blue-collar or farming	78	42
White-collar	25	80
	$P < 0.001$	

TABLE 11.7.   *Father's job satisfaction and probability of having a son planning college.*

Job satisfaction	Number of cases	% fathers with sons planning college
Satisfied	27	26
Dissatisfied	71	58
	$P < 0.05$	

3. Suppose you got the *same* pay, no matter *what* kind of work you did. Of all the kinds of work you can think of, what would you like best?

A satisfied response included choices of other working-class occupations as well as the subject's present job on any of the three questions. Since only three subjects gave a 'satisfied' response on all three questions, fathers who gave a 'satisfied' response on any two of the three questions were categorised as 'satisfied'. Over the whole sample, Table 11.7 shows that dissatisfied fathers were significantly more likely to have mobile sons than the relatively satisfied fathers.

Since foremen are more likely to be dissatisfied with their jobs than other skilled workers, it was desirable to examine the relationship of dissatisfaction to mobility within paternal occupational groups. Within the limits of a small sample, it can be seen in Table 11.8 that job dissatisfaction maintained its relationship to mobility within occupational groups.

If this same table is organised by holding the degree of job satisfaction constant and varying paternal occupation, we find an interaction effect between being a foreman and being dissatisfied with one's job.

TABLE 11.8. *Father's job satisfaction and son's educational plans at three levels of father's occupation.*

Father's occupation and job satisfaction	No. of sons planning college	No. of sons not planning college	Total	% Sons planning college[1]
Supervisory				
Satisfied	2	4	6	(33)
Dissatisfied	18	7	25	72
Other skilled				
Satisfied	3	9	12	25
Dissatisfied	5	5	10	50
Less than skilled				
Satisfied	2	7	9	(22)
Dissatisfied	19	17	36	53

1. Percentages based on fewer than ten cases are shown in parentheses.

When these factors occur together there is a sharp rise in the probability of having an upward mobile son.

SOURCES OF PARENTAL AMBITION: INTERPRETATION

Hypotheses concerning father's job dissatisfaction and maternal downward mobility as a possible source of college aspirations for a son were confirmed. The general hypothesis of a closeness to the middle class as a source of parental ambition showed mixed results. If we interpret occupational differences in terms of income, we can see that income is not sufficient to account for the comparatively low rate of mobility of sons of skilled workers other than foremen. The addition of the variable of job satisfaction indicated a possible inter-action effect between the superior income of the foremen and the foremen's job dissatisfaction. One might interpret the joint effects of income and job dissatisfaction in the following manner: When both income and job dissatisfaction are high, as in the case of foremen, there is an especially high probability of an upward mobile son; when income is high but job dissatisfaction low, as in the case of other skilled workers, there is a sharp drop in the probability of upward mobility; and when job dissatisfaction is high, but income low, as in the case of less than skilled workers, there is also a relatively low rate of upward mobility. A more refined measurement of job satisfaction and direct questions on income are needed before this interpretation can be tested.

An alternative interpretation of the high rate of mobility among sons of foremen is that the crucial factor is the marginal position of the foremen who—as many sociologists have pointed out—often represent managerial interests to the worker without being an accepted member of management's social class. This might be the source of the foremen's job dissatisfaction; it may also be that the close association with middle-class personnel is an additional force working to produce mobility aspirations.

The fact that mothers holding white-collar jobs had a higher probability of having a mobile son than mothers holding manual jobs lends strength to the association with middle-class personnel as a source of parental ambitions for a son's college education. People who associate with white-collar workers on the job may be particularly aware of the relationship between higher education and good jobs.

The second difficulty with the hypothesis of closeness to the middle class arose in the analysis of the relationship of subjective social-class identification to mobility. For future research, it would seem best to abandon this hypothesis in its most general form: the results indicate that it should be broken down into alternative modes of parental mobility orientation.

The above results suggest at least two distinct types of parental motivation: a *vocational orientation* and a *status orientation*. College attendance can be seen either as vocational training for certain desirable white-collar jobs (and many working-class parents do view college purely as a glorified trade school) *or* as a necessary attribute of middle-class status.

The following findings led us to conceptualise a vocational orientation as an independent source of parental motivation: (1) Occupational factors—father's job dissatisfaction, father being a foreman, and mother holding a white-collar job—were strongly predictive of a son's college aspiration; (2) Father's downward mobility was unrelated to a son's mobility. We can speculate that certain jobs involving close association with middle-class personnel lead to the conviction that college training is the necessary key to a satisfying job in today's occupational structure. Since relatively few mothers hold such jobs, a vocational orientation is necessarily more characteristic of fathers than of mothers.

Status orientation, on the other hand, is more characteristic of mothers than fathers. The concept of status orientation is based on these findings: (1) the striking relationship of downward mobility in mothers to college aspiration in sons; (2) the much weaker relationship of the same variables for fathers. We see the downward mobile mother as motivated by a desire to recover lost status; she is a prime example of a status-oriented parent.

PARENTAL BEHAVIOUR AND MOBILITY

Do parents of mobile sons provide their children with more encouragement and pressure for success than parents of non-mobile sons ? Analysis of all the responses to a series of open-ended questions on parental encouragement shows that *only certain types of pressures* are related to mobility. In general, occupational and educational plans for the future with accompanying encouragement are closely related to mobility while *reported responses to failures in school are not.*

Specific educational and occupational goals

The questions relating to parental encouragement were written in a funnel series; the first question, which was the most indirect, did not even imply college aspiration—'Did you ever think about your son's future when he was still a little boy ? If yes—what kind of plans did you think about?' The second question dealt with specific occupational plans upon entering high school, the third with the consideration of further education beyond high school, and the fourth specifically inquired about encouragement of further education. A Pressure Index was constructed of the tendency of the parent to respond to these questions with occupational and educational plans implying parental mobility aspiration and direct pressure towards these goals on the child.

TABLE 11.9. *Percentage of parents with low and high values on Pressure Index who have sons planning college.*

Values on Pressure Index[1]	Number of cases	% Parents with sons planning college
Mothers		
Low pressure	54	33
High pressure	49	66
	P<0·001	
Fathers		
Low pressure	61	36
High pressure	37	73
	P<0·001	

1. High—pressure responses to all four questions.
   Low—non-pressure response to one or more questions.

The Pressure Index shows a strong relationship to mobility; more generally, the more consistently a parent reports ambitious occupational and educational plans for his son from childhood onward and

both consideration and encouragement of the idea of further schooling the more likely he is to have a son who is planning on college.

In addition to the Pressure Index, which has an important occupational component, a purely educational index was constructed,
called the College Summary Score. One or more mentions of college
in response to each of the eight open-ended questions concerning
plans for the future and attitude toward school work received a score
of 1; the highest score received was 5. Table 11.10 shows that mothers
and fathers who have a high College Summary Score are much more
likely to have a son who is planning college than parents who have a
low College Summary Score.

TABLE 11.10.   *Percentage of parents with low and high values on the College
Summary Score who have sons planning college.*

Level of College Summary Score[1]	Number of cases	% Parents with sons planning college
Mothers		
Low score	46	22
High score	57	75
	$P<0.001$	
Fathers		
Low score	51	31
High score	47	70
	$P<0.001$	

1. Low—college mentioned once or not at all.
   High—college mentioned more than once.

A third measure of parental ambition was the range of jobs which
the parent found acceptable for any of these children when presented
with the task of sorting cards with jobs on them. The number of jobs
out of a group of relatively unpopular occupations[1] which the parent
finds acceptable would seem fairly good measure of the strength and
specificity of parental ambition. Working-class parents who indicate
that they would feel disappointed if *any of their children* took a working-
class job can fairly be said to have mobility aspirations. The data
showed that the fewer working-class jobs the parent finds acceptable
for any offspring, the higher is his probability of having a mobile son.

In addition, on a direct question as to what job the parent would
like this particular son to have when he is around forty years old, the

1. The jobs which fewer than 50 per cent of the parents found acceptable were
as follows: policeman, garage mechanic, machine operator, clerk in a store,
streetcar motorman, filling station attendant, taxi driver, clothes presser in a
laundry, street sweeper.

parents of the mobile sons were significantly more likely to choose a middle-class job requiring college than the parents of the non-mobile sons.

In review, the four parental predictors which have a significant relationship to mobility thus far are (1) an index of pressure starting in childhood for a middle-class occupation, (2) a score representing the saliency of the idea of college in the parents' minds, (3) a tendency to find few if any working-class jobs acceptable for any child of the family, and (4) a specific choice of a middle-class job requiring a college education for the son in question. Roughly speaking, the common factor in these findings is that they represent specific long-term occupational or educational goals in the minds of the parents. An important qualification is that the data consist of parental reports of long-term goals made to an interviewer at a time in the boy's career when he has made the crucial decision about college. Whether parental goals would work equally well as predictors for boys of grade school age remains to be determined.

Response to school failure

In contrast to the success of the predictors described above, responses to questions dealing with reaction to a poor high-school report card were quite unrelated to mobility. Since poor performance in high school is quite detrimental to parental hopes of college, it would seem reasonable to predict that parents of mobile sons would disapprove more strongly and take more drastic measures than parents of non-mobile sons. Even with the reported level of high-school performance held constant (performance is an excellent predictor of mobility in this and other studies), there was no relationship between the degree of disapproval of a poor report card in high school and the probability of mobility (Table 11.11).

MUST PARENTAL INFLUENCE OCCUR BEFORE HIGH SCHOOL?

The failure of response to high-school performance to relate to mobility is here interpreted as a matter of timing of parental pressure. Many of the parents of non-mobile sons appear to put the pressure on suddenly in the latter high-school years. Highly stressful family situations are often produced in this manner; because the boy's performance and general motivation have already degenerated beyond the point of no return, the net result of parental efforts and nagging is a complete breakdown of the parent–son relationship.

8*

TABLE 11.11.   *Degree of disapproval of a poor report card and probability of a son planning college: holding performance constant.*

	High school performance	Degree of disapproval	Number of cases	% Parents with sons planning college
Mother	Poor or average	Strong	34	38
		Mild	11	36
	Above average	Strong	42	55
		Mild	13	76
Father	Poor or average	Strong	39	49
		Mild	9	(33)
	Above average	Strong	33	58
		Mild	16	44

The success of occupational and educational plans, reportedly held since the boy's childhood, as predictors of mobility implies an early socialisation for mobility. Since we know that school performance from about the fourth grade onward is predictive of mobility and that attitude toward the school setting is a predictor of school performance for working-class boys, we can speculate that the influence of the parents on the probability of mobility takes place at a very early stage when basic attitudes toward school work are being formed. The crucial role of the parents may be to send the child to school with a receptive attitude toward the values and norms advocated by the school personnel. If this is the case, any attempt on the part of parent to alter school performance after some critical point, may well be quite futile in increasing the probability of mobility.

PATTERNS OF PARENTAL ATTITUDE AND BEHAVIOUR

The prediction of a more favourable attitude toward college on the part of parents of mobile sons than the parents of non-mobile sons was supported by the data, *when all five attitude scales were used*. If we compare the scores on all five scales for each parental matched pair and decide that the pair who are more favourable towards college on the majority of the scales are the parents of the mobile son, we will assign parental couples correctly for thirty-two of the forty-eight matched pairs. Correct assignment is far better than would occur by chance.

SUMMARY AND CONCLUSIONS

This study of the origin of upward mobility aspiration investigated ways in which working-class parents influence their sons to attend college. Two groups of high-school boys of working-class background, one of which was definitely planning on college and the other of which was definitely not planning on college were selected. These two groups of fifty boys each were matched on intelligence and school. A standardised interview was then administered to the mother and father of each of these boys in their homes.

The first type of parental influence examined was background characteristics viewed as sources of parental ambition. In line with predictions, the following parental factors showed a significant relationship to a son's mobility: father is a foreman; mother holds a white-collar job; father is dissatisfied with his job; and mother is downward mobile from a white-collar background. These results suggested two independent types of parental motivation, a *vocational orientation* emphasising the desirability of certain jobs requiring a college education and a *status orientation*, emphasising the college degree as a key to middle-class status. Vocational orientation appeared to be more characteristic of fathers and status orientation was more characteristic of mothers.

The second type of parental influence was the behaviour of the parent: concrete pressure and encouragement of the boy. Parents of mobile sons reported more deliberate encouragement of college, starting in the boy's childhood, and were more likely to have a middle-class occupational aspiration for their son than parents of non-mobile sons. Behavioural pressure for good performance during high school failed to relate to mobility. We concluded that parental pressure is more crucial during the early years when attitudes toward school are being formed.

The third type of parental influence examined was the attitude toward a college education, as measured by five Guttman scales. Parental favourability toward college was closely related to a son's mobility when all five scales were used.

In review, we see the origin of mobility aspiration in a long-term socialisation process involving alternative patterns of motivational sources, general attitudes and timing and techniques of encouragement by the parent. Further research will examine the process at an earlier point in time with special attention to development of measures for unique features of alternative patterns of mobility.

12

Linguistic development and Educability*

Denis Lawton

The study of parental ideology is one means of considering, in depth, the relationship of family, class and education. A second approach is the study of linguistic development. In this chapter, Dr Lawton begins by drawing a distinction between the demographic mapping of educational opportunity and the subcultural analysis of educability, going on to consider social-class variations in motivation, socialisation patterns and language development. He discusses the evidence for the suggestion that language is more than simply a means of communication, and that perhaps it both reflects and shapes perception and experience, with obvious implications for schooling. This is now a fundamental line of analysis in the study of educability but one which is inextricably linked with the others described in Part Five.

Before the 1939–1945 war the problem of equality of opportunity in this country was seen largely as a question of securing equality of *access* to educational institutions, especially to grammar schools. In the postwar years, however, when many hoped that the problem had been solved by the 1944 Act, sociologists have increasingly tended to draw attention to the more difficult questions of *retention* of pupils by the school, and *performance* of pupils at school. The problem of access is, of course, not yet solved—even with the replacement of grammar schools by comprehensive schools. All the reports since the war have shown gross discrepancies in the quality of schools in different areas, but we know how this problem could be solved given the financial resources. Once children have been allocated to equally good primary or secondary schools, however, it will still be evident

* This paper was specially written for this volume.

that not all children will perform equally well or will stay on at school for an equally long period to take advantage of what education has to offer them. The obvious answer to why these differences in attainment exist is that some children are more intelligent than others. But this is a much less satisfactory answer than it used to be. We now have to ask 'what do we mean by intelligence in this context?' 'Is it innate or acquired?' If, as Sir Edward Boyle suggested in the Newsom Report, intelligence can be acquired at school, then we are in a completely circular argument: those pupils who do well at school are intelligent; who are the intelligent? those whom the schools make intelligent. That is one of the complications to this kind of postwar argument; the other main difficulty is that we know from the evidence that measured intelligence simply does not determine educational success—pupils of fairly modest I.Q. ratings do well at school; some pupils of high measured I.Q. perform very poorly. Let us examine, very briefly, what evidence we have on the two aspects of the postwar problem. Both of them appear to be, to some extent, connected with social class: working-class children tend to be the under-achievers.

First, the question of retention of pupils by a school (what the Americans refer to as the drop-out problem—pupils who do not complete high school). The *Early Leaving* Report, the Crowther and Robbins Reports all showed that large numbers of working-class pupils of high measured ability left school 'early'. This was thought to be a loss both to the pupils themselves, as they were developed far below their optimum capacity, and to the national economy. Why did so many pupils, mostly working-class pupils, opt out of school? A number of reasons have been suggested: the purely physical difficulties—overcrowding at home making homework difficult; questions of attitude—pupils and parents not really thinking in terms of the value of education; finally suggestions that schools themselves were partly guilty—rejecting rather than accommodating working-class children from a subculture somewhat alien to the values of the school.

Next the question of *performance*, which is to some extent very closely connected with the problem of retention. This was clearly a problem also in the 1954 *Early Leaving* Report and it was still one of the problems mentioned in the Robbins Report 1963. Those working-class pupils who were graded as the top one-third in ability at the eleven-plus rating got poorer G.C.E. results five years later than some middle-class pupils who were only marginally grammar-school material at eleven-plus. Why should there be this kind of relationship between social class and 'educability'? Apart from the factors mentioned above in connection with the retention problem, an easy answer is to dismiss the whole of this as a simple matter of motivation: some children do well because they want to; others, although bright, fail because they lack interest and motivation. This is, of course, much too naïve. It merely leads to two other questions: what do we mean by motivation? Why should motivation be correlated with social class?

Even a simple definition of motivation is no straightforward task, as Professor Peters well demonstrates in his book *The Concept of Motivation* (1958). There is extrinsic motivation—being persuaded to do something by various forms of rewards and punishments; intrinsic motivation—the desire to do something worth while for its own sake; and finally social motivation—the desire to do something because it is regarded as an approved activity by an admired person. This is a very complex area and all that a sociologist can do is to examine motivation as a subcultural variable. As long ago as 1948 Allison Davis made a plea for linking the study of education with subcultural differences: 'In order to help the child learn the teacher must discover the reference point from which the child starts . . . his cultural environment and his cultural motivation.' Social anthropologists inform us that different people with different environments and different traditions view the world quite diversely. Some, like the Navaho for example, apparently see themselves in a very passive way: they are acted upon by the gods, or fate, or nature—they feel themselves to have little control over their own destiny. Others see themselves much more as dominators of their environment, conquering the forces of nature, overcoming difficulties, finding solutions and expecting to find solutions to all problems, refusing to accept adversity as inevitable. Western European and American culture is very much of the latter kind. Ours is a rational universe governed by scientific laws. The more we obtain an understanding of the laws the more we can master our environment. This has increasingly become the dominant feature of our society. But different subcultures within societies have a greater or lesser degree of attachment to this principle. It might be that certain religious sects are more 'fatalistic' than others. Florence Kluckhohn (1954) contrasts the Spanish–American fatalistic attitude to nature as opposed to the mainstream of United States' culture. Certainly a number of studies of life in England have shown interesting differences between communities in this respect as well as in many related areas which might have some educational consequences.

It is perhaps misleading to think of these subcultural differences simply in terms of social class: most recent studies have agreed that divisions within what has traditionally been referred to as working class are greater than any clear contrast with the middle class; but it is still useful to use the term 'traditional working-class' areas in contrast to those in more marginal positions and who are perhaps living on new housing estates. A number of studies of these traditional working-class communities, such as Liverpool's dockland (*Ship Street*) or Yorkshire coal areas (*Coal is Our Life*) or the Young and Willmott study of Bethnal Green in London, seem to agree on a number of factors. Such communities tend to be inward looking, with a social structure based largely on ascribed roles, having short-term goals rather than long-term planning; traditional patterns of behaviour are regarded as 'right' without question, they are not discussed rationally but a high degree of conformity is insisted on. Josephine Klein (1965) sums up this kind of mental state as 'cognitive poverty', and in the children tested it showed itself as a low level of imagination and aesthetic appreciation, a mistrust of the unfamiliar, a dislike of anything abstract, a low rate of explanatory behaviour and curiosity. If all this appears to the middle-class observer as a different way of regarding the world, this might be important or trivial. The question is does this different view of the world really matter? Is it in any sense an inferior kind of perception? Anthropologists as well as sociologists are very sensitive about this kind of value judgment, and we must specify inferior for some particular purpose. If we specify inferior in terms of benefiting from current educational programmes, then there is little doubt that children socialised into such subcultures are at a definite disadvantage in our schools. An important part of this socialisation process is, according to Klein, that in these communities the present is dominant. Future plans are seen as of little relevance—deferred gratification is *not* part of the way of life. In the up-bringing of children 'sensory dominance' is the key. Behaviour is guided more by immediate stimuli, current feelings and wishes than by a consideration of remoter consequences.

LANGUAGE AND SOCIALISATION

What part does language play in these developmental processes? For at least the last ten years sociologists have become more concerned with questions of language. It is important for at least two major reasons. The first is that language is an important medium of socialisation. The majority of a child's culture is transmitted to him by means of language—he is told what is permissible and what is offensive, and he is told *about* a vast amount of our transitional culture. It might be expected then that differences in linguistic behaviour would be closely connected with other cultural characteristics. Those who use language a great deal in their daily lives, for a variety of purposes and with a great deal of skill, may bring up their children in a way quite different from those who live in a largely non-verbal world. The second reason is that language is not simply a means of expressing thought, it is a dynamic element in the process. The language we use to some extent structures, inhibits or facilitates certain kinds of expression. Differences in the linguistic behaviour of adults, then, may have a direct effect on the perception of their children. This is a disputed point which will have to be argued more fully later in this chapter.

The area of language, socialisation and education is, therefore, a very important one and a very complex one. Before we can proceed with an analysis at that level we should examine the evidence for the existence of differences between the kind of traditional working-class community I have been referring to and the rest of English society, especially the more educable middle classes. There have been a large number of studies of children's language and language development over the last fifty years or so. Some of these studies have been concerned to set up developmental norms in language—stages which the average child could be expected to reach at a given age. This task is itself an extremely difficult one, and until recently such studies only achieved success over a very limited field and were handicapped by not having an adequate grammatical framework to operate with (the traditional latinate grammar is of very limited value for this purpose). Nevertheless some progress was made and a high level of agreement reached between various studies. One matter on which the majority agreed was that certain groups of children tend to be 'retarded' as measured by the norms. These groups include institutionalised children, twins, children from large families and working-class children. In the case of institutionalised children, this kind of retardation can be predicted as early as a few months of age when institutionalised children's babbling is much less close to the phonemes used in adult speech than that of children brought up in a normal family environment. Social-class differences of this kind do not appear until a child is about eighteen months old, but as children get older other differences begin to appear: the length of response or sentence length in a given situation has been used by a number of investigators, as well as various measures of grammatical complexity. An objection might be raised at this point stating that it is obvious that the speech of working-class people is different from middle-class speech—everyone knows that, so why waste money doing research on such an unnecessary issue? The answer is that the researchers have been concerned to discover *not* that there are speech differences, but the answers to two rather more difficult questions. First, exactly what is the nature and extent of these differences; secondly, how important are they—that is, to what extent is communication and even thinking limited by certain kinds of language? Both these questions have proved to be very difficult to answer.

As regards the nature of the differences, one point should be made immediately. It is not simply a question of vocabulary. Many of the early investigations of language did in fact show that working-class children at any given age tended to have a much smaller vocabulary than middle-class children, and this did impede their comprehension and expression. But if this were the *only* problem it would be very easily solved. Extension of vocabulary in a foreign language or one's native tongue is a very simple process indeed compared with learning to use unfamiliar structures. It is probably no exaggeration to say that vocabulary extension or learning lexical items is the simplest one per cent of the language learning process. There is no space in this paper to give details of what the structural differences are—I have summarised the literature elsewhere (Lawton, 1968).

As for the question about how important these differences in linguistic development might be, there are two kinds of theoretical approaches: the anthropological evidence and the psychological view. Both of them are concerned with the general question of the relation of language to thought.

ANTHROPOLOGICAL EVIDENCE

The anthropological evidence is relevant at this point because it is concerned mainly with the general issue of language and culture. To what extent, if any, is the culture of any particular society dependent on the structure of its language? If it could be stated that there was an important relationship, then this would support the view that in our society subcultural language differences might have important cognitive implications. In other words we may not only be dealing with a problem of inadequate control over language, but also of the existence of different kinds of language which forces its speakers to *think* in a different way.

It has sometimes been suggested that linguistic relativity or linguistic determinism (the view that language structures thought)· began with the American, Benjamin Lee Whorf. In fact the view is much older than that. The nineteenth-century German philosopher Von Humboldt claimed that 'man lives with the world about him exclusively as language presents it'. An equally extensive claim for the importance of language was later made by the American Sapir:

> The real world is to a large extent unconsciously built up on the language habits of the group. The worlds in which different societies live are distinct worlds, not merely the same world with different labels attached. We see and hear and otherwise experience very largely as we do because the language habits of our community predispose certain choices of interpretation.

Whorf finally established the view that language is not merely a vehicle for thought but an objective reality which completely interpenetrates experience: 'We cut up nature—organise it into concepts —and ascribe significances as we do, largely because of the absolutely obligatory patterns of our language.' Unfortunately the evidence in support of the Whorfian thesis is both complex and inconclusive. The task of proving or disproving such a view has proved very difficult.

Completely opposed to this linguistic relativity view is that of the linguists who maintain that anything could be said in any language. This view can in fact be shown to be demonstrably true, and was a healthy reaction to the unscientific nature of the earlier writers on non-European languages—missionaries, traders, etc.—who sometimes spoke naïvely of primitive tribes, primitive languages and primitive thinking. Clearly this was a grossly oversimplified view and it has certainly been established that the language structures of pre-literate societies are by no means simple or in any sense primitive. It has taken linguistic anthropologists some time to resolve the difficulty of these two conflicting views, but by 1964 Dell Hymes was able to clarify the whole area by declaring that what is of interest to anthropologists is not what *could* be said but what *is* said, and by implication what can be expressed easily as opposed to what can be expressed only with difficulty and only with much linguistic con tortions. Even pidgin, which is normally used for very concrete trader transactions, can be adapted to much more abstract purposes, as Roger Bell (1966) has demonstrated, but in order to translate something like 'the basis of catholic teaching' a certain amount of ingenuity is required to produce 'ars bilong tok katolik'. John Gumperz has also pointed out that in India educated speakers tend to switch freely from one language to another when discussing urban subjects, often inserting entire English phrases into their Hindi discourse.

Another facet of this view is that it is probably an oversimplification to say that language channels thought; it is much more likely that language is a function of social structure and that an interaction of language and social structure channels thought. Even this may well be too simple a model, since social structure is itself constantly being strengthened and reinforced by linguistic forms; so possibly the model should be:

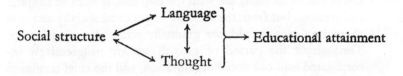

Examples which illustrate the relation between social structure, language and thought tend to be of a fairly elementary nature, but they may serve to make the point. Conklin (in Hymes, 1964) mentioned the case of sex differences among the Hanunoo where there is a noticeable difference in the colour vocabulary of men as compared to women. Men excel in ranges of reds and greys; women excel in blues. In this case the differences in discrimination were clearly due to differences in occupational function of the men as compared with the women—reds and greys were useful in hunting, blues were the colours commonly used for dyed fabrics. Another example is provided by Frake (also in Hymes, 1964). In order to participate in ordinary conversations among the Subanun of Mindano, Frake found it necessary to master the terminology of folk botany and medicine. He discovered that Subanun medical law and medical jargon were not esoteric subjects, and that even children could distinguish fungus skin infections which were not even differentiated by Western medical science. Frake implied that because they possessed the necessary vocabulary children in this society could diagnose diseases. Perhaps a more acceptable interpretation would be that the ability to diagnose is not simply a function of the knowledge of the word but of the social organisation of that tribe. It would be naïve to say that the child recognised the disease because he knew the word; it would be more realistic to say that he knew the word because the social structure of the Subanun was such that every man was his own doctor and that diagnosis of ailments was a very common topic of everyday conversation. In both examples social structure clearly has an important effect on linguistic usage in those particular societies and in each case the linguistic usage had some behavioural effect.

This kind of anthropological approach to language is very close to the work of some modern British linguists, for example, Halliday, Strevens and MacIntosh (1964). This school of linguists is very much in the tradition of J. R. Firth who was himself influenced to some extent by the work of such anthropologists as Malinowski. Here the linking concept between language and social structure is *role*.

> Every one of us starts life with the two simple roles of sleeping and feeding, but from the time we begin to be socially active at about two months old, we gradually accumulate social roles. Throughout the period of growth we are progressively incorporated into our social organisation, and the chief condition and means of that incorporation is learning to say what the other fellow expects us to say under the given circumstances . . . We are born individuals. But to satisfy our needs we have to become social persons, and every social person is a bundle of roles or personae, so that the situational and linguistic categories would not be unmanageable (Firth, 1935).

Halliday and others have developed this line of thought further by means of the concept *register*. A register can be defined as a variety of language which is distinguished according to *use*, in other words a variety of language which could be regarded as appropriate for different kinds of situation. Dixon has defined register in this way: 'A separate register can be recognised whenever a set of formal patterns correlates with particular arrangements of situational features.' By this definition there will be, for example, a scientific register, an economics register, a journalistic register, an ecclesiastical register, etc. A speaker will switch from one register to another according to the total situation: what he is talking (writing) about, in what kind of total event; according to the medium of communication; according to the role relations involved (formal, informal, intimate, etc.). It is quite clear that some individuals who play different roles at various levels in social structure will have a greater familiarity with certain registers; similarly some individuals will have a much wider range of registers at their disposal. Part of the task of a school is to introduce pupils to linguistic registers which may be quite unfamiliar to them in their daily lives, for example, scientific register. A further difficulty arises here, however, because we have to ask to what extent lack of familiarity with a register implies ignorance of the form of knowledge. To what extent is it possible to understand science, for example, without knowing the 'appropriate' way of communicating scientific knowledge. Obviously no general answer can be given to this question. Some aspects of the register might be purely conventional, other aspects might be obligatory. It will also differ from one register to another. Some registers will involve no real 'understanding' of new concepts and processes, for example, journalistic register. Once again, however, it is important to point out that vocabulary differences, although the most obvious feature of many registers, are not necessarily the most important, and lexical items are certainly the easiest feature of a register to learn.

The weight of the evidence then does suggest that language differences do have a certain influence on thought processes. Not necessarily making certain kinds of thinking impossible, but certainly making them more difficult. The real problem in education is likely to be extending pupils' range of control over the potentialities of their own language. This is no easy task because it involves learning new roles and extending the pupils' vision of society.

PSYCHOLOGICAL EVIDENCE

Psychologists now seem to be generally agreed that although some kind of thinking is possible without language, such thought is limited in nature. In particular the more abstract forms of thought seem to be beyond the scope of those who do not possess language. In extreme cases of linguistic deprivation it is much easier to see the limitations imposed on human beings by this lack of language. Deaf children and partially hearing children betray a number of deficiencies in their thinking processes unless through special teaching they have achieved a high degree of proficiency in language. It has been observed that deaf children tend to be inflexible in dealing with novel situations, and find difficulty in organising data, tend to use trial and error techniques in problem solving rather than critical planning; certain kinds of classifying tasks also present great difficulties to the deaf.

When they are older other problems appear: symbolising the future and long-term planning are very difficult; they are less advanced socially and tend to lack imagination in artistic work.

Some researchers might regard it as an invalid procedure to compare the thought processes of deaf children, who have a very serious language deficiency, with institutionalised or working-class children, for whom some would prefer not to talk in terms of 'deficiency' at all, but rather of dialect differences. In America, this controversy has reached the point where some theorists would wish to deny that linguistic factors are at all important in the so-called 'deprivation' problem. The view of these writers, following Hunt, is that what is lacking in the environment of 'deprived' children is concrete physical stimulation. In other words, it is a question of *sensory deprivation* rather than *linguistic deprivation*. If this were true then blind children should present a very considerable educational problem, since they are not only deprived of visual experiences but also handicapped in their movement by their lack of sight. Their sensory deprivation is enormous and their intellectual progress ought to be much inferior to that of deaf children. However, the evidence shows the exact opposite: blind children tend to make similar scores to normal children on I.Q. and attainment tests, whereas deaf children are usually about ten points below the normal I.Q. range and are retarded across the whole range of attainment—mathematics as well as English. Another interesting comparison is to examine social-class differences among deaf children. We have already seen that almost every study of normal children has shown differences in attainment of working-class and middle-class children. But this does *not* hold for deaf children. This would seem to indicate that it is the linguistic–verbal environment of working-class homes which is deficient rather than the sensory stimulation. In this respect the problems of deaf and other kinds of deprived children are similar in kind, though obviously different in degree.

Much of the experimental evidence in this field has been provided by Russian psychologists, most notably of all by Luria. Luria's view, supported by a great deal of experimental evidence (Simon, 1957 and 1963), is that abstracting and generalising verbal activity is the key to the systematisation of experience which plays so vital a part in cognitive activity, and that it is this quality which differentiates not only men from animals, but also normal children from those with various forms of cortical deficiencies. (See Lawton, 1968, chapter iv, for a much fuller discussion of this area.)

We have seen that there is a great deal of evidence that there are differences in middle-class and working-class language. We have also seen that some language differences do have an effect on thought processes. Can we now assume that our own society's social-class differences are important in this way? Or are they completely trivial in nature? We are told, for example, that working-class children have to learn their language against a high 'noise' background in congested living conditions. We are told that in such conditions mothers frequently do not have time, energy or opportunity to give adequate responses to their children's questions. How important are such social differences? The contribution made by Basil Bernstein to this field was that he demonstrated that some social-class language differences were certainly non-trivial in nature. It may be of interest to recount his experimental procedure to illustrate this point. Bernstein made use of tape-recorded discussions on capital punishment in order to test whether the linguistic differences between working-class boys and middle-class boys were of a completely unimportant kind, like the omission of aspirates and other dialect differences, or whether such differences were linked to the *content* of the discussion and to cognitive processes. One method he used to analyse the differences was an adaptation of Dr Goldman-Eisler's technique for evaluating speech by measuring 'hesitation phenomena'. Goldman-Eisler had conducted an experiment in which a number of individuals had been asked to look at some captionless cartoons, first describing exactly what they saw, second summarising what they thought the point or joke was—abstracting the message. She showed that these two kinds of tasks called for quite distinct forms of speech. The more concrete, descriptive speech was 'fluent' in the sense of consisting of relatively unpaused utterances, the hesitation phenomena were short and infrequent. On the other hand, the abstract, summarising speech was associated with much longer pauses and more frequent pauses. She labelled the descriptive passages with a low rate of hesitation 'well organised speech', and the abstract, heavily paused passages were referred to as 'now-organising speech'. The obvious implication was that in the abstract passages a higher level of 'verbal planning' was required, hence more 'thinking time' was used in the form of pauses.

Bernstein predicted that in his discussion group situation the working-class talk about capital punishment would be of a different kind from the middle-class. He predicted that working-class speech would be less heavily paused, that is to say it would be descriptive rather than abstract and would involve less verbal planning. This prediction was found to be correct, and the two kinds of speech could also be distinguished by a number of structural differences. This was a very important development of work on social class and 'educability'. Earlier studies had suggested a relationship between social class and such personality traits as impulsiveness etc., but Bernstein was now able to measure social-class differences objectively. He also provided an interesting theoretical framework to account for these social-class differences. He suggested that speech could be divided into two 'codes': Restricted Code and Elaborated Code. These two codes are seen as functions of different social situations. Restricted Code, which is used by both working-class and middle-class speakers, is the mode of expression adapted for communication between intimates—individuals whose communication is based on a set of 'closely shared identifications', those who have a great deal in common and therefore have no need to make explicit matters which can readily be taken for granted. This Restricted Code will therefore tend to be the means of communicating much of the verbal intercourse in family life; it will also be common among groups of teenagers; or in a very extreme form among the inmates of prison. In all these social relationships the verbal sequences will tend to be of the well-organised, well-learned kind—readymade utterances loosely strung together but expressed fluently. Very little verbal planning is required; it has all been said before. The content of this kind of communication will tend to be concrete, descriptive or narrative rather than abstract. The function of Restricted Code is much more likely to be 'social' than 'intellectual'. Its purpose is to reinforce social relationships rather than to communicate ideas or knowledge, and it is often punctuated by expressions such as 'isn't it?', 'wouldn't you?' etc.—what Bernstein refers to as sociocentric sequences.

The Elaborated Code, on the other hand, might be one of wide variety of speech activities, but will be much less 'predictable' than Restricted Code. The speakers will tend to be in a less close relationship and they will find it necessary therefore to be much more explicit; much less can be taken for granted. Speakers have to select more carefully from a wider range of choices both lexical (single words) and grammatical. The Elaborated Code is not only the medium for the communication of complicated information or novel ideas, it is also the vehicle for individuated responses, adapted for the unique individual rather than geared to group solidarity. Such communication will require a high level of verbal planning, and will need more pauses and longer pauses for its generation. It will tend to consist of more complex grammatical structures—subordinate clauses, adjectives, qualifiers. It will include more expressions of doubt and uncertainty.

Part of Bernstein's theory was that whereas middle-class speakers tend to be able to switch from Restricted Code to Elaborated Code according to the social context (according to *who* is being spoken to or *what* is being communicated), some members of lower working-class families will be limited to a Restricted Code, by reason of their position in the social structure. This has a number of educational implications for such working-class children: there will be various kinds of difficulties of communication between pupils and teachers; there will be difficulty in dealing with abstract concepts which become more necessary as the child gets older; the working-class child will be accustomed to make immediate responses and will tend to display a low level of curiosity—especially in abstract problems. Many of these characteristics will be interpreted by the teacher as bad manners, lack of cooperation, poor application to work, poor interest or motivation.

The Bernstein theory provides us with a much superior springboard for action than vaguer notions of culture clash or poor motivation. It brings us very much nearer to possibilities of solving the problem. My own research in this field was partly a duplication of Bernstein's discussion group situation, and partly an extension of the inquiry into other kinds of language situation (see Lawton, 1963, 1964, 1968). I found that the characteristics of a Restricted Code carried over into the writing of working-class boys who found written expression on abstract topics especially difficult. Perhaps the most interesting result, however, came from the last part of my study, in which working-class and middle-class boys (matched for intelligence) participated in an individual interview situation. They were given the opportunity of expressing themselves on some very easy and straightforward topics, for example *describing* their earlier experiences of schools and teachers, but they were also asked questions on quite *abstract* matters such as 'What is the purpose of education?' or 'Why are criminals locked up?' This was designed as the crucial situation in the experiment, in which it might have been expected that greatest differences would emerge between the working-class and middle-class boys. In fact, although there were some differences between the groups in this situation, they were smaller than the social-class differences in either the written work or in the discussion situation.

My interpretation of this was an optimistic one: when the working-class boys were in a situation with a friendly and sympathetic interviewer in which they were *forced* to make an abstract response or remain silent, they showed that they could communicate this kind of abstract information, although they obviously experienced some coding difficulty and were not particularly happy. But unlike the written tasks and the discussion in which they had some choice of action, in the interview they either had to respond or undergo the distasteful experience of remaining completely silent. They chose to respond as best they could and their replies were not very different from those of the middle-class boys either in form or in content. This led me to the conclusion that, at least with this particular sample of working-class boys, the potentiality was present of using an elaborated code, but when given a choice, working-class boys would not exercise that option but would tend to revert to the kind of language most familiar to them, i.e. narrative, descriptive, anecdotal material. In other words it may be that working-class pupils lack practice and therefore facility in this kind of elaborated code expression, but they may *not* lack the potentiality. One of the things that Bernstein showed was that this ability was not associated with I.Q.; I would claim that this part of my study has shown that working-class boys of only average I.Q. can come very close to an elaborated code usage when the context unambiguously requires it and when they have no satisfactory 'easier' alternative. This may well have important implications for classroom organisation and grouping procedures. It would seem to support those who wish to make learning groups much more flexible by team teaching etc. I would suggest that the most important need for some children is to have the opportunity for regular face to face contact with a teacher on an individual basis, similar to the tutorial sessions arranged at some public schools. This may be difficult to organise but it is by no means impossible and it may be of crucial importance.

Are there any other signs that might justify an optimistic attitude towards this problem? The Newsom Report not only focused attention on this problem but also made some constructive suggestions, for example, that all teachers should study sociology, and that every teacher should be concerned with the pupils' ability to communicate:

> There are . . . some objectives which can and ought deliberately to be pursued through every part of the curriculum. Very

high in this list we should place improvement in powers of speech: not simply improvement in the quality and clearness of enunciation, . . . but a general extension of vocabulary, and with it, a surer command over the structures of spoken English and the expression of ideas. That means seizing the opportunity of every lesson, in engineering or housecraft or science as well as in English, to provide material for discussion—genuine discussion, not mere testing by teacher's question and pupil's answer.

This would seem to be very sound advice, but some teachers, especially perhaps those not completely committed to a middle-class way of life, will be uneasy about their moral or social right to interfere with the pupils' subculture by attempting to change their language. This is a very important point. It is essential that any child's language, however unsatisfactory it may appear to the teacher, should be respected by the teacher as a valid form of expression. It is the only means by which many pupils can communicate with their own family and neighbourhood friends; a pupil should therefore never be made to feel that the way in which he speaks is 'wrong' or 'ugly'. There is no scientific justification for either of these judgments. At the same time, if we want pupils to benefit more fully from the education which they are offered, they must be encouraged to extend their range of control over language. There will come a time when the teacher will perhaps want to indicate that certain kinds of expression are not *appropriate* in certain contexts, but the pupil should also be left with the clear impression that other forms of English are perfectly appropriate for situations more familiar than the classroom context. Any form of teaching is an 'intrusion' into or 'interference' with the life of a child, but that is what education is all about. What must be ensured is that any intrusion is a justifiable one—unfortunately teachers in the past have tended to make intrusions on very shaky grounds, criticising children for dialect pronunciation or trivial points of etiquette rather than concentrating on extending the child's experience in ways which would have important cognitive consequences. But if we take a falsely romantic view of working-class language, or of working-class life in general, we not only ignore the possibility of individual development but also we will abandon thousands of young people to a traditional working-class socialisation process which will prepare them for a world which may no longer exist by the time they are adults. Already routine manual jobs are disappearing rapidly and the jobs which will become available will require a different kind of person—a person with a far higher control over language and a higher level of symbolic comprehension. This is not necessarily making them into middle-class children, it is simply adequately equipping them for a place in the second half of the twentieth century.

REFERENCES

BELL, R. (1966), 'Pidgin languages', *New Society*, **8**, no. 209, 481–3.

BERNSTEIN, B. B. (1962), 'Linguistic codes, hesitation phenomena and intelligence', *Language and Speech*, **5**.

BERNSTEIN, B. B. (1965), 'A socio-linguistic approach to social learning', in *Penguin Survey of the Social Sciences,* ed. J. B. Gould, Penguin Books.

DAVIS, A. (1948), *Social Class Influences upon Learning*, Harvard University Press.

DENNIS, N. *et al.* (1956), *Coal is Our Life,* Eyre & Spottiswoode.

DIXON, R. (1966), *Language*.

FIRTH, J. R. (1935), 'On Sociological linguistics', in Hymes (1964), see below.

GOLDMAN-EISLER, F. (1961), 'Hesitation and information in speech', in *Proceedings of 4th London Symposium on Information Theory.*

GUMPERZ, J. (1961), 'Speech variation and the study of Indian civilisation', in Hymes (1964).

HALLIDAY, M. *et al.* (1964), *The Linguistic Sciences and Language Teaching,* London, Longmans.

HUNT, J. MCV. (1961), *Intelligence and Experience,* New York, Ronald.

HYMES, DELL, ed. (1964), *Language in Culture and Society,* New York, Harper.

KLEIN, J. (1965), *Samples from English Cultures,* Routledge.

KLUCKHOHN, F. (1961), *Variations in Value Orientations,* Chicago, Row, Peterson.

LAWTON, D. (1963), 'Social class differences in language development: a study of some samples of written work', *Language and Speech*, **6**, part 3.

LAWTON, D. (1964), 'Social class language differences in group discussions', *Language and Speech*, **7**, part 3.

LAWTON, D. (1968), *Social Class, Language and Education,* Routledge.

LURIA, A. R. (1961), *The Role of Speech in the Regulation of Normal and Abnormal Behaviour,* Pergamon.

PETERS, R. S. (1958), *The Concept of Motivation,* Routledge.

SAPIR, E. (1921), *Language,* New York; reprinted Hart-Davis, Harvest Books, 1963.

SAPIR, E. (1961), 'Culture, language and personality', *Selected Essays,* eds. D. G. Mandelbaum and L. A. Berkeley.

SIMON, B., Ed. (1957), *Psychology in the Soviet Union,* London, Routledge.

WHORF, B. L. (1956), *Language, Thought and Reality,* ed., J. B. Carroll, New York, Wiley; London, Chapman & Hall.

YOUNG, M. and WILLMOTT, P. (1957), *Family and Kinship in East London,* Routledge.

13

Social class, values and behaviour in school*

Barry Sugarman

A third approach to the study of family, class and education in depth is the analysis of basic value orientations and of their influence on educability. In this chapter Dr Sugarman begins with a brief discussion of the sociological concept of culture. He then proceeds to discuss the subcultures of a simple, two-level model of social class with particular reference to belief systems. Significant social-class differences in basic attitudes towards time, towards activity, and towards individualism are discussed, and the interrelationship with socialisation patterns, the development of achievement motivation, and of language development are also noted.

CULTURE

When we compare *homo sapiens* with other animal species, we see that man is found living in a far greater variety of environments than is any other animal. He lives in equatorial heat and polar cold, in dense forests and in sandy deserts, on mountain sides and on open plains. Not surprisingly, man has many different modes of living. He is found as hunter and as farmer, as herdsman and as fisherman, as villager and city-dweller. Many and varied are the ways in which man has adapted himself to his environment.

Yet differences in environment alone are not sufficient to explain his varied ways of living. In *similar* environments different groups of men have created quite different ways of life. The climate and topography of southern California is very much like that of peninsular Italy, but life in Los Angeles is very different from Naples; the physical environment of Israel is much like that of surrounding Arab countries, but life is drastically different on opposite sides of the border; the same is true of West Germany and Poland. And so we

* This paper was specially written for this volume.

9

could go on. Again, the physical environment has not changed significantly in the last few centuries and yet in Britain, America and many other countries, the way of life has changed beyond recognition.

Any account of the variations in the way that men live must therefore take account of more than the physical environments in which they live. It must take account of the 'culture' of the group, referring to the basic essentials in the way of life that characterises this group of people and which is passed on from one generation to another by *learning*. The young swallow is born already possessing the skills and knowledge necessary for its basic survival. By genetic inheritance it has at birth instincts that tell it when and where to migrate, how to find food, build a nest, select a mate, protect its young. The human infant, by contrast, is born helpless and has to learn from parents and other older members of the group how to conduct itself.

The term 'culture' is used in two closely related senses. We talk of man having culture, while other animals lack it, and we talk too of *the* English culture or *the* Samoan culture. What we have here is a more general and a more specific application of the same idea. Culture, whether in its general or specific sense, is *learned* and it is *shared* by members of the same social group or community. When describing a specific culture, what one is trying to do is to characterise the way of life of a whole group of people or a whole society, ignoring the personal peculiarities of individuals. Thus it is possible to describe 'how they live' in Samoa, in a Welsh mountain village, or in a London suburb; the daily routine, the customs, rules, beliefs, rituals and so forth. Three main areas of a culture are usually distinguished. One is the *material culture* and technology, including the kinds of houses people live in, the kinds of tools, implements and weapons they use, the clothes and adornments they wear. Another area of any culture consists of their *values and normative rules,* governing what they consider right and wrong. The third main area concerns the *ideas and beliefs* these people have about how the world works, that is, their notions of science and metaphysics.

Infants and other new members of a society learn its culture as a condition of being accepted as full members. They learn to think and act as other members do, though within these broad patterns there usually remains scope for some individuality. Cultural patterns are thus learned and shared within each society. At one and the same time, they give the members a common frame of reference or basis for mutual understanding and differentiate them from the members of other societies. The term 'cultural variability' refers specifically to this fact—that the cultures differ, sometimes quite greatly, from each other. Variations in material culture are readily observable. We find cultures where tools are almost unknown, where people gather the fruits of nature as they come—fruits, nuts and roots. We find others where hunting and/or fishing provides a more abundant livelihood and there is some technology for making weapons or traps and knowledge of fire, cooking and the processing of the inedible parts of the animal. Societies with settled agriculture, where plants and/or animals have been domesticated, represent a most important stage of evolution, for here surplus produce is possible and so part of the population can be released from the production of food to specialise in other crafts producing comforts, such as fancy clothing, pottery, jewellery, art works and ritual.

Variations between cultures in the prevailing norms of what is good and bad conduct are of special interest to us. Some examples of this phenomenon are common knowledge among those who have travelled abroad. What is considered perfectly proper holiday dress for a woman in England is considered indecent in Spain and southern Italy; what is considered polite friendliness from a man towards a woman in England will be considered intolerably 'forward' throughout most of the Middle East and will be considered 'reserved' in North America. Norms of acceptable conduct between men and women thus vary in these sorts of ways. Behaviour on the sports field that the Englishman considers unsportsmanlike may be considered quite acceptable elsewhere in the world, and the behaviour of the Englishman in protesting about it considered prudish and 'sissy'. Again, the English institution of the queue is unknown abroad. What the English abroad regard as appalling rudeness, the pushing and shoving to get on a Paris or a New York bus, is normal and acceptable behaviour to people brought up in these other cultures.

'Norms' and 'values', though closely related, must be distinguished from each other. *Norms* define certain kinds of behaviour as approved or disapproved. *Values* are more abstract notions underlying norms, notions of the desirable or what should be desired. One value is likely to be exemplified in several norms. For example, the value of 'respect for privacy' might be exemplified in a norm against entering into immediate conversation with strangers, as well as in the lack of censure against those who build fences around their homes. Because of this element of abstraction and inference involved in defining values, it may be that the outsider sociologist understands the values of a certain culture better (at least in the sense of *explicitly* understanding) than do most of the members who have been brought up in that culture. But that could not usually be said where understanding the norms is concerned.

Cultures also vary in the beliefs that prevail, referring here to beliefs about the nature of the world rather than beliefs about what is *morally* right or wrong. This is most easily illustrated by reference to variations over historical time. In medieval times throughout most of Europe men believed that the earth was flat and hence that if one travelled too far one would fall over the edge; they believed that the sun revolved round the earth. In these same countries today virtually no one believes in the flat earth theory and no educated person believes that the sun revolves round the earth.

THE SUBCULTURES OF SOCIAL CLASSES[1]

In most societies it is found that the members are stratified into different status groups or social classes. They classify each other in some such terms and sociologists have seized upon this fact as an aid to analysis. Correlating social class, conveniently measured in modern societies by occupation, with customs and norms, it has been found that it is helpful to think of certain subcultures as typical of different social classes. Of course, there are overlaps where families lie close to the borderline or where they are in the process of changing their social class, but on the whole the notion of class subcultures has been found attractive and helpful by sociologists. People who grow up in one social class rather than another learn a subtle complex of assumptions, ideas, tastes and norms which they share with those who grew up in the same social class but not with those who grew up in a different one. Class equals tend to have the same ideas about many things such as what does and does not constitute good table manners, proper dress, the right way to speak to adults, a proper bedtime for children, which things take priority over doing homework and which do not, and so forth. Those of another social class or home background are likely to have different ideas about these things. We must pay special attention to the manner in which the characteristically different life experiences of different social classes result in their members developing views of life, with different images of the world or assumptions about how it operates, and different values or

1. The following section draws quite heavily on J. Klein, *Samples from English Cultures* (1965).

normative orientations concerning preferred and prohibited forms of conduct.

For the purposes of this discussion it should suffice merely to suggest the outlines of the subject. We shall simplify it by using a breakdown into just two classes: a *higher status* level in which the middle class swamps the much smaller upper class and a *lower status* level, the two corresponding very roughly to the manual versus non-manual workers dichotomy.

The subculture of the higher status level involves a wider knowledge about a wider range of subjects than that of the lower status level. It is not just that the higher status person has more highbrow interests and perhaps does *The Times* crossword. It is also that the higher status person knows more about the matters that actually affect the whole population, such as the working of the educational system as it affects their children, taxation, birth control, politics because they tend to read more magazines, the more 'serious' or informative newspapers and listen to more of the informative radio and TV programmes. Higher status persons also express more interest in politics than those of lower status and more interest and concern over their children's school careers. They are less often 'Don't knows' than those of lower status. As well as being better informed the higher status person is more prepared to appraise the sources of his information and prevent himself from being cheated either financially or intellectually. He is far more likely than the lower status individual to be a subscriber to *Which?*. He is also more sophisticated in his understanding of cause and effect in the world around him and in his insight into the motivations of people.

Those who grow up in the higher status level start to acquire skills in the use of language and the more complex forms of conceptual thought even before they begin school, while the children of lower status families usually do not. With this handicap the latter perform more poorly in school than their peers from higher status homes, especially on tests set in verbal form. This theory is put forward by Basil Bernstein (1965), who argues that this handicap consists not in the smaller vocabulary of the lower status child but rather in the way he combines his words into sentences. Again, it is not just that his grammar is poor but more that he is restricted to short, descriptive, stereotyped and often incomplete sentences. He is unable to express meanings of any complexity or subtlety, to indicate how one event depends on others, results from others, precipitates others; to convey intentions, motives or feelings other than the most obvious. He cannot express these shades of meaning and in his social milieu he does not hear them expressed by others. They exist for him only in the world of school, in the world of books and those mass media that he selectively ignores. That is to say that they do not exist for him. To those who come from the lower status subculture, meanings expressed in this more subtle and complex language of subordinate clauses and qualifiers are alien and incomprehensible. If this is so, it implies that the experience of life is profoundly different in the two subcultures.

Those who live in the subculture of the lower status group, given their less adequate intellectual comprehension of the world around them, tend to find the world extremely confusing, uncertain and with little patterning or regularity. Not only does it seem beyond the grasp of a person's mind at the present but he cannot see the possibility of reducing some part of this complexity to order and understanding how it works. Far from being a predictable affair, the environment is constantly throwing unexpected threats in his face. This is equally true for the physical and the social world but the latter is more relevant to our present concern. In the experience of lower status people there probably is more impulsive behaviour, certainly in the behaviour of parents to their children. On top of this, behaviour that is actually quite patterned and predictable does not seem so to them because of their generally poor level of comprehension. Hence one of the differences between higher and lower status subcultures lies in the degree or orderliness and patterning which the world seems to them to possess.

Higher status people do not believe in just contemplating the patterns of nature, though; they believe that one can and should influence them. Man can master his environment, he can control events for his own benefit. He can dam rivers, make fortresses, cultivate crops, manufacture products, raise loans, write to his M.P., organise pressure groups. And to do so is laudable. Among lower status people, daunted by the mysteries of nature and society and lacking confidence in the possibility of achievement, a more fatalistic outlook prevails. Max Weber (1958) and others have held that the value of activism emerged on a socially significant scale only with the Protestant Reformation and has been transmitted from one generation to the next among the middle classes.

In the subculture of the lower status level there is seemingly less concern with the possible long-term consequences of their present actions than one finds among higher status people. Those of lower status live more for the present, the future is not very important to them. Even in so far as they are aware of future consequences they are not as likely as those of higher status to let this affect their present behaviour. In the latter background it is taken for granted that a good future requires some sacrifice now and that this deferment of gratification is both prudent and meritorious (Schneider and Lysgaard, 1953). Children from higher ranking homes learn to ration out their sweets rather than eating them all at once, save their pocket money, refrain from being rude to people they do not like or from expressing other socially unacceptable feelings such as anger, boredom or impatience; they give up valuable time that could be spent watching TV or reading comics to do homework. It is not any specific behaviour pattern that is significant but the general characteristic of taking into account the *future* consequences of present actions and letting them influence what one does now.

Particularly at the age of adolescence and early adulthood (before marriage) is there a contrast between the perspectives embodied in the subcultures of higher and very low status groups. In the very low group there is considerable tolerance for the young if they want to abandon school work and have a good time now, since there is a generally held assumption among these people that adult life is destined to be a hard struggle so they might as well enjoy themselves while they can: 'You're only young once.' They do not see any future pay-off for sacrifices made in youth. To them, unlike the higher group, the future is fixed and cannot be changed so far as they can see.

There is a significant congruence between the general emphasis on future orientation found in the higher status group and the career pattern which these young people expect to follow. Whereas the manual worker reaches full earning capacity quite quickly depending on his level of skill, and then remains on a plateau, the white-collar worker proceeds more gradually but may continue to increase his earning power throughout his working life. The rate at which it increases varies and is affected by the way he acts. He can speed it up by studying for extra qualifications, or by demonstrating to his boss an attitude of outstanding dedication, or by just working harder. Knowing this is likely to reinforce quite strongly the belief in future orientation, or deferred gratification, among those oriented to middle-class careers.

We have now examined several themes that differentiate between the basic outlook on life characterising those who occupy higher and lower status levels. These were: knowledge and comprehension of the world around, verbal and conceptual sophistication, assumptions about the patterning and controllability of the environment, and the values of activism *versus* fatalism and future *versus* present orientation.

Let us now turn to consider how the class-related differences in outlook on life which we have discussed may result from differences between social classes in the patterns of family life. Specifically we shall examine various aspects of the parent–child relationship as it differs between higher and lower status families.

For a child to have a high level of linguistic facility implies that at least one of his parents (or perhaps a substitute parent such as a grandparent) has spent a good deal of time in talking to him, and has treated him as a 'person' in the sense of someone whose questions and ideas, though naïve, are to be taken seriously. Indeed, this kind of child-centredness (or intellectual indulgence of the child) seems to be an important element of the higher status background in its own right. It may well be that this is the real factor underlying the often-remarked association between size of family and parents' social status, size of family and child's academic success. Not only are parents who successfully restrict the size of their families likely to have more characteristics of the higher status subculture, but they also have the time and inclination to give a lot of attention to their children.

In the higher status family, parents treat their children less impulsively and this helps them to grow up as less impulsive individuals. The child is not spontaneously clouted for doing something annoying and/or forbidden, though he or she may well be physically punished. The difference between higher and lower status families seems to lie less in the frequency of physical punishment than in the choice of situations in which to apply it and the atmosphere in which it is applied. The higher status parent does not punish just because the child has made a mess or a noise or some other kind of nuisance; he or she punishes because the child has done something which, if permitted to develop, would lead to an undesired behaviour pattern (Kohn, 1959). The factor of parental consistency is worth special mention. It is essential to the higher status type of parent–child relationship because we have postulated that this involves training the child to follow *rules* of conduct. Rules necessarily imply consistency. Parental (rule-governed) consistency is a necessary condition for the child to learn similar behaviour. Deferred gratification does not pay and will not be learned unless the future reward can be confidently expected. Parental inconsistency from one time to another, sometimes rewarding and sometimes not, prevents the development of a future orientation.

Higher status parents set higher standards for their children, or at least they expect things of them at earlier ages than other parents. Moreover they carefully grade the standards of achievement that they set their children, so that they are high enough to stretch them but not so high as to induce despair. In this way these children get their motivation to try hard at a wide range of 'problems' or 'challenges' (not necessarily competitive ones) such as those presented in the classroom, which leave other children cold and uninterested. Higher status parents are less authoritarian than lower ones and permit their children more say in decision-making. The father and mother also share power between themselves instead of one dominating as is more usual among the lower status families. Strodtbeck has shown that authoritarian fathers tend to have sons who are low on the value of activism (Strodtbeck, 1961).

To summarise, it is suggested that among the features differentiating the parent–child relationship in the high status family from that in the low status family are the following: the relationship between parents and children is consistent in the standards of conduct which are defined in terms of general rules; it is child-centred in that much time is spent on the care of the child and in 'taking him seriously'; it is non-impulsive in the sense of rewarding and punishing not on impulse but only after considering the likely effect on the child's character development; it involves standards of conduct and performance that get progressively higher, but not arbitrary demands for instant obedience by an all-powerful parent.

SOCIAL CLASS, VALUE ORIENTATIONS AND BEHAVIOUR IN SCHOOL

Is it possible to measure the extent to which people hold values? In particular, is there any relationship between the holding of these values and the behaviour of pupils in school? In this section we shall look at some findings of studies directed at these questions, including one by the present writer (Sugarman, 1966).

Attempts to specify values that characterise a middle-class culture or way of life may be traced back to Max Weber. He saw the middle-class entrepreneur of the industrial revolution as essentially different from earlier kinds of businessmen. This new 'spirit of capitalism' involved a moral compulsion to hard work and a sober, calculating

9*

approach to all decisions based on a long-term view, together with immense confidence in one's own ability to make and move things. Earlier forms of business enterprise had depended, according to Weber, less on these qualities and more on the use of force, political intrigue and impulsive decisions. Although the middle class is no longer based on private enterprise to its former extent, it may be that some of its more generalised values are still found among a largely salaried middle class. Florence Kluckhohn (1961) has characterised the values of the American middle class in terms of a fivefold conceptual scheme. Human nature is assumed to be a mixture of good and evil; man is believed to have mastery over nature; the future is heavily emphasised relative to present and past; activism is preferred to meditation; familism is rejected for individualism. Let us assume that, in these broad terms, English middle-class culture is similar to its American counterpart.

A study by Strodtbeck (1961) in New Haven (Connecticut) found that pupils who were over- and under-achievers relative to their I.Q.s differed significantly in their responses to various values statements. These fell into two sets which he identified with 'mastery over nature' and 'individualism'. A study by Rosen (1956) in the same city found that these values were related to whether or not pupils aspired to go to college but not to their school marks. (Unlike Strodtbeck he did not hold I.Q. constant.) Another study conducted by Jayasuriya (1954) in London tried to measure *three* of the Kluckhohn value dimensions, adding future orientation. As it happened, my study found this new variable (with certain modifications) to be the most predictive of all. In his own study, Jayasuriya did not correlate values with academic achievements but with their social-class origins. He found that middle-class boys actually did score more highly on average than the working-class boys on the supposedly middle-class values. However, working-class boys in grammar schools had values that approximated the middle-class average and middle-class boys in secondary modern schools had values that approximated the working-class average.

The values items in the questionnaire used for the present study were based on those used by Jayasuriya and suggested by Kluckhohn. One value suggested by her and others as characteristically middle class is a strong *orientation to the future*. To score highly on this value someone answering the questionnaire would have to say 'disagree' to statements such as 'There is no sense in worrying about the future so long as you are doing all right now'. And they would have to agree to statements such as 'You have to give up having a good time now to do well later on', and 'Most times it is better to be tactful and diplomatic instead of saying just what you think'. A second value postulated to be middle class and used here is the belief that one can and should try to *master the environment*. To score highly on this value one would have to reject statements like 'One must learn to take life as it is without always trying to improve things', and 'The greatest source of happiness in life is to be satisfied with whatever you have'. The third value used in this study is *individualism*. To score highly on this dimension one would have to reject statements like 'It is best to be like everyone else and not stand out from the rest' and endorse others like 'Nowadays you have to look out for yourself before helping your parents'. This collection of sixteen 'agree–disagree' items formed part of the questionnaire that was given to the entire fourth year at four boys' secondary schools in Greater London (two secondary moderns, one grammar and one comprehensive school). Some of the principal findings were as follows:

'Over-achievers' or pupils whose academic work is better than most of those with similar I.Q.s tend to have high aggregate scores on these values while under-achievers tend to have low scores. (However, this is not true in the grammar school studied, where even the under-achievers had very high values scores.) Of the three dimensions of values used here, future orientation seems to be the one most strongly related to achievement when I.Q. is controlled (except in the grammar school again).

TABLE 13.1. *Achievement and values (combined).*

| Value scores | Achievement relative to I.Q. | | | | | |
	Over		Middle		Under	
Low	(0·20)	30	(0·29)	50	(0·44)	64
Middle	(0·34)	51	(0·39)	66	(0·29)	42
High	(0·45)	67	(0·32)	55	(0·28)	41
		148		171		147

P<0·001   C = 0·21

Teachers' ratings of the boys' general conduct is similarly related to aggregate values scores especially for future orientation. This relationship between conduct and values, however, is not as strong as that between achievement and values.

TABLE 13.2.   *Conduct and values (combined).*

Value scores	Conduct ratings					
	Good		Middle		Poor	
Low	(0·25)	37	(0·33)	54	(0·37)	80
Middle	(0·34)	52	(0·29)	47	(0·36)	78
High	(0·41)	62	(0·38)	62	(0·26)	57
		151		163		215

P<0·02   C = 0·15

Father's occupation bears only a tenuous relationship to son's values for this sample. Combining all schools together, there is a slight relationship between father's occupation and son's aggregate value score, but it is not statistically significant. Of the three components, only future orientation is significantly related to father's occupation.

TABLE 13.3.   *Father's occupation and future orientation.*

Future orientation score	Father's occupation							
	Unskilled manual		Skilled manual		Routine manual and foremen		Prof. managerial and Med./Big bus.	
Low	(0·43)	42	(0·40)	56	(0·38)	51	(0·30)	34
Middle	(0·42)	41	(0·29)	40	(0·33)	45	(0·38)	43
High	(0·14)	14	(0·30)	42	(0·29)	39	(0·32)	37
		97		138		135		114

P<0·05   C = 0·17

Thus, these boys' values are less closely related to their social class *origins* than they are to their *present* behaviour (notably academic achievement) and hence to their career prospects and *future* social-class position. This is what one would expect in a society with social mobility between generations. This is not to say that the homes of these pupils do not influence their values though, for we find that the intellectual quality of the home background is clearly and significantly related. This feature of the home was estimated from pupils' answers to questions about how many books are in their homes, what newspapers their parents take and whether their parents ever take or send them to plays, concerts and museums.

TABLE 13.4.   *Intellectual quality of home and values.*

	Intellectual quality of home					
Values scores	*High*		*Middle*		*Low*	
Low	(0·23)	43	(0·34)	73	(0·43)	59
Middle	(0·31)	57	(0·32)	70	(0·38)	53
High	(0·46)	85	(0·34)	74	(0·19)	26
		185		217		138

P<0·001   C = 0·22

These findings have implications for the problem of differential educability. It is not social class *per se* that results in the deteriorating performance of working-class pupils relative to their middle-class peers of similar ability. 'Social class' is just a shorthand way of referring to a complex of factors that are sometimes correlated with occupation. One of these factors that has a concrete effect on school achievement is the intellectual richness of the home background, as we have seen. We can go further and suggest one of the ways in which this causal factor may operate, namely through its influence on the values of the young. The kind of home in which children grow up affects both the values they hold (concerning how one should behave in general) and also the way they actually do behave in school. It seems that differences in the intellectual quality of the home actually *cause* differences in the values and behaviour of the children who grow up there. It is not so clear, however, whether differences in values *cause* differences in behaviour, or the reverse, or whether both are just different aspects of one common phenomenon such as the tendency to think and act in a future-orientated way.

Even if differences in values are not to be taken as a cause of differential educability, though, they clearly represent a significant dimension of the problem. Just to know with some confidence that the under-achiever *is* lacking in these values is a significant increase in our knowledge. It suggests, for one thing, that if the school is to equalise opportunities it may need to influence pupils on the level of their generalised value-commitments. How this might be done is not easy to say, but at least the nature of the problem is clarified.

REFERENCES

BERNSTEIN, B. (1965), 'A socio-linguistic approach to social learning', in *Penguin Survey of the Social Sciences,* ed. J. Gould, Penguin Books.

JAYASURIYA, D. L. (1954), 'A study of adolescent ambition, level of aspiration and achievement motivation', unpublished Ph.D. thesis, University of London.

KLUCKHOHN, FLORENCE R. and STRODTBECK, F. L. (1961), *Variations in Value Orientations,* Chicago, Row, Peterson.

KOHN, M. L. (1959), 'Social class and the exercise of parental authority', *American Sociological Review,* **24,** 352–6.

ROSEN, BERNARD L. (1956), 'The achievement syndrome', *American Sociological Review,* **21** (April), 203–11.

SCHNEIDER, LOUIS and LYSGAARD, S. (1953), 'The deferred gratification pattern', *American Sociological Review,* **18** (April), 142–9.

STRODTBECK, F. L. (1961), 'Family integration, values and achievement', in *Education, Economy and Society,* eds. A. H. Halsey, J. Floud and C. A. Anderson, Collier-Macmillan.

SUGARMAN, B. N. (1966), 'Social class and values as related to achievement and conduct in school', *Sociological Review,* **14** (Nov.), 287–301.

WEBER, MAX (1958), *The Protestant Ethic and the Spirit of Capitalism,* New York, Scribner.

14

Social class and family life*

Olive Banks

The purpose of Part Five has been to review recent attempts to explore the relationship of family, class and education at a micro level. Professor Cohen has suggested the importance of 'parental ideology', the adjustments to the work situation made by fathers, for example, which may affect their perception of the value of education for their children. Dr Lawton outlines the key contribution of linguistic development in educability, and Dr Sugarman has indicated the possible existence of social-class differences in basic attitudes towards time, activity and individualism. It may be that a social-class gradient in the possession of these basic value orientations has a fundamental influence upon both parental ideology and linguistic development, we do not yet know. What is clear, however, is that all three aspects of the home motivational environment interpenetrate, and that they seem to operate through class-linked child-rearing practices, an area already touched upon in several chapters and discussed more fully by Professor Musgrove in Chapter 10. In this concluding paper, Dr Banks briefly reviews some of the principal sources of social class variations in attitudes and values, going on to consider patterns of child-rearing, the heterogeneity of the social classes, and the extreme complexity of analysis at this level. Dr Banks's contribution thus summarises many of the issues raised in Part Five and concludes that while we must not ignore the influence of school and peer group, future research into the relationship of family, class and education will need to focus on the mechanisms of socialisation, on an interdisciplinary basis.

* Reprinted from *The Sociology of Education*, Batsford, 1968, pp. 102–10, by kind permission of the author and the publisher.

The attempt to explain how it is that working-class families hold different values from middle-class families, and behave in different ways towards their children, depends essentially upon the development of a theory to explain how their different life chances and life experiences predispose them towards different views of the world around them and of their place in it. This problem has always interested sociologists, and there is no space here to review all the work, both theoretical and empirical, which has been done in this sphere. All that will be attempted is to draw attention to those aspects of it which appear to be particularly relevant to the problem of achievement. In general, attention has been focused upon three different aspects of working-class life, all of them to some degree interrelated. They may be briefly summarised as material life chances, working conditions, and opportunities for status.

Traditionally, those in working-class or manual jobs have earned less than those in middle-class or non-manual occupations. Moreover this is still largely true, in spite of a rise in the standard of living of the working classes, and some overlap between certain highly paid workers and certain types of non-manual employment. Working-class employment has also been characteristically insecure. Not only has it been more liable to unemployment during periods of depression, but also few manual workers are employed on more than a weekly basis. This contrasts with the typical monthly, quarterly or even permanent tenure of most non-manual jobs. Manual workers also have less chance of advancement in their jobs.

Within the work situation itself there are also important differences which may have implications for working-class attitudes. Manual work is frequently carried out in unpleasant working conditions. It may be dangerous, dirty, or physically strenuous. Frequently it involves long hours, or shift work. Often it is less intrinsically rewarding, and perceived as such, even when it is highly paid. It is also less likely to involve authority, responsibility or power. Finally, many studies have shown that manual work is low in the prestige or status hierarchy of all modern societies.[1]

It is reasonable to expect that these radically different life and work experiences will be reflected in the attitudes of the working classes both to work itself and to other aspects of their lives, and there have been many attempts to show that this does indeed occur. It has been

1. G. Routh, *Occupation and Pay in Great Britain 1906–1960*, Cambridge U.P., 1965. See also J. H. Goldthorpe *et al.* 'The affluent worker and the thesis of embourgeoisement', *Sociology*, 1 (1967), 12–31.

argued, for example, that the working class will value different aspects in their working situation, prizing such qualities as security more than other aspects of the job, and there are a number of studies which show that this is the case. In a widely based international comparison using national sources, Inkeles has shown that those in higher-status occupations report more job satisfaction and are more likely to want a job which is interesting and stimulating. They are also less likely to want security or certainty in a job and are more willing to take risks to get promotion.[1]

The lack of security, combined with lack of opportunity, are also likely to influence the expectations of the manual worker. He may well lower his aspirations to what seems meaningful or reasonable in his circumstances, and this may influence his hopes not only for himself but also for his child. Many studies have in fact shown that the working classes are less ambitious for their children.

The deprivation of the manual worker, both in his working situation and in his material standard of living, is also seen as profoundly influencing his view both of himself and of the world around him. In particular he is less likely to share in the middle class, achieving orientation described by Kluckhohn. His own lack of power to alter his situation, his uncertainty about the future, his sense of insecurity, will, it is suggested, lead him to see the world as dominated by luck or chance,[2] rather than under his control. He is not likely to spend time planning for a future which is not only unpredictable but largely out of his hands. He will naturally gravitate towards the getting-by attitude described by Kahl, and he will do this because of his own experiences in coming to terms with his own environment. Neither is he likely to share in the individualistic approach of the middle classes. 'Getting ahead' for the manual worker 'must rest in the progressive increase of the rewards which they gain *from their present economic role*'.[3] For this reason he is likely to emphasise collective or group mobility through trade union representation and trade union power.

The low status ascribed to manual work, and especially to unskilled work, may also influence the worker's own self-esteem. He may

1. A. Inkeles, 'Industrial man: the relation of status to experience perception and value', *American Journal of Sociology*, July 1960. See also E. L. Lyman, 'Occupation differences in the value attached to work', *American Journal of Sociology*, 1961.
2. See, for example, A. W. Gouldner, *Patterns of Industrial Bureaucracy*, Routledge, 1955, pp. 117–36; and F. M. Katz, 'The meaning of success. Some differences in value systems of social classes', *Journal of Social Psychology*, 62 (1964).
3. Goldthorpe *et al.*, *op. cit.*

accept the opinion of others as to his lack of ability and may transfer this to his children. High ambition in such circumstances may appear as inappropriate or even absurd. Parents with such an attitude may not only fail to encourage their children to achieve; they may not even recognise the achievement of their children unless it is drawn to their attention.[1] Recent work on the child's self-concept of ability has suggested not only that it is related to achievement but that parents are an important source of the child's self-image.[2]

It has also been suggested that the material, power and status deprivation of the working-class parent will affect his actual handling of the child. Kohn, for example, specifically relates parent–child relationships to differences in the conditions of life, and particularly the occupational conditions of the different social classes. It is, he suggests, the greater degree of self-direction present in middle-class occupations which leads them to value self-direction in their children and so to encourage in their children such qualities as curiosity and self-control. Working-class parents, on the other hand, stress such qualities as honesty, obedience and neatness, because in their working lives what is mainly required of them is that they should follow explicit rules laid down by someone in authority.[3] A small study by Roy also suggests that the home environment itself may be a factor in working-class disciplinary practices. She found an increase in the permissiveness of child-rearing attitudes as the number of rooms in the house increased.[4]

The most thorough-going attempt to relate the occupational situation of the family to the socialisation of the child is the recent study by McKinley, which combines an extensive review of the literature with data of his own, based on a questionnaire given to adolescent boys. As a result of his own work and his interpretation of research findings in this field, McKinley argues that 'the greater punitiveness and the more common rejection of the child by parents in the urban lower classes is a consequence of the parent's greater frustration and stronger feelings of threat. The parent's aggression is

1. See, for example, the descriptions of working-class parents in B. Jackson and D. Marsden, *Education and the Working Class,* Routledge, 1962, p. 88.
2. W. B. Brookover and D. Gottlieb, *A Sociology of Education,* New York, American Book Co., 2nd ed., 1964, pp. 468–77.
3. M. L. Kohn, 'Social class and parent–child relationships: an interpretation', *American Journal of Sociology,* Jan. 1963.
4. K. Roy, 'Parents' attitudes toward their children', *Journal of Home Economics,* 62 (1950), quoted in W. C. Becker, 'Consequences of different kinds of parental discipline', in *Review of Child Development Research,* eds. M. Hoffman and L. W. Hoffman, New York, Russell Sage Foundation, 1964, vol. 1, p. 171.

displaced from the frustrating system (the power and reward structure of industrial society) to the relatively powerless child.'[1] The frustration of the lower-class father leads him not only to aggressive behaviour but to withdrawal from the family and an attempt to gain status in some alternative behaviour system, such as sexual prowess, masculinity and the adult male peer-group. This in turn has important influences on the pattern of identification with the two parents. The lower-class boy is likely to identify with the mother rather than the father, which may lead to adolescent rebellion in an effort to escape this identification. The inadequacy of the father will also mean that the peer-group is likely to be of particular importance for the lower-class adolescent as he seeks a masculine model. This general picture is in sharp contrast to the family situation of the upwardly mobile, which is characterised by moderate socialisation techniques, shared parental authority and identification with the father. McKinley's study, therefore, is an important attempt to relate aspects of occupational status, socialisation processes, and achievement behaviour. However, we cannot fully assess its significance without further research in all these areas.

So far in this discussion we have treated social class as if it were a homogeneous category. In fact, this is very far from the case, and studies in the differences within social classes show them to be both complex and heterogeneous. This serves to emphasise the importance of research into intra-class differences. Although much fewer in number than those concerned with comparison between classes, the researches carried out in this field are sufficient at least to indicate certain important areas to which further attention should be paid.

One of the main ways in which to differentiate between working-class jobs is in terms of skill, and it has been shown several times that the children of skilled workers perform better at school and are more likely to go on to higher education than are the children of the unskilled. This finding holds even when ability is held constant. Within the middle classes there is a similar distinction between the upper and lower strata.[2] There is also evidence, from the same studies, that skilled and semiskilled workers have higher aspirations for their

1. D. G. McKinley, *Social Class and Family Life*, Glencoe, Illinois, Free Press, 1964, p. 54.
2. See, for example, the Crowther Report, H.M.S.O., 1959; J. Floud, A. H. Halsey and F. M. Martin, *Social Class and Educational Opportunity*, Heinemann, 1956. Similar data for the U.S. is summarised in W. B. Bookover and D. Gottlieb, *A Sociology of Education*, 2nd edn. New York, American Book Co., 1964, chap. 7. See also R. Turner, *The Social Context of Ambition*, San Francisco, Chandler, 1964.

children than unskilled workers, and the upper-middle than the lower-middle classes. Some studies have also suggested that foremen as a group stand in an intermediate position between the middle and the working classes.[1]

There is, therefore, clear evidence of differences both within the working classes and the middle classes, corresponding to the level of skill demanded in the job. In the absence of sufficient evidence we can unfortunately only speculate as to why these differences occur. The more favourable position of the skilled worker or foreman relative to the unskilled worker, in terms of the status of the job, its chances of promotion and, usually, its material rewards, offers several possible reasons for the working-class differences that have been found. The lower-class family may well have fewer expectations for the future and so lower aspirations for themselves and their children. They may have less self-esteem and be less self-confident. They tend to have larger families, and to be less well-educated, which will increase their chances of using Bernstein's public language forms. They are also less likely to have acquired achieving values as a consequence of their particular life experiences, either during their own childhood or later. Within the middle classes those in lower-middle-class occupations will be differentiated from the upper-middle classes by their earnings, their status and their education level. This may well reflect upon the horizons they set for their children.

On the other hand, we cannot overlook the possibility that the cause of the difference is of a much more complex and subtle kind, arising not as a consequence of their class position but as one of its causes. The foremen and skilled workers are likely to include far more upwardly mobile individuals than the unskilled workers, and so are those in the upper-middle rather than the lower-middle occupations group. It is at least possible that the personality and value orientations which helped the upwardly mobile families to succeed will also be passed to their children. Smelser, for example, in a study of upwardly mobile, stationary, and downwardly mobile families concluded that 'achievement at the level of the family was influential in the development of such personality factors as strength, power, self-direction and distance from others'.[2]

On the other hand, other workers have emphasised downward

1. See, for example, Floud, Halsey, Martin, *op. cit.*; E. G. Cohen, 'Parental factors in educational mobility', *Sociology of Education,* 38 (summarised in Chapter 11 of this volume).
2. W. T. Smelser, 'Adolescent and adult occupational choice as a function of socio-economic history', in *Sociometry,* 26 (1963).

mobility, and especially maternal downward mobility as an important factor in school achievement and parental ambition. Cohen, for example, found that mothers who had married downward from a white-collar background had a higher probability of having a son planning to go to college than mothers who came from a manual-worker background. This was also true of mothers holding white-collar rather than manual jobs. Fathers' downward mobility was, however unrelated to the sons' plans for entering college.[1] Floud, Halsey and Martin also found that mothers whose occupation before marriage was superior to that of their husbands were more likely to have children who were successful in the eleven-plus than other mothers.[2] Kohn, in his study of parental values towards the upbringing of children, found that working-class mothers holding white-collar jobs were closer to the middle class than other working-class mothers, and so were those with relatively high educational attainment.[3] Such mothers therefore are not only likely to be motivated by a strong desire to regain status; their close association with the middle classes through their social origin, their job or their educational background, has provided them with the necessary knowledge, and quite possibly values, which will ensure for their children a successful school career. Cohen, for example, concludes that 'we can speculate that the influence of the parents on the probability of mobility takes place at a very early stage when basic attitudes towards school work are being formed. The crucial role of the parents may be to send the child to school with a receptive attitude toward the values and norms advocated by the school personnel.'[4] Such mothers, of course, are also more likely to use Bernstein's formal language.

In discussing fathers, emphasis is more often placed upon blocked mobility, or mobility pessimism. Swift, for example, found that 'with the middle class, the father's dissatisfaction with his job and its prospects related significantly to the likelihood of his child's success in the eleven-plus'.[5] Cohen found for her sample that working-class fathers who were similarly dissatisfied were more likely than other fathers to have sons planning to go to college.[6] Kahl found that his

---

1. E. G. Cohen *op. cit.* See also I. Krauss, 'Aspirations among working-class youth', *American Sociological Review*, vol. 29 (1964), 869.
2. Floud, Halsey, Martin, *op. cit.*, p. 88.
3. M. L. Kohn, 'Social class and parental values', *American Journal of Sociology*, 64 (1959).
4. Cohen, *op. cit.*, p. 422.
5. D. F. Swift, 'Social class and achievement motivation', *Educational Research*, 8, in no. 2 (1966), 93.
6. E. G. Cohen, *op. cit.*

'getting ahead' fathers were unhappy and dissatisfied with their occupational status.[1] This would appear, indeed, to be a factor of some considerable importance, but we still need to know whether it operates simply as a determinant of parental ambition vicariously expressed through the child, or whether, as Kahl's argument would suggest, it operates at a deeper level. The 'mobility pessimism' itself, that is to say, may be the result of strong achievement values or an achievement drive which has for some reason been blocked.

At the same time Harrington has suggested that when blocked mobility leads to frustration, and pressure on the child to succeed *in place of* the parent, the result is likely to be unfavourable for the child's mobility. 'The family in which educational success is too much the price of parental approval to be enjoyed for its own sake', she argues, 'is unlikely to throw up creative ability, and where the child is treated as an extension of the parental self-image, self-direction cannot be expected'.[2]

This review of working-class family life serves therefore to underline the general conclusions already drawn, that our only hope to understand more about class differences in achievement is by a greater understanding of the general socialisation process. We need to know how the child acquires not only the values and skills of his group but, even more significantly in a society where education is a major key to social mobility, the ability and the motivation to learn new skills and new values. This requires, it is hardly necessary to add, more than the sociological approach alone. It is an interdisciplinary concept and requires interdisciplinary methods, and in particular an emphasis on the relationships between personality and social structure. If, however, sociology is to make its full contribution it is vitally necessary that it should go beyond the descriptive studies of social-class differences with which it has frequently been content in the past, and consider, as it is indeed beginning to do, the actual process of socialisation itself.

The family is of course the earliest and the most important area in which socialisation occurs. Yet, however important the family is, and has been shown to be, it would be false to assume that it is the only factor in explaining either inter-class or intra-class differences in educational achievement. The school itself is a socialising agency of

1. J. A. Kahl, ' "Common man" boys', in *Education, Economy and Society*, ed., A. H. Halsey, J. Floud and C. A. Anderson, Collier-Macmillan, 1961, pp. 348–66.
2. M. Harrington, 'Parents' hopes and children's success', *New Society*, 26 Nov. 1964, p. 9.

some considerable importance, in which the teachers and the peer group each play their part, a part which may reinforce or may conflict with the influence of the family.

For this reason the sociology of education has come to pay increasing attention to the school. Jean Floud pointed out in 1961 that although home and school in interaction determine educability, the school has been neglected. 'Little has been done to explore with any thoroughness or in any detail the explicit and implicit demands of life in school to which we find pupils responding selectively in terms of their differing social experience outside its walls.'[1]

Since then a number of sociologists have turned to the study of educational institutions, and in particular there has been considerable interest recently in the study of the school as an organisation. At the same time work has been undertaken into the peer group and the adolescent culture, and into the teacher's role. A beginning has therefore been made in the creation of a sociology of the school.

1. J. Floud, 'Sociology and education', in *The Teaching of Sociology to Students of Education and Social Work,* Sociological Review Monograph No. 4, 1961, p. 64.

Author Index

Abel-Smith, B. and Townsend, P., 67n
Abrams, M., 6
Acton Society Trust, 66n
Anderson, C. A. and Schnaper, M., 202n
Annan, N., 202n
Association of Education Committees, 81
Ault, H. K., 81

Banks, O. L., 23, 51n
Bantock, G. H., 104
Barber, B., 23, 24
Becker, W. C., 258n
Bell, R., 231
Ben-David, J., 70n
Bendix, R., 66n
Berkowitz, L., 20
Bernstein, B. B., 22, 47, 68n, 102, 235, 237, 245, 260, 261
Blaug, M., Peston, M. H. and Ziderman, A., 7
Blishen, E., 113
Blyth, W. A. L., 10, 97
Boocock, S. S., 3
Bordua, D. J., 141n
Bronfenbrenner, U., 196n
Brookover, W. B. and Gottlieb, D., 258n., 259n
Brown, D. R., 192n
Butler, N. R. and Bonham, D. G., 67n

Carlsson, G., 65n
Caro, F. G., 19
Carter, M. P., 15, 16
Central Advisory Council for Education (England)
   (1954, Early Leaving), 4, 5, 10–11, 45n, 50, 52, 55n, 74, 80, 83, 200, 225
   (1959, Crowther Report), 4, 21, 35, 37, 38, 44, 50, 52, 53, 225
   (1963, Newsom Report), 50, 59n, 225, 238
   (1967, Plowden Report), 4, 22, 103, 158, 159, 160, 181, 183
Child, I. L., 194n
Church, R., 114n

Clegg, A. B., 99, 102
Clements, R. V., 66n
Cohen, A. K., 130, 134, 140n, 141, 142, 143
Cohen, E. G., 23, 260n, 261
Cloward, R. A. and Ohlin, L. E., 142n
Collins, H., 83
Committee on Higher Education (Robbins Report), 4, 11, 50, 52n, 55n, 56, 57, 58, 59n, 64n, 225
Conant, J., 99
Conklin, 231
Coombs, P. H., 4

Dale, R. R., 83
Davis, A., 194n, 226
Dennis, N., 227
D.E.S., 69n, 86n
Dixon, R., 232
Douglas, J. W. B., 11, 64n, 68n, 75, 100, 101, 186, 187, 189, 192
Douglas, J. W. B., Ross, J. M. and Simpson, W. R., 4, 11, 12, 21, 22
Duncan, S. M., 159, 160

Eggleston, S. J., 13, 107
Elder, G. H., 11, 193n, 198n
Empey, L. T., 20
Erickson, C., 66n

Ferguson, T., 136
Firth, J. R., 232
Floud, J., 22n, 52n, 59, 60, 62, 263
Floud, J. and Halsey, A. H., 64n
Floud, J., Halsey, A. H. and Martin, F. M., 34n, 36n, 42, 43n, 55n, 77, 83, 185n, 189n, 193n, 259n, 260n, 261
Frake, 231
Frankenberg, R., 93
Fraser, E., 7, 41n, 76n, 81, 84, 193

Galton, F., 186
General Register Office, 67n
Getzels, J. W. and Jackson, P. W., 191n
Girard, A., 41n, 44n
Glass, D. V. 35, 37, 51n, 65n
Glass, D. V. and Grebenik, E., 67n
Goldman-Eisler, F., 235

Goldman, R. J., 24n
Goldthorpe, J. H. and Lockwood, D., 16, 93, 98
Goldthorpe, J. H., Lockwood, D., Bechhofer, F. and Platt, J., 17, 18n, 256n, 257n
Gouldner, A. W., 257n
Gray, J. L. and Moshinsky, P., 4
Greenald, G. M., 76, 77
Gumperz, J., 231

Halliday, M., 232
Hallworth, H. J., 194
Halsey, A. H. and Gardner, L., 186n
Hargreaves, D. H., 19
Harrington, M., 262
Herriott, R. E. and St. John, N. H., 18, 102
Himmelweit, H. J., 24, 185
Hollingshead, A. B., 105
Hyman, H. H., 19
Hymes, D., 230

Inkeles, A., 24, 257

Jackson, B. and Marsden, D., 13, 68n, 99, 101, 192, 258n
Jackson, E. and Crockett, H. J., 65n
Jayasuriya, D. L., 13, 250
Jones, C. V., 75

Kahl, J. A., 5, 19, 20, 43n, 206, 207, 209, 257, 261, 262
Katz, F. M., 21, 257n
Kelsall, R. K., 52, 53, 56, 62, 66n, 201n
Kent, N. and Davis, D. R., 190, 192
Kerr, M., 197, 227
Klein, J., 15, 16, 18, 227, 244n
Kluckhohn, F., 226, 250, 257
Kohn, M. L., 248, 258, 261
Krauss, I., 13

Lavin, D. E., 24n
Lawton, D., 22, 24n
Lees, J. P. and Stewart, A. H., 187
Lewis, B. R., 76
Lindsay, K., 4
Lipset, S. M. and Bendix, R., 24n, 65n, 212n
Lockwood, D., 17
Luria, A. R., 234
Lydall, H. F., 67n
Lyman, E. L., 211, 257n
Lynn, R. and Gordon, I. E., 195n

McClelland, D. C., 20, 39, 198n, 199n

McCord, J., McCord, W. and Thurber, E., 140n
McKinley, D. G., 258, 259
Marsden, D., 23
Matza, D. and Sykes, G. M., 19
Mays, J. B., 10, 94, 96
Merton, R. K., 133
Metcalfe, O., 76, 79, 84
Miller, H., 6
Miller, S. M., 65n
Miller, W. B., 140n, 141
Ministry of Education (1947) *School and Life*, 112n
Morris, J. N. and Heady, J. A., 67n
Musgrove, F., 20, 21, 23, 105, 196n

Newcomb, T. M., 138
Newfield, J. G. H., 58n
Newson, J. and Newson, E., 194, 195
N.F.E.R., 76, 81
Nicholson, J. L., 67n
Nisbet, J. D., 41n
N.U.T., 69n

O.E.C.D., 5

Pareek, U., 20
Parsons, J., 104
Peaker, G., 159
Peters, R. S., 226
Peyre, C., 34n, 35n

Raynor, J. M., 18
Rodman, H., 19
Roe, A., 199n
Rogoff, N., 9, 14, 106
Rose, G., 16
Rosen, B. C., 21, 250
Rousseau, J. J., 198
Routh, G., 256n
Roy, K., 258

Sampson, E. E., 188n
Schachter, S., 187
Schneider, L. and Lysgaard, S., 247
Schools Council, 4, 21
Sewell, W. H. and Armer, J. M., 107
Sexton, P. C., 9
Shaw, M. C., 197n
Sherif, M. and Sherif, C. W., 142n
Simon, B., 234
Simpson, H. R., 156
Simpson, R. L., 13
Smelser, W. T., 260n
Spinley, B., 197
Stott, D. H., 77
Strodtbeck, F. L., 197n, 249, 250
Sugarman, B. N., 5, 21

Svalastoga, K., 4, 65n
Swift, D. F., 8, 24, 24n, 98, 261

Thorndike, R. L., 8
Tipping, D. G., 67n
Torrance, E. P., 192n
Tumin, M. M., 6
Turner, R., 259n

Waller, W., 139n, 147n
Warner, W. L. and Abegglen, J. C., 199n
Webb, J., 102, 143n
Weber, M., 246, 249, 250
Westergaard, J. H., 67n

Westwood, L. J., 24n
Whalley, G. E., 75
Whiting, J. W. M. and Child, I. L., 196n
Whorf, B. L., 230
Willmott, P., 12n
Wilson, A. B., 13
Wilson, R., 16n
Wiseman, S., 8, 24n, 103
Wolfle, D., 70n

Young, M. and McGeeney, P. J., 24n
Young, M. and Willmott, P., 227

Zigler, E., 23n

Subject Index

Achieved roles, 92
Achievement motivation, 20, 196–8, 249, 250
Activism, 12–13, 17–18n, 20 et seq., 249
Age-earnings profiles, 7
Ascribed roles, 92, 227
Association, 92

Birth order, 186–8

Catchment area, 92–3
Child-rearing patterns, 23
  (See also Middle Class, Working Class)
'Cognitive poverty', 227
Community, 91 et seq.
Comprehensive education, 47, 69–70, 133
Contextual studies, 8–14, 91–148
Creativity, 191
Culture concept, 242–3
Culture conflict, 96, 139

Demographic studies, 4–8, 31–87

Economics of education, 6
Edge Hill College of Education, 102
Educability, 5, 33 et seq., 45 et seq., 68, 224, 226, 253, 263
Education
  and the economy, 31
  and income, 6, 9
  and talent, 34
Educational opportunity, 5, 32 et seq., 59, 200, 224
Embourgeoisement, 17
  (See also Working Class)
Emotional disturbance, 84, 85
Emotional environment of home, 190–3
Extrinsic motivation, 226

Famille éducogène, 40–1
Family migration, 192–3
Family roles, 119–121
Family size, 21, 22, 41–3, 76–9, 184–6

Fatalism, 226
  (See also Middle Class, Working Class)
France
  Social class and education, 4, 35
Future-orientation, 20 et seq., 46, 227, 247 et seq.
  (See also Middle Class, Working Class)

Hesitation phenomena, 235
'Higher Horizons' project, 103
Home facilities, 79–82

Individualism, 20 et seq., 250
Inner urban areas, 8, 10, 69, 94–6, 109–26, 181
Intelligence tests, 36, 45, 55, 64, 154–6, 185, 187, 225
Interdisciplinary study, 24 et seq., 262
Intrinsic motivation, 226
Irish Republic
  Family size, 22
    (see also Roman Catholics)
  Social class and education, 5

Japan
  Social class and education, 4
Jews, 15, 193, 197–8, 209

Kirkby, 115

Language and socialisation, 227–9
Leicester University, 103
Linguistic Codes
  elaborated, 22, 236 et seq.
  restricted, 47, 68, 236 et seq., 245, 260, 261
Linguistic deprivation, 234

Marginality, 217
Matched pairs, 206
Middle Class
  and grammar school entry, 35, 37, 38, 42, 54, 60, 200
  and parental interest, 152 et seq.
  and university entrance, 54, 62, 200
  child-rearing practices, 194–6, 248, 258

Middle Class—*continued*
  communities, 97
    (*See also* Suburbs)
  language, 235
    (*See also* Linguistic Codes)
  leaving age, 5, 44, 169
  school performance, 45, 56, 72 *et seq.*
  'sunken', 192, 261
  values, 18 *et seq.*, 134–5, 244 *et seq.*,
    250, 257
'Mobility pessimism', 262

Navaho, 226
Need-achievement
  (*See* Achievement motivation)
Neighbourhood values, 10
Netherlands
  social class and education, 4
Norms and values, 243
Norway
  social class and education, 4
Nursery education, 182

Parental education, 7–8, 42, 74–6,
  162–4
Parental encouragement, 164 *et seq.*,
  188 *et seq.*, 208
'Parity of esteem', 50, 133
Peer group, 3, 13, 128 *et seq.*, 259
Poverty, 39–40, 76, 81, 170
Projective tests, 197
Protestant ethic, 132, 246

Roman Catholics, 15, 22, 43, 121, 185

Schools,
  grammar, 34, 35, 37, 38, 42, 54, 60,
    72 *et seq.*, 200
  social climate of, 10, 11
Social Class
  and family size, 42
  and personality, 24
  and society, 132
  subcultures (*See* Working Class,
    Middle Class)
  two-level model, 18, 20, 245

Social mobility, 64–6, 205 *et seq.*
Social motivation, 226
Streaming, 11, 12, 69, 79, 127 *et seq.*
  (*See also* Schools)
Subcultural studies, 14–23, 151–202,
  205–63
Suburbs, 9, 10, 12, 16, 93, 227
'Success ethic', 19, 21, 132 *et seq.*, 142n
Sweden
  social class and education, 4

Teachers' assessments, 64
Teacher's role, 10, 95, 102, 136, 142
'Teacher/social worker', 102

United States
  social class and education, 4, 5

'Value-stretch', 19
Verbal planning, 235

Working Class
  and grammar school entry, 35, 37,
    38, 42, 54, 60, 72 *et seq.*, 200
  and parental interest, 152 *et seq.*
  and status frustration, 141, 207, 258
  and university entry, 54, 62, 200
  child-rearing practices, 194, 248, 258
  children's aspirations, 20
  cultural heterogeneity, 14–18
  deferential, 16–17
  deprived, 15–16, 93, 114
  insecurity, 256–7
  language, 235
    (*See also* Linguistic Codes)
  leaving age, 4, 5, 11, 44, 169, 200, 225
  'privatised', 10, 12–13, 15–18, 93, 98
  school performance, 4, 11, 45, 56,
    72 *et seq.*
  traditional, 15–16, 93, 114, 227
  values, 18 *et seq.*, 207, 244 *et seq.*, 257

Youth Employment Service, 117, 124